IBM's PERSONAL COMPUTER

Second Edition

Chris DeVoney

Contributors
Douglas Ford Cobb
P. D. (Pete) Moulton

Que Corporation
Indianapolis

P5

Cover art: Dick Held
Artwork: Linda Holman
Design: Paul Mangin
Typeset by Que Corporation

Manufactured in the United States of America

Published by Que Corporation
7960 Castleway Drive
Indianapolis, Indiana 46250

First Printing, May, 1983
Second Printing, July, 1983

About the Author

Chris DeVoney is the technical director of Que Corporation and the author of the first edition of this book. Mr. DeVoney received his B.S. degree from the University of Gloucester. He founded Marcum Consulting and, prior to joining Que, implemented a major POS reporting network of microcomputers for a 24-store retail chain. Mr. DeVoney has also served as technical consultant to two retail computer stores and has been employed in the microcomputer industry since it began in 1975.

Mr. DeVoney is president of the Indianapolis Small Systems group and has been active in forming other computer professional organizations. He has conducted workshops for IBM Product Center personnel on operating systems and the IBM Personal Computer.

Editorial Director
David F. Noble, Ph.D.

Editors
Diane F. Brown, M.A.
Virginia D. Noble, M.L.S.

Managing Editor
Paul Mangin

IBM's Personal Computer

Table of Contents

Acknowledgments

The writers of this book wish to thank the following people, whose efforts made this book possible:

Joe Hancock, Rex Hancock, Marianne Carter, and the staff of Com-puterLand of Indianapolis, Indiana, for loaning many different pieces of equipment and software.

Kevin Wandryk, Carmen Governale, and the staff at Digital Research Inc., for providing information and assistance on its products.

William McAllister of the IBM Product Center, Indianapolis, Indiana, for his valuable assistance.

William McCloud of the IBM Products Center, New York, New York, for his assistance with the IBM COBOL section.

Larry Hanger of MicroLink, Inc., for his assistance on the Intel iAPX family of products and future products.

Chris Larson, Mark Ursino, and Tandy Towers at Microsoft, Inc., for providing information and assistance on its products.

The staff of the Sears Business Center, Indianapolis, Indiana, for making an Expansion Unit available for examination.

Maura Smith and Al Irvine at SofTech Microsystems for providing information on its products.

And thanks to all those listed in the first edition of this book for their valuable contributions.

INTRODUCTION

Welcome to the second edition.

The first edition of *IBM's Personal Computer* was published in February, 1982, just three months after the first IBM Personal Computers were shipped. It was the first book to be published about the IBM Personal Computer and has become a standard guide to the machine. Coming as it did at the very beginning of the Personal Computer story, the first edition contained observations about the machine and speculations about the impact it would have on the personal computer marketplace.

The introduction of the IBM Personal Computer changed the microcomputer world. And the Personal Computer itself has changed in some exciting ways since its debut. In fact, so many new things are happening with the Personal Computer that, although we call this a second edition, it is almost a completely new book. This book examines the IBM Personal Computer system in substantial detail. It discusses all of the new hardware and software developments that have occurred in the past year and a half. Because much of what was speculation in the first edition is now established fact, this book also contains our observations about the trends that have been created by the Personal Computer and the importance of the Personal Computer to the entire microcomputer industry.

Chapter 1, "The Personal Computer Comes of Age," traces the development of the IBM Personal Computer. This chapter comments on the tremendous importance of the Personal Computer to the personal computer industry and includes some new speculations about the future of the Personal Computer.

Chapter 2 describes the System Unit and the Keyboard of both the original Personal Computer and the new Personal Computer XT.

The unique aspects of the Personal Computer, including its extensive memory-expansion capability, the keyboard, and the 16-bit CPU, are treated in detail. IBM's new Expansion Unit and the Fixed Disk storage option are also discussed.

The Personal Computer's peripherals are treated in chapter 3. They include: the Monochrome and new Color Displays, their printers and adapters, the CRT controller, the Color/Graphics Monitor Adapter, and the Asynchronous and Bisynchronous Communications Adapters.

The operating systems for the Personal Computer are described in chapter 4, with emphasis on PC DOS, CP/M-86, and the UCSD p-System. PC DOS V2.0 is discussed at length.

Chapter 5 covers IBM's language software library. BASIC, Pascal, COBOL, FORTRAN, and other languages available for the Personal Computer are reviewed here.

The business software library is reviewed in chapter 6. This chapter can help you decide which IBM program will best satisfy your particular applications needs. The new additions to the business library, including Multiplan, Peachtext, and the BPI family of accounting software, are presented in this chapter. Chapter 6 also discusses IBM's unusual position regarding third-party software.

Chapter 7, "Communications with the IBM PC," explains the principles and techniques of microcomputer communications as they relate to the IBM Personal Computer. This chapter was written by Pete Moulton, the Communications editor of *Personal Computer Age* magazine and expert in the area of data communications.

The appendix on Personal Computer BASIC commands lists the commands used by the Personal Computer and the Personal Computer XT and compares them with standard BASIC.

Enjoy the book!

CHAPTER 1

The Personal Computer Comes of Age

The development of IBM's Personal Computer began late in the summer of 1980 when IBM chairman John Opel, who has since retired, and president John Carey, now chairman, authorized Phillip D. Estridge to form the Personal Computer development team.

Almost exactly one year later, on August 12, 1981, the IBM Personal Computer was announced. Even before the first units were shipped, the excitement began to build over IBM's entry into the microcomputer world.

Mike Markkula, then president of Apple Computer Company, said that the announcement was "the legitimizing of the microcomputer industry." Apple Computer placed full-page advertisements in *The Wall Street Journal* that said "Welcome, IBM." Apple's warm welcome reflected its awareness that although IBM would be a worthy competitor, all of the participants in the microcomputer industry would benefit from having IBM as a neighbor.

Ben Rosen, president of Sevin-Rosen Partners, Inc., and ex-publisher of *The Rosen Electronics Letter,* identified the IBM announcement as the fourth milestone in the eight-year-old microcomputer industry. He accorded the same significance to the IBM announcement as he did to the MITS/Altair introduction of the first personal computer kit in 1975; the first major, assembled (appliance) personal computers from Commodore, Radio Shack, and Apple in 1977; and the first breakthrough in personal computer software, VisiCalc®, which was introduced in 1979.

Most industry insiders knew that the IBM Personal Computer would be important. Nevertheless, almost every observer underestimated the dramatic success of the IBM Personal Computer. Apparently, even IBM significantly underestimated the potential of its product. Future Computing, a Dallas, Texas-based consulting firm, predicted in August, 1981, that the IBM Personal Computer would generate 1 billion dollars in sales for IBM by the end of 1984. In fact, that mark will be achieved before the end of 1983, one year earlier than expected. Estimates of the number of installed IBM Personal Computers vary, but many insiders expect the number to reach 500,000 by the end of 1983.

A Look at IBM

In an industry that was started by very small companies with extremely clever technical people, varying business capabilities, and marginal financial resources, the entry of IBM was quite a shock. IBM's gross sales in 1982 exceeded 29 billion dollars, which earned it a place in the top ten among U.S. corporate giants.

IBM's *profit before taxes* for 1982 was nearly 6 billion dollars, which is greater than the *gross sales* of many companies that are recognized as corporate giants. IBM's *after-tax* profits of 3.6 billion dollars were more than the *gross sales* of most of the manufacturers in the microcomputer industry. For example, Apple Computer, the largest microcomputer-only computer company had 1982 sales of less than 1 billion dollars.

Partly because of its tremendous financial resources, and partly because of its well-honed business machinery, IBM is a strong competitor in most of the markets in which it participates. IBM owns the lion's share (according to some sources, as much as 70 percent) of the mainframe computer market as well as a large part of the minicomputer market, despite strong competition from a number of large, well-managed firms. In fact, some describe the IBM name as being synonymous with "computer."

Many observers felt that the size of the company would be an obstacle to IBM when it decided to produce a personal computer. IBM had developed a reputation for being stodgy and slow moving. Other observers questioned whether the relatively small size of the IBM Personal Computer market would discourage IBM from entering the personal computer area. After all, even if the Personal Computer generated 1 billion dollars in annual sales for IBM, the product would only account for about 3 percent of IBM's total business.

To the surprise of these observers, IBM demonstrated remarkable desire, agility, and flexibilty in planning, designing, and implementing the Personal Computer product plan.

Teaching Big Blue New Tricks

In many ways, the Personal Computer represented a major departure for IBM from its traditional business policies. IBM has always had the reputation of not being interested in products developed by third-party manufacturers for IBM computers (the "not invented here" attitude). In the case of the Personal Computer, however, IBM recognized that it was entering a marketplace that had already developed some important standards, and that the success of the IBM Personal Computer would depend on IBM's accepting some of those standards.

The need to cooperate with third-party software and hardware vendors was increased by the extremely tight timetable of the Personal Computer project. The development team was given only one year to conceive, design, and develop IBM's Personal Computer. Considering that IBM normally requires four years to launch a new product, the one-year limitation was severe.

The first stop on the third-party vendor tour was Bellevue, Washington, home of Microsoft Corporation. IBM contracted with Microsoft to develop the new computer's operating system. This system, PC DOS (or MS DOS in its generic form) has since emerged as the new "industry standard" operating system in the 16-bit world. Microsoft's popular BASIC language was also selected as the primary programming tool for the Personal Computer.

IBM also acquired applications software from outside vendors. The VisiCalc program was selected as the Personal Computer's electronic spreadsheet. IBM clearly knew that the success of its new machine would depend in part on its ability to run VisiCalc. The Personal Computer's vast memory resources and fast calculation speed make it an ideal spreadsheeting tool.

Similarly, the accounting software for the new machine was licensed from Peachtree Software of Atlanta, Georgia. The new computer's word processor was Information Unlimited Software's EasyWriter™.

Even some of the Personal Computer's hardware was purchased from outsiders. The disk drives were purchased from Tandon Corporation. The IBM 80-column dot-matrix printer was manufactured for IBM by Epson.

This trend toward purchasing certain components for the Personal Computer instead of manufacturing them has not abated. A variety of new software products has been announced since the Personal Computer was first introduced. All of these products were acquired from outside vendors. These products include the Multiplan™ electronic spreadsheet, the BPI Systems family of accounting software, and Peachtree's Peachtext™ word processor.

Looking back, the decision to use outside suppliers for the Personal Computer was wise. First, this decision allowed the project to be completed on schedule. It is extremely unlikely that the one-year timetable would have been achieved if all development work had been done in-house. Second, the Personal Computer ended up incorporating much of the finest technology available at the time. This trend continues as IBM keeps selecting the best third-party products to bear the IBM logo.

Distribution

IBM also took advantage of the young industry's established distribution channels. Although IBM has sold the Personal Computer through its own retail outlets since its introduction, the machine has also been available through ComputerLand stores, Sears Business Centers, and a variety of smaller chains and independent computer stores.

From the beginning, IBM has maintained a very high standard for its dealers. A store can become a Personal Computer dealer only after passing a thorough checkout by IBM.

It is interesting to note that it took IBM longer to complete its dealer network than it did to design and produce the computer. This care in selecting dealers is consistent with IBM's traditional "marketing first" orientation. By being very selective, IBM has managed to keep the quality of the dealer base very high and thus can offer its retail customers a level of service that is hard to match.

Nearly 800 dealers carry the IBM Personal Computer. This number includes 350 ComputerLands, 40 IBM Product Centers, 45 Sears Business Centers, and more than 300 independent dealers. The dealer network is still expanding as IBM, Sears, and ComputerLand open new stores and as more independents are granted dealer status. IBM has also made the Personal Computer available to value-added resellers through the IBM VAR program. Only nine VARs for the Personal Computer have been named to date, but this number should increase in the near future.

Software

Another break with IBM tradition is the Personal Computer software submission program. Early in the development of the Personal Computer, IBM established a Software Submission Group and a Personal Computing Publishing Department. These groups were designed exclusively to acquire and publish quality software for the Personal Computer. Although the program suffered at first from restrictive submission rules and a low cap on potential royalty income for software authors, it represents IBM's interest in opening up the Personal Computer to the industry at large.

The IBM Approach

Although IBM broke with tradition in a number of ways by introducing the Personal Computer, the company retained the basic strengths that have made it the dominant force in the computer industry. More than one industry observer has commented about IBM that "they do things right." Certainly this statement applies in the case of the Personal Computer.

In an interview in *ISO World* magazine, Don Estridge, leader of IBM's Personal Computer project and now vice president of the Systems Products Division, said: "We started off with ideas that were just that. One of them was 'Let's build the best product that we know how to build.' We never believed that, just because the product was a personal computer or just because it was to be purchased in a retail store, the customer would accept from IBM anything less than IBM quality."

The Personal Computer did suffer some early problems, however. Users complained about the awkward location of the shift key on the keyboard. The disk drives on the first machines had a capacity of only 160,000 bytes, not sufficient for many business applications. This problem was solved by the introduction of DOS 1.1 and the adoption of double-sided disk drives in June, 1982.

These minor flaws should not obscure the overall attention to high quality that has been apparent throughout the life of the IBM Personal Computer. It was and remains an outstanding personal computer, carefully designed, well implemented, and professionally supported. This attention to high quality was a major factor in *Info-World Magazine's* decision to name the IBM Personal Computer its hardware product of the year for 1982.

The Effect on the Marketplace

The IBM Personal Computer has had a major impact on the entire microcomputer industry. One estimate claims that the Personal Computer has actually expanded the personal computer marketplace by 25 percent. Portia Issacson of Future Computing believes that the Personal Computer doubled the 1982 revenues of the dealers who sell it. Along with the Apple II and the TRS-80 series of computers, the Personal Computer is an industry leader.

The Personal Computer has also changed the market in other ways. IBM's attention to quality control has raised the level of quality consciousness throughout the industry. IBM's choice of a binder enclosed in a cloth slip case for its software made that packaging the industry standard.

One comment frequently heard when the Personal Computer was introduced was that IBM was "too late" in the marketplace. In retrospect, IBM's entry into the market was perfectly timed. By waiting for the software and hardware technology to mature and the distribution channels to stabilize, IBM was able to move smoothly into a ready market. In fact, IBM launched the second wave of the consumer computer industry.

The Personal Computer's Mini-Industry

Like the Apple II before it, the IBM Personal Computer has created a "mini-industry" of start-up companies that produce hardware and software products for the machine. IBM has encouraged this development from the beginning of the Personal Computer project. The

Personal Computer is, by design, an open system. The full technical specifications of the computer have been published by IBM. This means that anyone with sufficient training to understand the specs can create hardware and software for the computer. IBM clearly realized that although this policy would make it easier for other computer manufacturers to emulate the Personal Computer, the loss of revenue from this source would be far outweighed by the gain from having large numbers of third-party software and hardware vendors.

Companies like Tecmar, Davong, Quadram, and hundreds of others produce a variety of memory boards, disk drives, communications devices, and other expansion boards for the Personal Computer. Estimates of the number of firms involved in this mini-industry vary. The June, 1983, edition of Que Corporation's *IBM PC Expansion & Software Guide* lists more than 2,200 products from more than 600 vendors. About 500 of these products are hardware expansion devices.

Opening the 16-Bit Doors

The IBM Personal Computer was the first serious 16-bit computer in the marketplace. Its success has been so dramatic that it has carried the entire industry into the 16-bit world in little more than a year. In fact, it was primarily the success of the Personal Computer that prompted *InfoWorld's* November 29, 1982, issue to ask, somewhat prematurely: "Is 8-Bit Dead?"

The Personal Computer is shifting the industry's perception about what is an "adequate" computer. In 1981, a 64K computer was considered sufficient for most functions. Today, many users feel that 128K or 256K are required for success with a computer.

The Personal Computer has created new opportunities for software manufacturers as well. Thanks to the Personal Computer's vast memory capacity, programmers need no longer cram their code into 64K of memory. According to Bill Gates, chairman of Microsoft Corporation, "The main reason for the 16-bit micro being advantageous is the increased address space. That sounds like a technical issue, but what it boils down to for the end user is that we can do more complex software, with a better end-user interface, in a more transportable form than we have ever been able to do in what I call the '8-bit world.'"

The New Software Standard

As mentioned above, MS DOS has become the de facto, industry-standard operating system in the 16-bit world. The most common configuration for new computers is to emulate the IBM Personal Computer by using an Intel 8088 processor and MS DOS. One industry observer estimates that 75 percent of the new software being developed is being written for this combination. In fact, the success of the Personal Computer has even brought a measure of standardization to the previously helter-skelter world of 5 1/4" disks.

Because more powerful hardware has the capability to use more powerful software, the introduction of the IBM Personal Computer made possible vast improvements in the realm of applications software.

The IBM Personal Computer has lead to the development of exciting applications software, such as Lotus' 1-2-3 and Context Management Systems' MBA. These programs are among the first to take full advantage of the IBM Personal Computer's advanced features, especially its massive memory. The programs combine spreadsheeting, graphics, and a data base into a single managerial software tool. Both programs require more than 64K of memory just for the program code. These programs are possible only because of the power of the 16-bit address space.

Even more exciting systems and applications software are just around the corner. In late 1983, VisiCorp will begin shipment of its new operating environment, Visi^{on}™. Conceived as a tool that will simplify the use of microcomputers and link togeher all of the common business computer applications, This may be the most important new software product of the year. It will be available initially only for the IBM Personal Computer.

Similarly, Digital Research is already delivering its new single-user, multitasking operating system, Concurrent CP/M-86™. Concurrent CP/M looks and behaves much like the familiar CP/M operating system, but allows up to four different applications programs to run simultaneously on a single computer. Only one application is invisible at a time, but the others can be retrieved with the touch of a single key. Concurrent CP/M will vastly increase the power and practicality of the IBM Personal Computer.

In applications software, there seems to be no limit on what can be achieved. One exciting program developed for the 16-bit world is Microsoft's Flight Simulator. This program realistically simulates the flight characteristics of a small aircraft and includes a full set of instrumentation. What is really exciting about the program is its attention to the external factors—things like wind, weather, and time. The sophistication of this program is possible only because of the power of 16-bit processors.

Unfortunately, the development of new 16-bit software for the Personal Computer and its look-alikes is proceeding rather slowly. Only a handful of new programs take full advantage of the potential of 16-bit computers. In fact, the majority of software available for the Personal Computer has been converted from the 8-bit world. This group includes the popular programs VisiCalc, SuperCalc™, Word-Star™, and dBase II™.

This scarcity should change, however, as time passes. The longer the IBM Personal Computer is in the marketplace, the more new software will emerge to take full advantage of its power.

IBM-Compatible Computers

The popularity of IBM's Personal Computer has created a market for "IBM look-alike" computers. These personal computers, including the Compaq™ Portable computer and the Hyperion™, are riding the crest of two of the biggest waves in the microcomputer industry: portability and the IBM Personal Computer. Because IBM seems to be in no hurry to introduce a portable, these look-alikes should enjoy considerable success over the next few years.

Other IBM-compatible computers have been announced by both start-up and established firms in the industry. These computers fall into two classes. The first includes machines designed to emulate precisely the IBM Personal Computer. This group is best typified by the Columbia Data Systems computer. The Columbia claims to be completely compatible with the IBM Personal Computer, but also offers multiuser capabilities that the IBM Personal Computer does not have.

The other group is made up of machines that use the Intel 8088 processor and MS DOS, but which are not identical to the Personal Computer. This large family includes some of the biggest names in the computer world. Digital Equipment Corporation's Rainbow is one example. The Rainbow also offers the option of an 8-bit Z80 microprocessor, enabling the machine to use both 16-bit and 8-bit software. Other computers that fit into this category are the Wang™ Laboratories Professional™, the Vector Graphics™ System 4™, and the Zenith Data Systems Z-100™.

Even without IBM's name and marketing power, a number of these new look-alikes are finding a niche in the marketplace. Part of this success stems from demand from dealers who want to sell IBM Personal Computers but who are unable to achieve official dealer status because of IBM's selective dealer policies. These dealers are choosing IBM look-alikes as an alternative to the Personal Computer.

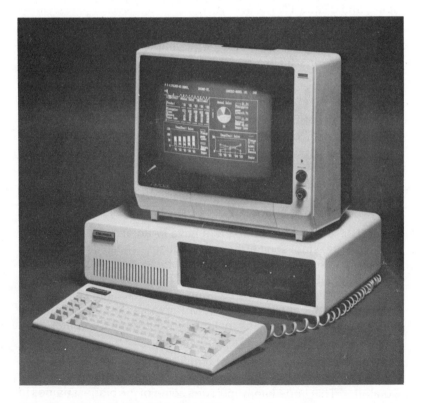

1.1   The Columbia Data Systems MPC

1.2   *The Texas Instruments Professional*

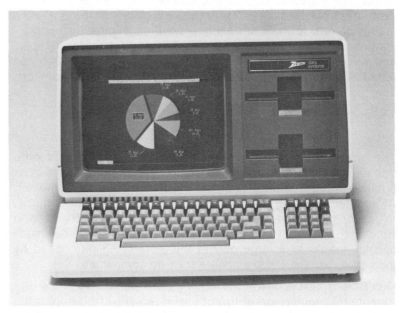

1.3   *The Zenith Data Systems Z-100*

The Competition Heats Up

The competition between the participants in the professional computer marketplace is starting to get "red hot." Although IBM commands more than 20 percent of the total personal computer market, the other participants are working hard to capture smaller but still significant shares. The recent introduction of the TI Professional at a price of $2,595 and the 15 percent price cuts announced by IBM in April, 1983, have set off a wave of price reductions throughout the marketplace. In April, 1983, alone, Apple lowered the price of the 128K Apple III by $500 to $2,495, and Wang dropped the price of the Professional by $100 to $2,595.

The net result of these price cuts is that it is now possible to purchase a personal computer with a video display, one disk drive, and 64K of memory for about $2,500. A fully equipped system with hard disk and expanded memory can be obtained for about $5,000.

Although a price war is unlikely in the professional computer marketplace, the trend is clearly toward lower prices and higher performance. This is especially true in the case of the look-alikes, which, unlike IBM Personal Computers, can be obtained at significant discounts from retail price. The pressure is clearly on the look-alike manufacturers to maintain a price advantage over the market-leading IBM Personal Computer. Thanks to its high volume of sales and the resulting production scale economies, IBM will probably be able to match price reductions made by any of its competitors, keeping the pressure on.

Publications

The growth of the IBM Personal Computer market has created opportunities for a third group of entrepreneurs: magazine and book publishers that produce products related to the Personal Computer. At least five monthly magazines address the Personal Computer: *PC, Personal Computer Age, PC World, Softalk for the IBM PC,* and *Reference.* Most of these publications have been extremely successful, thanks in a large part to the advertising purchased by third-party hardware and software start-up companies.

Que Corporation is one of the leading book publishers in the IBM Personal Computer market. In fact, the first edition of this book is the best-selling title about the Personal Computer. Que's *IBM PC*

Expansion & Software Guide is the leading reference guide to third-party hardware and software for the IBM Personal Computer.

The Personal Computer XT and DOS 2.0

In March of 1983, IBM introduced the first major revision of the basic IBM Personal Computer: the Personal Computer XT. Although both the inside and the outside of the XT look very much like the original Personal Computer, the XT represents a major step forward in the Personal Computer product line.

The XT incorporates several hardware changes. It includes eight expansion slots instead of the five in the Personal Computer. This means that the new machine has a much greater capacity for add-in boards than has the original Personal Computer. The extra expansion slots replace the cassette port, which has been dropped.

In addition, the XT is the first IBM product to use the new-generation 64K RAM chips. The XT supports 256K of memory on the motherboard of the computer. No expansion cards, therefore, are required to make the jump to 256K.

The last exciting feature of the XT is IBM's new Fixed Disk drive. This Winchester-type drive has a capacity of 10 megabytes, allowing the Personal Computer to perform easily tasks like accounting and data base management. The power requirements of the Fixed Disk have necessitated the addition of a new power supply on the XT.

Chapters 3 and 4 contain detailed descriptions of the Personal Computer XT and all the newly announced IBM peripheral hardware products.

Another important new product from IBM is DOS V2.0. Usable with any Personal Computer, DOS V2.0 contains special drivers for the XT's Fixed Disk that make it particularly suited to the XT.

Although DOS V2.0 is similar to the earlier versions of DOS, DOS V2.0 also differs from those versions in some important ways. For example, DOS V2.0 resembles the UNIX™ operating system, using a hierarchical file structure much like that used by UNIX. This allows groups of related files to be consolidated under subdirectories—a technique that is especially useful on hard disk systems where a simple directory yields a long list of file names.

DOS V2.0 includes other features that support the use of IBM's new Fixed Disk. For example, the new DOS contains BACKUP and RESTORE commands that facilitate the backup of massive hard disk files. DOS V2.0 also includes installable device drivers that allow hard disks and other peripherals made by third parties to be used with the Personal Computer. DOS V2.0 has a treat for floppy disk users as well. The new system allows the IBM Personal Computer disk drives to store 360K of information on each disk, instead of the 320K maximum under DOS V1.1.

IBM claims that the majority of programs written for DOS V1.1 will run under DOS V2.0 without difficulty. Some programs may have trouble, however. Users will find that although DOS V2.0 is familiar (it contains all of the commands found in DOS V1.1), some time will be required to learn all of the new, advanced features.

DOS V2.0 represents an evolutionary step in PC DOS toward the UNIX operating system. This step is a significant one in the development of PC DOS. (Chapter 4 has a thorough discussion of DOS V2.0.)

A Look at the Future

What does the future hold for the IBM Personal Computer? One thing seems almost certain—that IBM will continue to increase its share of the market. Associated with this increase will be a growth in the number of firms that produce hardware and software expansion devices for the IBM Personal Computer. IBM has set a course that could make it the dominant force in the personal computer industry.

New Computers

Amazingly, IBM has achieved its strong market position by selling a single, business-oriented computer. To date, Big Blue has ignored large segments of the marketplace, including the lucrative home and portable markets.

IBM may introduce a home computer costing less than $1,000 in the near future. In fact, rumors about a new computer from IBM, code-named Popcorn, have already appeared in prestigious magazines and newspapers like *The Wall Street Journal*. Because IBM keeps corporate secrets well, no one outside the company knows exactly what the "Popcorn" computer will look like.

Entering the under-$1,000 home computer marketplace would require yet another change of direction for IBM. The home computer marketplace is even further from IBM's traditional area of expertise than the business market of the original Personal Computer. This time around, however, no one is underestimating the power of IBM. The companies that now control the home computer marketplace—Commodore, Apple, Texas Instruments, and Radio Shack—are preparing themselves for the arrival of IBM.

Some industry observers think that IBM will wait to make the move into this market. They note sales statisics which show that about 30 percent of all Personal Computers are being sold primarily for home use. These observers point out that IBM already holds a significant share of the home market even without a home computer.

IBM may also develop its own portable version of the Personal Computer. The success of Bytec's Hyperion and the Compaq portable have proven that there is real demand for portable machines. A portable version of the IBM Personal Computer would be a good complement to the original Personal Computer and the Personal Computer XT.

IBM Software

Some industry experts are predicting that IBM will soon introduce its own line of applications software for the Personal Computer. Because the personal computer market is so large and growing so rapidly, the market for Personal Computer software is extremely attractive. IBM certainly has the resources to gain a significant share of this market. Although the terms of IBM's license agreement with its major software suppliers are not public knowledge, there is little doubt that it costs IBM a good deal in royalty expenses to sell some of these products. In-house development would help reduce that cost.

On the other hand, IBM has benefited tremendously by selecting outside software for the Personal Computer. IBM may decide that it is in its interest to continue to select the best outside software for the Personal Computer, rather than to develop new products in house.

The Best Is Yet to Come

Navy Captain Grace Hopper, the original author of COBOL and one of the pioneers of computing, claims that the current state of the art in computing is comparable to the position of the Ford Model T in automobiles. If this comparison is true, just think of the exciting developments the future of computing holds.

IBM has been the market leader in the computer industry since the beginning. In all likelihood, IBM will be the leader in the future as well. The creation and nurturing of the IBM Personal Computer has shown that IBM has the resources, the skill, and the flexibility to grow and change with the market.

The Personal Computer and its descendants will continue to serve important roles in future computing. This and later editions of *IBM's Personal Computer* will help you stay informed as the market and the Personal Computer change.

CHAPTER 2

The System Unit, the Expansion Unit, and the Keyboard

The IBM Personal Computers (nicknamed the PC and the PC XT) are remarkable achievements, incorporating the latest technology in a microcomputer system that is a blend of simple mechanical design and technical complexity. The outward appearance of both machines is sleek and futuristic, and the construction is simplicity itself. With only a screwdriver, a person can dismantle the Personal Computers or the Expansion Unit. But once open to close scrutiny, the Personal Computers are found to be highly complex machines, whose circuitry not only contains both past and recent semiconductor developments, but also provides for future developments.

This chapter covers the System Unit and the Keyboard Unit, the two essential hardware components of the Personal Computer. Included in this discussion is the Expansion Unit, whose characteristics are similar to the System Unit. No attempt is made to describe the electronic circuitry of these three major pieces of hardware. The focus, instead, is on their use and potential.

Since the first edition of this book, IBM has introduced both an updated version of the original Personal Computer and the Personal Computer XT. Throughout this second edition, the terms *original* Personal Computer, *current* Personal Computer, and Personal Computer *XT* are used to distinguish a particular version from the other two.

The term *Personal Computer* is used whenever information applies to either the original version or the current version. If the discussion pertains to all three versions of the machine, the terms *Personal Computers* or *Personal Computer systems* are used.

Pictured (from top to bottom) are the IBM Color Display, the Personal Computer System Unit, the Expansion Unit, and the Keyboard Unit.

In any discussion of hardware, the reader should not lose sight of the importance of software. Fundamentally, a computer system consists of both hardware and software. Together, they form a unified computing system to do a set of tasks. By itself, computer hardware is useless.

Hardware and software are intimately related. Occasionally, this intimacy makes it difficult to determine whether praise (or blame) should be directed to a system's hardware or software. This problem is especially a possibility for the Personal Computer systems when their operating systems, particularly PC DOS and its BASIC language, are tailored especially for the Personal Computers. The intimate bond between hardware and software can be seen further when certain features of the hardware, such as the Keyboard Unit, are dependent on the operating system or other software that is used. If this close bond is kept in mind throughout the following discussion, the importance of the hardware will be kept in perspective.

The Personal Computer Systems

Two components are essential to all of the Personal Computers: the System Unit and the Keyboard Unit. These two pieces give the Personal Computer systems their unique character and identity. The major peripherals are optional: a video display, or displays; and a printer. Other components extend the capabilities of the computer: memory boards, display and printer adapters, disk drives and adapters, communications adapters, and more. Most of this equipment is optional.

The Personal Computer XT is different because it has a double-sided, double-density floppy disk drive; a 10 megabyte (million byte) hard disk; adapters for both disk units; and the Asynchronous Communications Adapter as standard equipment.

The overall styling of the Personal Computers is streamlined. Each device has rounded corners and a sleek, low profile. All major units of the system—the System Unit, Keyboard Unit, Expansion Chassis, IBM displays, and printers—are colored two-tone buff.

The Personal Computer, including two floppy disk drives and either IBM printer, weighs 66 lbs. (29.7 kgs.), putting it in the middle-weight class. The heaviest piece is the two-drive System Unit, weighing 29 lbs. (13 kgs.). Although many other "appliance" computers are lighter, the Personal Computer can be transported easily in several trips. Luggage manufacturers have responded to the Personal Com-

Pictured are the System Units for the Personal Computer (above) and the Personal Computer XT (below). The right-hand drive in the XT unit is the 10M IBM Fixed Disk.

puters by offering carrying cases for each major component, making the Personal Computers even more transportable.

The Personal Computer XT, including its floppy and hard disk drives and IBM printer, weights only 3 lbs. more than the Personal Computer, for a total weight of 69 lbs. (31.2 kgs.).

The System Unit at a Glance

Purpose: To house the Personal Computers' major com-
                            ponentry

Dimensions: 5.5 in.   (142mm) height
                            19.6 in. (500 mm) length
                            16.1 in. (410 mm) depth

Weight:

  Personal Computer   21 lbs   (9.5 kg) without disk drives
                            29 lbs   (13 kg) with two mini-floppy drives

  Personal Computer XT   32 lbs   (14.5 kg) with mini-floppy & hard disk
                                     drive

Power Cable   6 ft.   (1.83 m) length

Contents:

  Personal Computer   1. System Board w/5 expansion slots
                            2. Cassette and keyboard jacks
                            3. Up to 2 mini-floppy disk drives w/adapter
                               (optional)
                            4. 63.5 watt power supply with cooling fan
                            5. Audio speaker

  Personal Computer XT   1. System board w/8 expansion slots
                            2. Keyboard jack
                            3. 1 mini-floppy drive and 1 hard disk
                               w/adapters
                            4. 130-watt power supply with cooling fan
                            5. Audio speaker
                            6. Asynchronous Communications Adapter

With light and modular construction, the Personal Computers, excluding a printer, individually fit well on a small desk. If the display is placed on top of the System Unit, the Personal Computer and Keyboard Unit occupy 480 square inches (1219.2 cm.2) of table space—roughly 3 and 1/3 square feet. An IBM printer takes up 176.4 square inches (448 cm.2), or just under 1 and 1/5 square feet. Most small desks have enough surface area for all three units, but some users may find this arrangement cramped.

The Personal Computers represent a serious effort to relate high technology to human physiology. The technical term for this relationship is *ergonomics,* a field of biotechnology in which biological constraints are addressed by engineering principles in the design of a machine. The term was coined in the aerospace industry by engineers designing fighter plane cockpits. In 1957, the Museum of Science and Industry in Chicago featured an exhibit that showed how machinery could be designed to accommodate the limitations of the human body. Although the term is not new, practical applications of ergonomics for the sake of comfort and ease of use are still relatively rare. IBM, whose Displaywriter and other systems are used throughout the world daily, took these concerns seriously in designing the Personal Computers.

The System Unit and the Keyboard Unit, which are the essential parts of the computer system, are the center of attention in this chapter. Also examined is the Expansion Unit, whose physical characteristics closely resemble those of the System Unit.

The System Unit

Every Personal Computer system, including the XT, has a System Unit, which is "the computer itself." The System Unit houses the System Board, which contains the microprocessor (the "brain"of the computer system); the ROM (read-only memory), or permanent memory; the RAM (random-access memory), which is both user memory and that reserved for certain adapters; 5 or 8 expansion slots, depending on the model of the computer; 2 bays for 5 1/4-inch disk drives (floppy or hard disk); the power supply; the audio speaker; and various connectors and ports.

In the System Unit and its contents are found the following five principal differences between the the Personal Computer and the Personal Computer XT:

- The ROM BIOS (RIOS)
- The expansion slots
- The power supply
- The standard disk storage
- The standard RAM memory and provisions for additional RAM

The interiors of the Personal Computer (above) and the Personal Computer XT (below). The front of the units face the bottom of the picture.

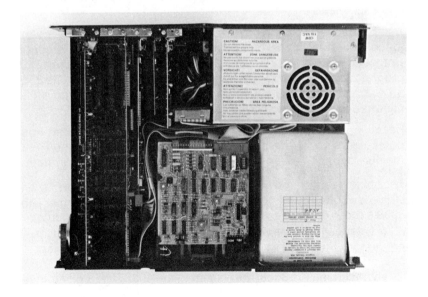

Also, a change has been made in the RAM memory of the current Personal Computer. How this RAM memory compares with that of the original version is discussed later in this chapter.

Two key parts of the System Unit remain the same for all Personal Computers: the CPU and the 8087 coprocessor.

The CPU

At the heart of every computer system is a central processing unit, abbreviated as CPU. Like the human brain, which regulates and controls the operations of the human body, the CPU regulates and controls the functions of every other part of the computer. In large computer systems, the CPU and the *ALU* (arithmetic logic unit) are usually a group of integrated circuits (chips) that accomplish one function. However, in small computers, the two units are combined in a single chip, a microprocessor.

In discussions of small computer systems, the terms *CPU* and *microprocessor* are often used interchangeably. This practice, however, is not always correct. A CPU is a microprocessor, but a microprocessor is not necessarily a CPU. Only one microprocessor, the CPU, has the responsibility of controlling the computer system. Any other microprocessors in the system control specific functions and equipment.

Another microprocessor, however, can take control of the computer for certain applications. For example, this happens in the Personal Computer systems if a Z80 CPU expansion board is used. When Z80 programs are run, the Z80 assumes control of the system. The Z80 *acts* as a second CPU, but for the sake of technical accuracy, this microprocessor should not be called the *CPU*.

Because of its role, the CPU is the most important element in a computer system. The power of the CPU, coupled with the RAM memory capacity, determines the computing power of the system.

The microprocessor used in the IBM Personal Computers is an 8088, developed by Intel™ Corporation of Sunnyvale, California. The 8088's roots go back to the early 1970s to Intel's 4004 calculator chip. Later generations were the 8008, 8080, 8085, and 8086 micro-processors. Further developments led to the iAPX family of micropro-cessors (the iAPX 86, 88, 186, 188, 286, and 386). All of the iAPX family, including the 8088, are related to the 8086. The significance

---

The Numeric Coprocessor at a Glance

Name: 8088

Construction: 40-pin plastic package; chip uses HMOS technology

Purpose: To supervise and control the computer system

Primary manufacturer: Intel Corporation

Date of introduction: 1979

Characteristics:
1. 4.77 Mhz system clock speed
2. 20 addressing lines — 1M memory addressing
3. 8 data lines
4. Separate Bus Interface and Execution Units
5. Software compatible with Intel 8086 CPU
6. Multiple levels of interrupts
7. 99 basic machine-language instructions
8. 650,000 operations per second, average (0.65 MPS)

---

of the 8086 and its relationship to Intel's other products requires a brief technical explanation.

Microcomputers "think" in binary digits, the basic building block of information in a computer. A *bit* is common computerese shorthand for *binary digit*. The most frequent grouping of bits is 8, which is the number of bits needed to express a *byte,* or one character. Many of a computer's internal processes work in pairs of bytes. The most frequent pairing is 2 bytes, or 16 bits.

Most 8-bit microprocessors (which include Intel's 8080 and 8085, Zilog's Z80, Motorola's 6800 and 6809, and MOS Technology's 6502) work directly with a maximum of 65,536 (64K) bytes of memory at one time. Although this number may seem large, a 25-page document or large accounting spreadsheet can quickly fill this memory space.

Most 16-bit microprocessors can *address* (directly access) from 262,144 (256K) to 16 million bytes of memory and share the work of addressing memory and executing programs between two internally separate units. These microprocessors can work at rates that are 2 to 15 times faster than their 8-bit counterparts. Some 8-bit microprocessors can work with more than 64K, but additional external circuitry is needed, and such arrangements generally do not have the speed of a 16-bit configuration.

The 16-bit 8088 is similar to the 8086 microprocessor. Both units have 20 separate pathways, called *addressing lines,* and can directly address up to 2^{20} (1,048,576) memory locations, or 1 megabyte, abbreviated as *M* or *MB.*

The major difference between the 8086 and the 8088 is the number of separate pathways, or *data lines*, that are devoted to transferring information to and from the CPU. One bit of information can be transferred along one data line. The 8086 contains 16 data lines and can transfer two consecutive bytes (16 bits) of information at one time. The 8-bit microprocessor has only 8 data lines and can store (place in memory) or fetch (retrieve from memory) only 1 byte (8 bits from the 8 data lines) at a time. This is one of the reasons why a 16-bit microprocessor can do more "work" than an 8-bit microprocessor during a given period of time.

The 8088 is a hybrid microprocessor. While still containing the 20 addressing lines of its "big brother" (the 8086), the 8088 CPU has only 8 data lines and transfers information between itself and the computer system 1 byte (8 bits) at a time.

The difference between the 8088 CPU and most 8-bit microprocessors is the use of separate units within the CPU to transfer and work on information. For example, the 8088, like the 8086, but unlike most 8-bit CPUs, incorporates a *Bus Interface Unit* for transferring information to and from the CPU. Another unit, called the *Execution Unit,* keeps track of the instructions the CPU executes. When an 8086 needs two bytes of information, the Bus Interface Unit handles the transfer of the two bytes. However, the 8088's Bus Interface Unit, which is slightly different from the 8086's, works harder by fetching two consecutive memory locations, one byte after the other, to provide the necessary information. After the two bytes are fetched,

A close-up of the 8088 CPU chip. (Photo courtesy of Intel Corporation.)

the Execution Unit "sees" one group of 16-bits, but is "ignorant" of the extra work performed by the Bus Interface Unit.

Another difference between the 8088 and 8086 CPUs is in performance speed. The 8088 is inherently slower than the 8086. Memory transfers in the 8088 are always 8-bit versus the frequent 16-bit transfers in the 8086. However, the average speed of the 8088 in the IBM Personal Computers is approximately 0.65 mps (million operations per second). This rate translates to about 650,000 data transfers, additions, subtractions, or other operations each second. The 8088 in the Personal Computers operates at a top speed that is six times faster than a comparable computer system using the Intel

Interrupt Vector Listing

Interrupt Number		Name	BIOS Initialization
0		Divide by Zero	None
1		Single Step	None
2		Non Maskable	NMI_INT (F000:E2C3)
3		Breakpoint	None
4		Overflow	None
5		Print Screen	PRINT_SCREEN (F000:FF54)
6		Unused	
7		Unused	
8		Time of Day	TIMER_INT (F000:FEA5)
9		Keyboard	KB_INT (F000:E987)
A		Unused	
B	8259	Unused	
C	Interrupt	Unused (Reserved Communications)	
D	Vectors	Unused	
E		Diskette	DISK_INT (F000:EF57)
F		Unused (Reserved Printer)	
10		Video	VIDEO_I O (F000:F065)
11		Equipment Check	EQUIPMENT (F000:F84D)
12		Memory	MEMORY_SIZE_DETERMINE (F000:F841)
13		Diskette	DISKETTE_I O (F000:EC59)
14	BIOS	Communications	RS232_I O (F000:E739)
15	Entry	Cassette	CASSETTE_I O (F000:F859)
16	Points	Keyboard	KEYBOARD_I O (F000:E82E)
17		Printer	PRINTER_I O (F000:EF02)
18		Cassette BASIC	(F600:0000)
19		Bootstrap	BOOT_STRAP (F000:E6F2)
1A		Time of Day	TIME_OF_DAY (F000:FE6E)
1B	User Supplied	Keyboard Break	DUMMY_RETURN (F000:FF53)
1C	Routines	Timer Tick	DUMMY_RETURN (F000:FF53)
1D	BIOS	Video Initialization	VIDEO_PARMS (F000:F0A4)
1E	Parameters	Diskette Parameters	DISK_BASE (F000:EFC7)
1F		Video Graphics Chars	None

Interrupt Vector Listing for the ROM BIOS from the Technical Reference Manual. *The various functions that the ROM BIOS handle are listed in the Name column. (Reprinted with permission from International Business Machines Corporation.)*

8080A microprocessor, one of the more popular microprocessors to date. In most cases, the user should find the speed of the Personal Computers more than sufficient.

IBM's Personal Computers directly attribute most of their unusual power to the use of the 8088 rather than an 8-bit CPU. The operating systems, the programming languages, and applications programs (covered in chapters 4 through 6) are greatly aided by the use of the 16-bit 8088 CPU.

The 8086 and 8088 microprocessors are worthy of praise, but some caution is appropriate concerning immediate and future applications. When the Personal Computer was first announced in 1981, most software was based on the 8080 8-bit CPU. This situation gave the owner of a microcomputer using 8080, 8085, or Z80 CPUs a wide range of software to fit many needs. However, neither the 8088 nor the 8086 can use directly most of this software! The native languages (machine languages) of the 8080 family and the Zilog Z80 family are different from the native language of the 8086/8088 CPU family. Even more incompatibility exists between the 8086 family and the 6800 and 6502 families of CPUs.

Most of the high-speed applications software, such as word processing, planning tools, and entertainment programs, are written in the native language of the CPU. Programs written in the native language for an 8-bit microprocessor must be converted to run on a 16-bit microprocessor. The subject of software compatibility is covered more fully in chapters 4 and 5.

The outlook regarding software for the Personal Computer is very bright. In the first year after the introduction of the Personal Computer, fewer than 100 different programs were available. Currently, 1,400 programs are available for the Personal Computers, and this number is growing at an astounding rate. Still, a potential buyer of software should determine whether a prospective program is compatible with the Personal Computer before purchasing the software.

An Empty Socket

The IBM System Board (discussed later) contains a 40-pin socket labeled "Aux Processor Socket" in the *Technical Reference* manual. The circuit lines to this socket are for the Intel 8087 math coprocessor. The significance of the math coprocessor becomes evident in a brief discussion of the inner functions of a CPU in a computer system.

A common assumption is that computers do mathematical tasks with lightning speed. *Number crunching* is the term frequently used for such tasks. In reality, computers perform mathematical functions slowly, compared to most other memory-based or CPU-based operations. A microprocessor can perform thousands of mathematical operations in one second, but only one or two bytes at a time. This restriction retards math performance.

Both 8- and 16-bit microprocessors readily add and subtract two-integer numbers. In math, an integer is any whole number—that is, any number without a decimal fraction. For computers, an integer is a whole number usually in the range from -32,768 to +32,767. Computers impose this restriction because the numbers in this range can be held in 2 bytes (16 bits) of memory, a natural number of bytes for the CPU. Since a 16-bit microprocessor has direct instructions to multiply and divide integer numbers, it can perform better than an 8-bit microprocessor.

Noninteger numbers slow down a microprocessor's calculation speed. A noninteger number is a real number outside the restricted range of integers, any number with a decimal fraction, or a number in scientific notation. Numbers such as 12.2, 3.1415, 1,024,567.68, and $6.23*10^{23}$ belong to the set of real numbers.

Most CPUs have no built-in instructions for handling real numbers. The CPU must be programmed to perform mathematical operations on these numbers, which individually occupy five to nine bytes of memory versus two bytes used by an integer number. Because the CPU must juggle more bytes of information for real numbers, they require extensive electronic manipulation. Integer numbers, stored in just two bytes, are directly manipulated, making integer number operations 10 to 100 times faster than real number operations.

Many programs, if written in high-level languages like BASIC or Pascal, need much time to manipulate the many bytes that represent real numbers. Most programs use real numbers, and a CPU must perform many instructions to add just two real numbers. When programs involve a significant amount of numbers, such as accounting, spreadsheet, scientific, or engineering software, there are noticeable delays while the computer calculates.

The Coprocessor

Minicomputers and mainframes suffer from numeric "stiffness," but on a different scale. To combat slow operation, many minicomputers and mainframes incorporate a *math processor* or *floating-point coprocessor*. This device has the circuitry to perform arithmetic functions internally rather than follow an external set of instructions. Math processors can "outcalculate" their associated CPUs by as much as 100 to 1. Because math processors are faster, their principal use in mainframes and minicomputers is to do a computer's main task: "crunch" numbers swiftly.

The 8087 Numeric Data Processor is the math processor for the 8086 family of CPUs, including the Personal Computers' 8088 CPU. Like their mainframe and minicomputer counterparts, these processor chips outperform their associated CPUs significantly.

The Coprocessor at a Glance

Name:	8087 Numeric Data Processor
Purpose:	To provide high-speed numeric operations in a hardware chip
Primary manufacturer:	Intel Corporation
Date of announcement:	1980
Characteristics:	1. Functions with the Intel 8086/8088 microprocessors
	2. Conforms to IEEE standards
	3. Performs operations on numbers that are 18 digits (integers) long and floating point numbers 16 to 80 bits wide
	4. Handles data transfer between processors
	5. Has built-in math instructions for add, subtract, multiply, divide, square root, absolute value, tangent, arctangent, and others
	6. Operates 15 to 100 times faster than 8086/8088 microprocessors performing similar instructions

The 8087 is often called a *numeric coprocessor*, or simply an *8087 coprocessor*. It has been constructed specifically for high-speed manipulation of numbers. Although the 8087 is a microprocessor, it is not the central processor of the computer system. This responsibility belongs to the 8088 CPU. However, the 8087 works with either the 8088 or the 8086. If there is proper software and a hardware switch has been activated, the 8088 of the Personal Computers transfers the number-crunching tasks to the 8087 and waits for the results. When they are returned by the 8087, the 8088 resumes its tasks. The 8087 is truly a *co*-processor; it does not control the computer system, but works with the CPU by doing numeric tasks.

The 8087 is another example of a point made earlier—that not all microprocessors are CPUs. Also, the 8087 demonstrates a trend in the computer industry: the use of "dedicated" microprocessors that work with a CPU to increase the speed of overall operation.

According to its specifications, the 8087 can outperform the 8088 by 100 to 1. The actual increase in speed varies according to the type of operation. An average improvement in speed of 25 to 1 is almost assured. This increase in "throughput" with the Personal Computers is dramatic.

Installing an 8087 coprocessor is simple. After the unit is turned off and the cover of the System Unit is removed, the chip is placed into the Aux Processor Socket to the right of the 8088 CPU on the System Board. For the Personal Computer, the second switch on the System Board's Switch Bank 1 is then turned off. For the Personal Computer *XT*, which has only one bank of System Board switches, switch 2 is turned off. After the cover is replaced, the 8087 is ready for use.

What software can take advantage of the 8087's capabilities is a different matter. Neither the 8086 nor the 8088 CPU uses the 8087 coprocessor automatically. A special set of machine-language instructions are used for the 8087 coprocessor. Most programs are "unaware" of the 8087 and will instruct the CPU rather than the coprocessor to compute numbers. Few operating systems, programming languages, applications programs, or other software immediately recognize and use the 8087 coprocessor.

There are exceptions, however. Some programming languages provide either separate subroutines or the ability to "search" for the coprocessor and use its features. (This subject is discussed further in chapter 5.)

Use of the 8087 numeric coprocessor may have some disadvantages. It draws 0.457 milliamps of current, which is almost one-eighth of the power supplied to the System Board in the Personal Computer. The maximum heat dissipation of the 8087 is three watts. By itself, the 8087 presents no difficulty, but in a system with many expansion cards, the 8087 can create two related problems: excessive power consumption and insufficient heat dissipation.

The power supply of the Personal Computer generates 67.5 watts, and the Personal Computer XT's power supply yields 130 watts. Depending on the number and kind of expansion cards that are used in the computer, owners may find the power supply inadequate should the 8087 coprocessor be used. This possibility is true more for the Personal Computer than for the XT because of the latter's greater power capacity. Some signs of trouble would be periodic lockup of the computer for no apparent reason, failure of the Personal Computer to complete its power-on test, a malfunction of the RAM memory, unreliable disk drive operations (particularly when writing information to the disk), or eventual burnout of the power supply. However, the use of most combinations of expansion boards with the 8087 coprocessor should *not* overtax the power supply.

Heat dissipation is the greater problem. The three-watt maximum rating of the 8087 can raise the temperature inside the System Unit by several degrees. The fan in the Personal Computer's power supply provides adequate air circulation if the expansion boards used do not generate much heat. Certain combinations of expansion boards with the coprocessor can raise the temperature inside the Personal Computer beyond a safe level. Unfortunately, experimentation by the owner will be necessary to determine if the 8087 will cause a thermal problem.

Summing up CPUs

Much of the IBM Personal Computers' performance advantage over other microcomputer systems results from the use of the 8088, 16-bit microprocessor.

With the 8088's large user-memory range (up to 1M) and processing speeds that are faster than most 8-bit microcomputer systems, the Personal Computers are very powerful machines for their size. With memory expansion and the use of the 8087 math coprocessor, the Personal Computers are capable of outstanding performance.

The System Board

The System Board, which is commonly called the *motherboard*, is the main circuit board of a microcomputer. Some computers use a motherboard that is simply a series of parallel lines for carrying electrical signals to and from various parts of the computer. Other microcomputer manufacturers place most of the computer's circuitry on the motherboard. The System Board of the Personal Computers uses this approach. When the motherboard holds most of the circuitry, the design of the computer can be compact.

The System Board of the Personal Computer is different from that of the Personal Computer XT. There are also differences between the original Personal Computer's System Board and the current version's. Each of these differences will be highlighted during the discussion of each major component.

The ROM

ROM, an abbreviation for read-only memory, is a type of preprogrammed memory that contains one or more programs vital to the computer's use. Often called *firmware* (software permanently housed in hardware), the contents of ROM remain when the power is removed, unlike most RAM (random-access memory), which loses its information with the loss of power. All computers use ROM memory to hold certain start-up programs, such as a routine that starts the disk drives, loads the operating system into memory, and transfers control to the now-loaded operating system. This routine is called a bootstrap program.

The Personal Computer's System Board has sockets for six 8K ROM chips. One ROM holds the RIOS (a contraction of ROM BIOS, which is discussed below). Four other ROMs hold the Cassette BASIC language interpreter. The sixth socket is not used. Originally, it was provided for expansion purposes.

(Actually, the sixth ROM socket was intended as a fifth socket for the Cassette BASIC language interpreter. When IBM asked Microsoft™, the author of IBM's BASIC, about the space requirement for Cassette BASIC, the reply was 32K. Assuming that additional space might be needed, IBM provided the sixth ROM socket. Microsoft's estimate was accurate, and the sixth socket has proved to be unnecessary.)

The Personal Computer XT has only two sockets for the ROM, and both are occupied. The RIOS is housed in an 8K ROM chip. The Cassette BASIC interpreter is held in a single 32K chip, even though the XT does not have a cassette port. The reason is explained later in chapter 5 on languages.

The ROM in all Personal Computers currently contains two major programs: a set of subprograms called the RIOS, and the Cassette BASIC interpreter.

Key to System Board

1. **Expansion slots**
2. ***Cassette connector**
3. **Keyboard connector**
4. **8088 CPU**
5. **Numeric coprocessor socket**
6. **Power connector**
7. ***DIP switch(es)**
8. **ROM BIOS (RIOS)**
9. ***Cassette BASIC ROM(s)**
10. ***RAM**
11. **Speaker connection**

*Denotes differences between Personal Computer and Personal Computer XT

A close-up of the System Boards for the original Personal Computer (left page) and the Personal Computer XT (right page). See previous page for the key.

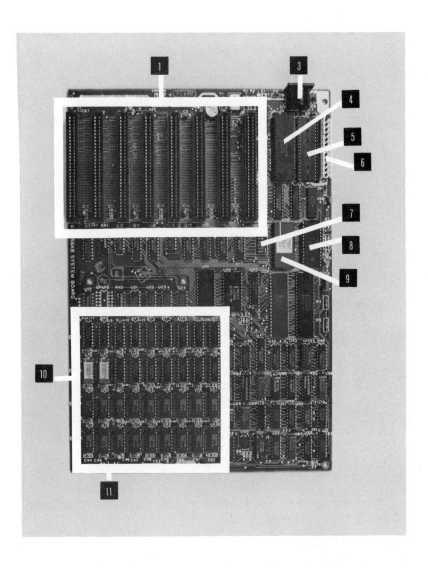

The System Board at a Glance

Purpose:	To house the microprocessor and coprocessor, ROM and RAM memory, DMA (direct memory access) circuitry, expansion slots, keyboard and cassette[1] interface, speaker, timing, and support circuitry.
Dimensions (approx.)	8½ in. (216 mm) width 11 in. (279 mm) length ⅛ in. (4 mm) depth

Functional sections:

1. Processor subsystem (8088 CPU/8087 Coprocessor and support chips)
2. ROM memory subsystem
3. RAM memory subsystem
4. I/O Channels (expansion slots)
5. Integrated I/O channels (speaker, keyboard, and cassette[1])

Differences between models:
Old PC vs. new PC[2]

1. 64K versus 256K maximum RAM on-board
2. New RIOS

PC vs PC XT[3]

1. 64K versus 128K RAM standard
2. 4 versus 1 ROM for Cassette BASIC
3. 5 versus 8 I/O Channels (expansion slots)
4. No cassette circuitry on XT

Notes:

[1] not available on XT
[2] new PC is Personal Computer manufactured after January, 1983
[3] comparison is between new PCs and XT (see note 2)

The RIOS

As indicated earlier, the term RIOS (pronounced RYE-ose) is an abbreviation of ROM BIOS. BIOS is an acronym for Basic Input/ Output System, a collection of programs that control the handling of characters between the microprocessor and other devices of the computer system (the keyboard, the video display, the printer, etc.). The word "basic" in BIOS should not be confused with the BASIC programming language, but means merely "fundamental."

The ROM at a Glance

Purpose: To permanently hold system programs

Primary manufacturer   Motorola
of chip:

Total system capacity: 256K

Current Use:

  Personal Computer   48K space on System Board
                            8K (one 8Kbit by 8-bit ROM) for RIOS
                         32K (four 8Kbit by 8-bit ROMs) for Cassette
                                BASIC. One empty socket for 8K expan-
                                sion ROM
               208K additional available through expansion
                                slots

  Personal Computer XT   40K on System Board
                            8K (one 8Kbit by 8-bit ROM) for RIOS
                         32K (one 32Kbit by 8-bit ROM) for Cassette
                                BASIC
               216K additional available through expansion
                                slots

  Programs in ROM: 1. RIOS (ROM BIOS or ROMed Basic In-
                             put/Output System)
                       2. Cassette BASIC Interpreter

There are two different sets of RIOS for the Personal Computer. Any Personal Computer purchased before January, 1983, uses one set. All other Personal Computer systems, including the XT, have the current version. The principal differences of the latter version are recognition of the IBM Fixed Disk, the Expansion Unit, and up to 640K of RAM memory.

The older RIOS for the Personal Computer is "ignorant" of the Fixed Disk and the Expansion Unit. The new RIOS contains a set of low-level subroutines for handling the Fixed Disk and the Expansion Unit. Also, the new RIOS allows the Personal Computer to recognize and use up to the full 640K of RAM memory. Previously, only 544K were usable.

The RIOS at a Glance

Purpose: To control the exchange of information between the CPU and peripherals

Author: IBM

Location: 8K ROM on System Board

Current programs:
Personal Computer[1]   1. Cassette operating system
                                 2. Power-up self-test
                                 3. Fundamental I/O routines for video display (monochrome and color), keyboard, printer, mini-floppy, and asynchronous communication adapters
                                 4. Graphic characters generator
                                 5. System configuration analysis (for memory size and peripherals)
                                 6. Time-of-day clock
                                 7. Print-screen routine
                                 8. Mini-floppy diskette bootstrap loader

Changes for Personal   1. Deletion of cassette I/O system
Computer[2] and XT   2. Change in system configuration analysis (recognition of hard disk and up to 640K RAM).
                                 3. Addition of fundamental routines for hard disk
                                 4. Addition of hard disk bootstrap loader

Notes: [1] Personal Computer manufactured before January, 1983.
                                 [2] Personal Computer manufactured after January, 1983 or updated Personal Computer with Expansion Unit.

Having the BIOS in ROM is a mixed blessing. After the Personal Computers are turned on, their complete RIOS gives them many more capabilities than other systems have without such a RIOS. However, a "ROMed"BIOS is less able to use new devices. Although provisions were made for adding new devices to the Personal Computers without changing the chip, a ROM change became necessary for the Fixed Disk and additional RAM memory.

A change in the RIOS requires a simple substitution of one ROM chip. Personal Computer owners who have a unit manufactured before January, 1983, must receive a ROM update before using the Expansion Unit, Fixed Disk, or more than 544K of RAM memory. This ROM update is provided with the Expansion Unit.

The Personal Computers' reserved ROM space of 192K allows boards to be placed in the expansion slots for additional intelligence. Adapter boards for peripherals can be intelligent, containing in ROM chips on the expansion board almost all the programming that is necessary for the peripherals' use. The software for complete application programs can be housed in ROMs, placed on a board, and mounted in an expansion slot. This kind of software, however, is quite fixed and hard to modify, so it is not used frequently.

Part of the RIOS conducts a self-test that lasts from 5 to 120 seconds. The length of the test is influenced somewhat by the number of peripherals in the system, but mainly by the amount of RAM memory. This test is made each time the system is turned on. A code number on the video screen reports any malfunction or major component (such as the keyboard) that is not connected. Provided that the malfunctioning or unconnected component is not the video display itself or its adapter, this code can help a repairperson or system owner to detect where a fault lies. The self-test also assures the user that the system is functioning properly after it is switched on.

The RIOS handles the characters on the screen; allows the keyboard a wide range of "editing" capabilities; and controls the time-of-day clock, the print screen function and printer, the start-up of the disk drive, and several other peripherals.

Technically, the RIOS contains the fundamental routines for using the following hardware:

    An Asynchronous (RS-232) Communications Adapter
    The Keyboard Unit
    The display
    A printer
    A graphics character generator
    Mini-floppy disk drives
    A hard disk drive

Also, the RIOS performs the following housekeeping functions:

    Determines the IBM (or IBM-like) options in the system

    Determines the amount of RAM memory in the system

Handles the day-of-year, time-of-day software clock

Handles the print screen function

Performs the power-on self-test

Boots the operating system from the mini-floppy or hard disk

Placing these programs of the BIOS into ROM is not a new concept. Before the Personal Computer was introduced, several microcomputer manufacturers needed to limit the size of these programs because of price considerations and the limited memory addressing (64K) of 8-bit microprocessors. Drastically lower prices for ROM memory chips have made it economical to use 8K ROMs in the Personal Computer and now the 32K ROM for Cassette BASIC in the Personal Computer XT. The Personal Computers' 1M memory addressing makes the devotion of 256K of memory space to ROM chips a trivial matter.

A final note about the 256K ROM space is in order. This space is not exclusively for ROM. For example, the Fixed Disk adapter uses some of the reserved ROM space for communicating to the system. Manufacturers should be cautious when constructing boards in this manner because conflicts among boards for memory addressing space can occur.

Those interested in additional information about the RIOS should purchase the *Technical Reference* manual. There are separate manuals for the Personal Computer and the Personal Computer XT. Either manual gives the complete assembly language listing of the appropriate RIOS, in addition to other useful aspects of the computer's hardware.

The RAM

A major misnomer in computer circles is RAM, the acronym for random-access memory. Almost all memory is randomly accessible, including ROM memory. IBM justifiably calls most RAM memory "user memory"; but, in a sense, RAM memory is better called "reusable" memory.

If a CPU is thought of as a person, RAM memory is like a blackboard, on which information can be placed temporarily and easily erased to clear the way for new information. In every computer system the RAM memory is a temporary, highly accessible, high-speed work

The RAM at a Glance

Purpose: To hold temporarily program and data informa-
                                  tion and to act as work space for the CPU.

Contents: 1. Sockets for four rows of nine chips
                                  2. 16K or 64K Dynamic RAMs
                                  3. Support circuitry for RAM

Capacity of System
Board:

  Older Personal
  Computer[1]

    Device used: 4116-type 16K bit by 1-bit Dynamic RAM[1]
                                  16K available per row
                                  250 ns. access time; 450 ns. cycle time

    Capacity: 16K (on row) filled standard
                                   16K-48K (one to three rows) filled optional
                                   64K total capacity of System Board
                                   480K additional RAM through expansion slots[2]
                                   544K total RAM space[2]

  Personal Computer
  and Personal
  Computer XT

    Device Used: 4164-type 64K bit by 1-bit Dynamic RAM[2]
                                  64K available per row
                                  250 ns. access time; 450 ns. cycle time

    Capacity:
    Personal Computer   64K (one row) filled standard
                                  64K-192K (one to three rows) filled optional

    Personal
    Computer XT   128K (two rows) filled standard
                                  64K-128K (one or two rows) filled optional

    Both systems: 256K total capacity of System Board
                                  384K additional RAM through expansion slots
                                  640K total RAM space available

The RAM at a Glance, cont'd

Characteristics:
1. Fast Dynamic RAM (DRAM) chips usable with Direct Memory Addressing (DMA).
2. Dynamic RAMs require refreshing (performed by independent System Board circuitry and transparent to CPU)
3. Ninth RAM chip used for parity checking
4. RAMs (both 16K and 64K) identical to those used in many other microcomputers.

Notes:
[1] Personal Computer manufactured before January, 1983
[2] Applies to systems using old RIOS. If new RIOS is installed, 576K of RAM available through expansion slots, new system total is 640K of RAM.

area that holds only one major item (for example, a program or its data) in a section of memory at a time. After a task is completed, the memory may be erased and new items placed in this work space. RAM memory is thus reusable memory.

RAM's work space is *volatile,* which means that if the power is removed, the contents of the chip are lost and RAM "forgets" what it was holding. Kinds of temporary programs that become lost may be accounting, planning, or data management programs; housekeeping utilities; or parts of BASIC, Pascal, FORTRAN, or other programming languages.

As indicated earlier, IBM calls most of the RAM memory "user memory" because it is reserved for the computer user's programs and data. However, some RAM memory is not user memory. The RAM memory on either the Monochrome Display or Color/Graphics Adapters is one example. This memory is *dedicated* for use by the adapter. The memory is accessible to the user, but not for programs or data. Throughout most of this book, the RAM memory discussed is user memory, not dedicated memory.

One of the axioms of computing is "the larger the RAM, the larger the task, or tasks, the computer can perform." Although disk storage (covered later in this chapter), CPU power, and speed greatly influence computer performance, larger RAM space is highly desirable.

All System Boards for the Personal Computers have four rows of nine RAM chips. Each row appears to have one chip too many because only eight chips are needed to create a row of bytes. (Each chip holds one bit of a memory location; 1 bit x 8 chips = 1 byte). The ninth memory chip in each row performs *parity checking,* which is a constant self-testing of the system's RAM memory. During parity checking, the individual "on" RAM bits are added, and the total is either an odd or even number. Then the "on" bits are tested again to see whether the total is still odd or even. If it is not, one or more of the RAM chips has "forgotten" what it was holding (an occasional phenomenon called *soft drop*). Parity checking is a worthwhile feature because it detects incorrect or garbled information and prevents it from being processed and stored.

The parity checking is performed by independent circuitry that tests each RAM memory location as it is read by the CPU. Should a RAM location fail this odd/even test, the "Parity Error" message is displayed on the screen and the current program is immediately aborted. The only way to reset the system after a parity error is to turn the power off, then on again.

The original Personal Computer's System Board has four rows of 16 K bits (16,364 memory bits) memory chips, commonly called, "16K RAM chips." The row farthest from the front of the system is soldered into place. The first three 9-chip rows are plugged into their sockets on the System Board, allowing a nontechnical user to expand RAM easily up to the maximum of 64K.

Both the current model of the Personal Computer and the XT have four rows of 64K bits (65,536 memory bits) memory chips, or "64K RAM chips"—four times the capacity of the 16K RAM chips! Like the original version of the Personal Computer, the row from the front of the system is soldered into place, providing 64K of RAM before expansion.

In the current Personal Computer with standard equipment, the first three rows of sockets are vacant. Up to three sets of nine 64K RAM chips may be installed, yielding a total of 256K on the newer System Board.

The standard Personal Computer XT starts with 128K of RAM by filling the last *two* rows. Two additional sets of nine 64K RAM chips may be added to bring the total to 256K, the same as that of the current Personal Computer. All Personal Computers thus allow easy expansion of RAM memory.

Close-ups of the RAM memory for the original Personal Computer (above) and Personal Computer XT (right). The placement of the RAMs on the current Personal Computer's System Board is the same as the original, but 64K RAM's are used instead of 16K Rams.

IBM originally offered 16K RAM chips for the System Board of the original Personal Computer. Shortly after it was announced, 32K and 64K RAM cards were made available. IBM now sells an expandable memory card that contains from 64K to 256K of RAM memory, using the newer 64K RAM chips. These 64K RAM chips are available for expanding also the RAM of the current Personal Computer and the XT.

The maximum amount of RAM space available for the Personal Computers is more than 512K. The 8088 CPU has a memory-addressing range up to one megabyte. Of the 1M, 256K is reserved for use by the system's ROM (read-only memory). Almost all of the remaining space may be used as RAM memory. However, 128K of this RAM space is dedicated to adapters, such as the Monochrome or Color/Graphics Adapters. The total amount of user memory available for programs and data is 640K. Whatever RAM space is not used on the System Board may be obtained by placing the appropriate RAM memory board(s) in the system's expansion slots—up to 576K for the original Personal Computer, or 384K for the later or updated versions of the system.

A new ROM chip containing the RIOS must be installed in the Personal Computer to use the full 640K of RAM on Personal Computers manufactured before January, 1983. Without this chip, the maximum RAM memory of any earlier Personal Computer is 544K. All models manufactured after this date, including the Personal Computer XT, can use up to 640K if that much is installed.

System Memory Map

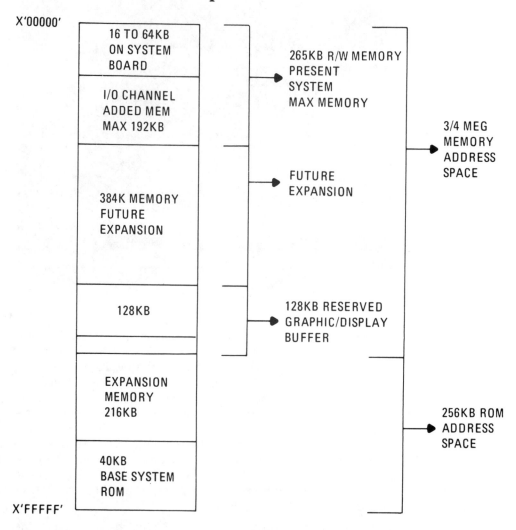

System Memory Map from the Technical Reference *Manual. (Reprinted with permission from International Business Machines Corporation.)*

A set of DIP (dual in-line position) switches on the System Board must be set for the amount of memory that is available to the system. The setting of the switches is checked by the RIOS after the power is turned on or when the system is reset. These switches are the only way to indicate to the Personal Computers how much memory can be used. Details for setting the switches are found in the *Guide To Operations Manual* for the Personal Computer and Personal Computer XT.

The memory capabilities of the Personal Computers have been expanded, but is larger RAM memory necessary, or even helpful? The answer to this question depends on the intended use of the Personal Computer. When the system was first introduced, 64K of RAM was sufficient for most tasks. As programs matured and became more complex, the need for more RAM space became apparent.

The first major program to use more than 64K of RAM in the Personal Computer was VisiCalc®, the popular electronic spreadsheet program. VisiCalc kept its models in the RAM memory of a computer, and the size of the models was restricted by the limits of 64K of user memory. Advanced VisiCalc users who wanted to create larger, more sophisticated models desired much greater RAM space. These experienced users welcomed a 256K version of VisiCalc. The new program itself occupied slightly more memory space than the 64K version, but the RAM memory space that was available for the models was almost six times larger, making more complex models possible.

During the past two years, 128K of RAM has become almost a de facto standard for 16-bit microcomputer systems. Some software publishers and serious users of microcomputers are pushing toward 256K+ as a standard. Several word-processing programs, such as WordStar™ or Benchmark™, use larger memory to edit directly large documents with less dependence on slower working disk storage. The following planning tools and multiple applications programs can flourish with 256+ of memory: Context Management's MBA™, Lotus Development's 1-2-3™, Micro Data Base Systems' Knowledge Man™, Microsoft's MultiPlan™, Sorcim Corporation's SuperCalc™ and SuperCalc²™, and VisiCorp's VisiCalc and Advanced VisiCalc®.

Developments in operating systems and other sophisticated programs indicate that 128K will be considered a minimum amount of

RAM memory. Some programs, of course, will require more than 256K.

Another reason for more RAM memory is that it makes possible the use of a RAM printer spooler and a RAM, or silicon, disk.

RAM printer spoolers are "background" programs, which means that they steal processing time from the CPU while it is idle. The printer spooler blocks off a section of RAM memory for use as a holding *buffer*. When activated, the CPU "prints" data to this high-speed spooler buffer. It, in turn, passes the characters to the slower working printer as CPU time becomes available. By "printing" pages of text into memory, the CPU becomes free sooner to continue its work with the applications program while the printer spooler program feeds the slower printer. The larger the buffer area, the sooner the CPU becomes free to handle its next task.

The RAM disk is a favorite item among performance-oriented users of the Personal Computer. Like the RAM printer spooler, the RAM disk has a reserved area of memory. After the RAM disk is properly set up and made ready, RAM memory becomes a silicon disk drive, allowing high-speed transfers of information from memory rather than from the disk drive. RAM disks are many times faster than their mechanical counterparts.

In both cases, a section of RAM memory must be devoted exclusively to the program's buffer. From 2K to 32K should be allocated to the buffer for effective use of the printer spooler. The RAM disk's area may be as large as the floppy disk it imitates; the devotion of 160K to 360K of RAM space is effective. The allocation of more than 386K of memory to a RAM printer spooler or disk is possible, but is "overkill." The use of this much memory for printer buffers or RAM disks is seldom necessary or practical. Yet, if desired, this option is available with the powerful RAM capabilities of the Personal Computers.

Because of the 8088 microprocessor, The Personal Computers have a large capacity for growth in memory space. Foresight in the design of the Personal Computers is demonstrated by the ease of RAM expansion. Adding extra RAM chips or RAM expansion boards readily expands the Personal Computers to meet the opportunities presented by sophisticated software requiring more than 64K of RAM memory. Such expansion is not easily accomplished, or even possible, with many 8-bit microcomputer systems.

I/O Channels, the System's Expansion Slots

At the back of each System Board and Expansion Board of the Expansion Chassis are several black or green printed circuit board edge connectors that are soldered into place. These are the expansion slots, or *I/O Channels* (their technical name). They are the doorways to the versatility and growth of the Personal Computers.

The number of expansion slots varies. The Personal Computer has five expansion slots, but the Personal Computer XT and the Expansion Unit each have eight slots. This difference in the number of expansion slots is one of the five major differences between the Personal Computer and the XT. (The other four are the XT's RAM memory, hard disk drive, larger power supply, and standard offering of a communication card.)

The expansion slots are extensions of the Personal Computers' *bus*, the metal pathways that carry power and computer signals between the various parts of the computer. When a card is plugged into an expansion slot, the card becomes part of the computer system. The 62 connections of each expansion slot allow the Personal Computers to use a video monitor, a printer, a modem, additional memory, disk drives, and many other devices.

All devices not part of the System Board (including the Expansion Chassis, but excluding the keyboard and cassette recorder) require the use of one of the expansion slots. Each outside device is called a *peripheral*, which is a unit connected to, and used by, the computer, but not actually part of the computer (or, more specifically, not part of the System Board). The computer and its peripherals combine to form the hardware of the *system*. Put simply, a peripheral is any part of the Personal Computers not located on the System Board.

The five expansion slots of the Personal Computer and the first six expansion slots of both the Personal Computer XT and the Expansion Unit run the depth of the unit, allowing cards up to 13 1/8-inches (33.3 cm.) long. The rightmost two slots in the Personal Computer XT and the Expansion Unit are "short" slots for cards as long as 5 inches (12.7 cm.). In both units these slots are shorter because they are located behind space reserved for the left-hand disk drive.

Another difference between the expansion slots of the Personal Computer and those of the Personal Computer XT and the Expansion Unit is in the space between each slot. The Personal Computer

---

The I/O Channels (Expansion Slots) at a Glance

Purpose:	To provide a pathway between the Personal Computer systems and additional devices
Primary Manufacturer:	Various (TRW/Cinch, Amphenol, Ansley, etc.)
Location:	Rear-left corner of System Board Rear-left corner of Expansion Board (Expansion Unit only)
Number:	Five full-length slots (Personal Computer) Six full-length and two short slots, eight total (Personal Computer XT and Expansion Unit)
Physical characteristics:	1. 62-pin DIP connectors (32 contacts by 2 rows) 2. 100 mil (0.1 in./2.54 mm) spacing between contacts 3. Printed-circuit board mounting
Other characteristics:	1. 8-bit bidirectional data bus 2. 20-bit (1M of memory) addressing bus 3. Four voltages available to slots ($+/-$ 5 vdc, $+/-$ 12 vdc) 4. OMA addressing 5. Six levels of interrupts 6. Device ready, memory refreshing, clock, and other signal provided
Differences in slots:	
Space between slots (center-to-center)	Personal Computer — 1 in. (2.54 cm) Personal Computer XT and Expansion Unit — $13/16$ in. (2.06 cm)
Length of board for slot: Full-length slots. Short slots:	$13\frac{1}{8}$ in. (33.34 cm) $+/-$ $\frac{1}{8}$ in. (0.32 cm) 5 in. (12.7 cm) $+/-$ $\frac{1}{4}$ in. (0.64 cm) Timing requirements more strict for 8th slot in Personal Computer XT and Expansion Unit.

---

allows 1 inch (2.5 cm.) between the centers of the slots. The Personal Computer XT and the Expansion Unit each allow 13/16 of an inch (2.06 cm.) between the centers of the slots. Therefore, adapter cards for the XT and the Expansion Chassis must be thinner.

Currently, many of the IBM adapter cards come in two versions: a PC version (indicated by a red dot on the box), and an XT version (marked by a blue dot). Functionally, the boards are identical. The only difference is that Personal Computer XT boards are usually thinner for the narrower slots. Boards for the Personal Computer may be used in the XT, but some boards will be too thick and will overlap another expansion slot, making that slot unavailable for some other board.

In both the Personal Computer XT and the Expansion Unit, the eighth (rightmost) slot is technically different from all the other expansion slots. The system timing requirements of the eighth slot are more sensitive than those of the other slots. Also, the eighth slot requires a special signal, which is sent by the mounted card through one of the I/O Channel's lines, to indicate that the card is in use. These requirements make the XT's System Unit and the Expansion Unit work properly. The result is that some non-IBM expansion cards cannot be used in this slot. When the Personal Computer XT is delivered, the Asynchronous Communications Adapter occupies the eighth slot. The Expansion Unit is delivered with a Receiver Card mounted in the eighth slot. XT and Expansion Unit owners are thus kept from placing in this slot an expansion board that does not fit these requirements.

When the Personal Computer is purchased, one or more of the expansion slots may be occupied. Most frequently, one slot will have an adapter for the selected video display, either monochrome or color. If a disk drive is purchased with the Personal Computer, a second slot will contain the mini-floppy disk adapter. The Personal Computer XT, as purchased, has three of its eight slots filled: one with the mini-floppy disk adapter, a second with the fixed or hard disk adapter, and a third with the Asynchronous Communications Adapter.

One design concept in the construction of the original Personal Computer was that of giving the owner freedom to choose the kind(s) of video monitors to be used: monochrome, color, or both. All Personal Computers also offer flexibility in the selection of printers and other devices. This flexibility, however, restricts the number of devices that can be used at one time without "outside aid."

Most serious owners of the Personal Computer will purchase the following options:

- A display and adapter
- A printer and adapter
- Two diskette drives and adapter
- One memory board

If the IBM Monochrome Display and IBM printer are selected, this combination uses three expansion slots. The IBM Monochrome Monitor/Printer Adapter controls both the display and the printer, and thus eliminates one adapter. If a color monitor is chosen, then separate Color/Graphics and Printer Adapters must be used. This combination takes up four slots. Four slots are also occupied if both the Monochrome and Color Displays are used.

If an Asynchronous Communications Adapter or Synchronous Data Link Control (SDLC) is added to either of the last two combinations, the Personal Computer expansion slots will be filled, leaving no room for further growth.

This problem is compounded if the Personal Computer's owner tries to add a letter-quality printer with or without the IBM Printer. The same is true if the owner wants to install a hard disk, 8-inch disk drives, or a variety of other devices.

One of the first complaints lodged against the Personal Computer was limitation of growth because of an inadequate number of expansion slots. Five slots simply are not enough for all uses of the Personal Computer.

The eight slots in the Personal Computer XT and the creation of the IBM Expansion Unit are a response to this complaint. The narrow expansion slots of the XT permit the use of three additional devices. By adding an Expansion Chassis, six more slots are made available. (This is discussed in the next section.)

The cramped expansion capability forced new design trends on board makers for the IBM Personal Computer. The "multifunction" board has become almost a standard among non-IBM board products. A *multifunction board* combines from two to six or more functions, or adapters, on the same board. Although specific features and prices vary, the most popular form of these boards is the multifunction memory board. The *multifunction memory board* typically holds 64K to 256K of RAM memory and has one or two serial connections, a parallel printer connection, and a time-of-day/day-of-year clock/calendar. These features are an innovative response to the potential disadvantage of limited expansion slots.

I/O Channel Diagram

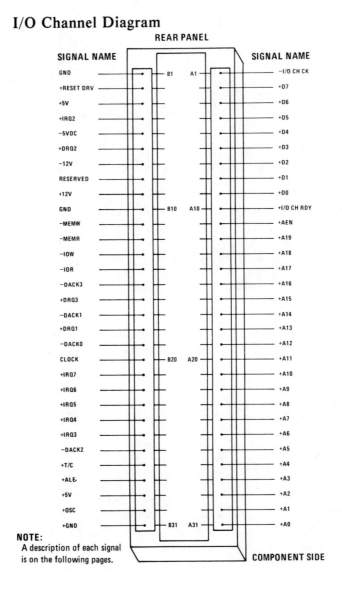

REAR PANEL

SIGNAL NAME			SIGNAL NAME
GND	B1	A1	−I/O CH CK
+RESET DRV			+D7
+5V			+D6
+IRQ2			+D5
−5VDC			+D4
+DRQ2			+D3
−12V			+D2
RESERVED			+D1
+12V			+D0
GND	B10	A10	+I/O CH RDY
−MEMW			+AEN
−MEMR			+A19
−IOW			+A18
−IOR			+A17
−DACK3			+A16
+DRQ3			+A15
−DACK1			+A14
+DRQ1			+A13
−DACK0			+A12
CLOCK	B20	A20	+A11
+IRQ7			+A10
+IRQ6			+A9
+IRQ5			+A8
+IRQ4			+A7
+IRQ3			+A6
−DACK2			+A5
+T/C			+A4
+ALE			+A3
+5V			+A2
+OSC			+A1
+GND	B31	A31	+A0

NOTE:
A description of each signal
is on the following pages.

COMPONENT SIDE

The I/O Channel (Expansion Slot) Diagram from the Technical Reference
Manual. *(Reprinted with permission from International Business Machines
Corporation.)*

A close-up of the top of the System Boards for the Personal Computer (top) and Personal Computer XT (bottom), showing the expansion slots. The number and distance between the XT's slots and the Expansion Unit's slots are identical. The ruler shows the 13/16-inch space between the slots. The space between the Personal Computer's slots is 1 inch.

With the available combinations of the Personal Computer, the Personal Computer XT, the Expansion Chassis, and multifunction boards, the limited expansion slots are not a limitation at all.

The technical aspects of the expansion slots, or I/O Channels, will not be described in depth in this book. Briefly, all lines necessary to make a peripheral "talk" to the computer, including the 1M memory-addressing and error-condition line, are available through the connector. (A detailed discussion of the expansion slots is found in the *Technical Reference Manual* for either the Personal Computer or the Personal Computer XT.)

Additional System Board Components

The System Board includes the following additional components: the power supply connectors, the audio speaker and connections, and the cassette port. This section briefly reviews two of these components: the speaker and the cassette port.

The Audio Speaker

The audio speaker is a 2 1/4-inch diameter, 8-ohm speaker that is supplied with a half-watt of power. Audiophiles have hooked the output connections to larger speakers for louder or fuller sound. A small, two-wire connector links the front of the System Board and the speaker. The speaker is powerful enough for office environments, and most chattering printers won't drown it out.

An interesting facet of the design of the Personal Computers is the attention to sound. The speaker circuitry produces tones from 37 to 32,000 Hz. (hertz, or cycles per second). Two separately controlled circuits provide the frequencies to the speaker. This arrangement allows the speaker to produce "polyphonic," or multiple, tones at one time. Although the music demonstration provided with the IBM Disk Operating System (DOS) and BASIC (the MUSIC program) is a little "tinny," the capabilities for generating sound are greater.

The Cassette Port

The cassette interface is located at the back of the System Unit of the Personal Computer. The Personal Computer XT does not have a cassette port nor any of the cassette interface circuitry. This is one of the major differences between the Personal Computer and the XT.

Cassette Interface at a Glance[1]

Purpose: To provide program and data storage with an
                            audio cassette recorder

Connector: 5-pin DIN (circular)

Location: Rear center of System Board (connector)
                            Mainly on rear of System Board (circuitry)

Signals[2]:   Motor control
                            Ground
                            Audio Out (into Personal Computer)
                            Microphone or Auxilary In (from Personal Com-
                            puter; level selectable by jumper at front of
                            System Board)

Speed: 1000-2000 baud (150 CPS average)

Notes: [1] Section not applicable to Personal Computer
                                XT
                            [2] Signal references are standard audio indus-
                                try names and represent sound from stand-
                                point of cassette recorder, not computer.

The demand for faster, more reliable storage of information has made the disk drive, floppy or fixed, the standard for the Personal Computers. The exchange of a cassette interface for more expansion slots in the Personal Computer XT is logical. This exchange may seem contradictory, however, because the Personal Computer XT still contains the Cassette BASIC language interpreter. (This will be explained in more detail in chapter 5.) The rest of this discussion applies to only the Personal Computer.

The cassette interface is a 5-pin DIN (circular) connector. It may be attached to any standard cassette recorder that has the necessary motor controls (start/stop) and audio levels.

Initially configured for a recorder's microphone jack, the System Board uses a small jumper, located near the front of the board, to allow two different audio output levels to the cassette recorder: "Microphone" and "Auxiliary In." If the auxiliary input jack of a cassette recorder is used, the jumper should be changed. The input circuitry of the cassette recorder can be damaged if improper levels of sound (technically, mismatched voltages) are applied to the cassette jack.

In the past, most business, educational, and private users of the Personal Computer selected disk storage. To date, only a handful of programs use the cassette port.

IBM does not even supply a cable for a cassette recorder. Although the DIN connector is not unusual, it is not generally used in either the audio or computer industry with a cassette port. The user will have to search for the proper cable to connect the Personal Computer to a cassette recorder.

The cassette interface provides a relatively swift recording rate of 1,000 to 2,000 baud, or an average of 150 cps (characters per second), comparable to the TRS-80 Model III™ and Color Computers, which operate at the same speed. Special characters (checksums) are also recorded (like all other cassette-using computers) and used to check the validity of the recording.

A Brief Summary of the System Board

The Personal Computers take advantage of the power available with the 16-bit microprocessor. The architecture of the Personal Computer's System Board allows the maximum amount of usable memory from the 8086/8088 family of microprocessors: one million bytes. The RAM of the original Personal Computer System Board is expandable to 64K; the later versions, Personal Computer and Personal Computer XT, are expandable to 256K, four times the amount available with the original model. The total space dedicated to user memory is 640K. Through the incorporation of the 8087 numeric coprocessor, the Personal Computer can perform "number crunching" at an accelerated rate. The 40K space dedicated to ROM is larger than many other personal computers' RAM space. This ROM contains enough system programs (including Cassette BASIC, RIOS, and the power-up self-test) to make the computer exceptionally "intelligent," even when it is first turned on.

The initial prospects for increasing the computer's performance through the expansion slots appeared to be limited. The computer industry's rally around the "multifunction" expansion boards, the increased expansion slots of the Personal Computer XT, the IBM Expansion Unit, and outside expansion chassis producers have all altered the conception of limited expansion.

The Personal Computers, excluding the XT, can use a cassette recorder for storage; however, such use requires locating the proper connecting cable. The speaker is a useful tool for all systems. It generates unique sounds and makes programs more responsive to the needs of the operator.

The Expansion Unit

The Expansion Unit provides additional expansion slots and storage capability. It has several characteristics that are similar to the Personal Computers' System Units, and even uses an identical cabinet. The back of the Expansion Unit, however, does not contain connectors for the Keyboard Unit or a cassette port, but it does have an a.c. connector for the IBM Monochrome Display.

The interior of the Expansion Unit is more like that of the Personal Computer XT than the Personal Computer. The unit uses a board with eight slots—six normal length slots and two short slots—that accommodate Expansion Board lengths up to 5 1/2-inches (14 cm.). Like all Personal Computer units, the Expansion Unit contains two spaces for 5 1/4-inch drives. It uses the same power supply as the XT, supplying 130 watts, compared to the Personal Computer's 63.5 watts. The Expansion Unit also powers all cards and disk drives installed in the unit. Unlike the System Unit, the Expansion Unit does not contain a System Board, but has an Expansion Board. It is used exclusively for optional upgrading of the system.

The Expansion Unit uses two unique cards: an Extender Card and a Receiver Card. The Extender Card may be placed in any slot of the Personal Computer, but should be placed in the eighth expansion slot of an XT unit. The Receiver Card should be placed in the rightmost slot of the Personal Computer's Expansion Unit. Each card uses a 62-pin, D-shaped female connector that protrudes from the back of the unit. The voltage-carrying lines of each connector are identical. A 56-line shielded cable, 39 inches (1 m.) in length and 2 3/8-inches (6 cm.) in circumference, connects the two cards. The cable is reversible: either end can be connected to the Receiver or the Extender Cards.

The Expansion Unit at a Glance

Purpose:	To provide additional expansion slots and housing for hard disk drives
Dimensions:	Identical to Personal Computer XT except 33 lb (14.9 kg) weight

Contents (both models):	1. Expansion Board
	    6 full-length slots
	    2 short slots
	    Independent oscillator and support circuitry
	2. Power Supply — identical to Personal Computer XT's
	3. Bays for two disk drives
	4. IOM Fixed Disk Drive
	5. Expansion Board (for System Unit)
	6. Receiver Board (mounted in Expansion Unit slot 8)
	7. Updated RIOS (for older Personal Computers)

Differences in models:	One model supplies Fixed Disk Adapter; other unit does not (for use with Personal Computer XT that is supplied with this adapter).

Careful observers may note a possible contradiction in the preceding paragraph. The expansion slots have 62 bus lines, which carry the electrical signals and power between the expansion slots and the rest of the System Board. Why are only 56 lines connected between the Expansion Unit and System Unit?

The explanation is simple. First, the Expansion Unit has its own Power Supply, which provides the necessary current for the unit to operate. This means that the five power lines—two +5, one -5, one +12, and one -12 volts d.c.—do not have to be connected. As a result, five lines are eliminated. Second, an independent 14.31818 MHz. (megahertz, or million cycles per second) oscillator (for expansion boards that require this signal) is also provided in the Expansion Unit. This high-speed signal does not "transport" reliably in the cable that connects the two units. Providing an independent oscillator in the Expansion Unit increases reliability and eliminates one more line from the cable. These are the six lines not used—five power lines and the oscillator line.

One understandable misconception is that the Expansion Unit provides eight additional slots. In fact, it provides only *six* extra slots when it is connected to any System Unit. The Expansion Unit requires one slot for the Extender Card (used with the System Unit), which reduces the number of free slots to four in a Personal Computer, or seven in the XT. The eighth slot of the Expansion Unit *must* hold the Receiver Card, again reducing the number of free slots.

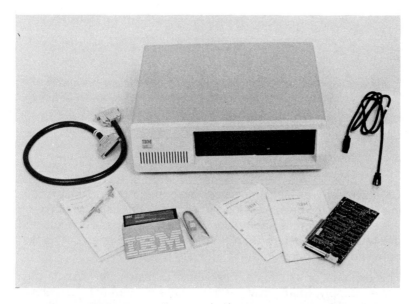

Pictured is the IBM Expansion Unit, including the 10M Fixed (hard) Disk. Moving clockwise from the unit, also pictured are the a.c. power cord, the Expansion Board for the System Unit, the instructions for installation, the new RIOS chip and chip extractor, the diagnostic disk for testing the unit, narrower brackets for boards mounted in the unit, and the connecting cable.

Receiver Card for the Expansion Unit.

After the Expansion Unit has been added, 10 slots are available for the Personal Computer (5 slots in the System Unit, plus 8 slots in the Expansion Unit, minus 2 cards for the Expansion Unit and 1 card for the Fixed Disk Adapter), or 13 for the Personal Computer XT (16 slots, or 8 slots each for the Expansion and System Units, less 2 slots for the required Expansion Unit cards and disk adapter cards and 1 for the serial adapter).

Only one Expansion Unit may be added to the Personal Computer systems. If it is added to a Personal Computer manufactured before January, 1983, an update to the System Board's ROM (RIOS) must be made. This ROM is provided with the Expansion Unit, along with a tool to remove the old ROM and detailed instructions.

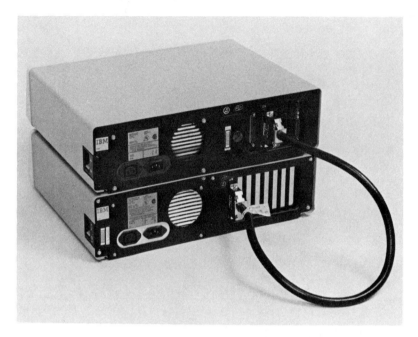

Pictured is the Expansion Unit (bottom) connected to a Personal Computer.

The Expansion Unit can house two 5 1/4-inch Fixed Disk drives because the Unit's power supply is constructed to support them.

Certain expansion boards may be placed only in the System Unit. A full description is rather technical. Briefly, the RIOS cannot use certain boards if they are not housed in the Personal Computers' System Unit. This and other requirements force certain boards to be placed only in the System Unit.

The following is a list of restrictions placed on IBM expansion boards for all Personal Computers.

For use in System Unit only:

   Monochrome Display/Printer Adapter
   5 1/4-inch Diskette Drive Adapter (mini-floppy)
   Any memory boards
   Color/Graphics Adapter (if only a color display is used)
   Extender Board

For use in Expansion Unit only:

Receiver Board

For use in System or Expansion Unit:

Asynchronous Communications Adapter
Game Control Adapter
SDLC Adapter
Printer Adapter
Prototype board (with some restrictions)
Color/Graphics Adapter (if not the primary display)
Fixed Disk Adapter

Only one Diskette Drive Adapter and one Fixed Disk Adapter are allowed in the entire system. With the Expansion Unit, however, any Personal Computer system can use two mini-floppy disk drives and two Fixed Disk drives.

Fixed Disks can be added to the Personal Computer only through the Expansion Unit. The power supply of the Personal Computer is insufficient to operate the Fixed Disk. Once an Expansion Unit containing one Fixed Disk is added, a second Fixed Disk can be added easily.

A Personal Computer XT owner wishing to use a second Fixed Disk must purchase the Expansion Unit and house both Fixed Disk drives in that Unit. There is no connecting cable for Fixed Disks located in different units. Such a cable, because of electronic constraints, would be unwise. The owner must remove the Fixed Disk and adapter board from the Personal Computer XT and place them in the Expansion Unit. The power supply of the Expansion Unit is sufficient for this arrangement. Now, an XT owner can mount a second mini-floppy disk drive in the System Unit. A special cable, provided with the second drive, allows the second drive to receive power from the first one.

IBM currently sells two versions of the Expansion Unit. The unit for the Personal Computer contains the Fixed Disk Adapter. The unit for the Personal Computer XT does not because the XT contains this adapter when purchased. In all other respects, the two models are identical.

At this time, mini-floppy disk drives cannot be placed in the Expansion Unit. The mini-floppy adapter board must be in the System Unit, and a cable to connect mini-floppy drives between different units is

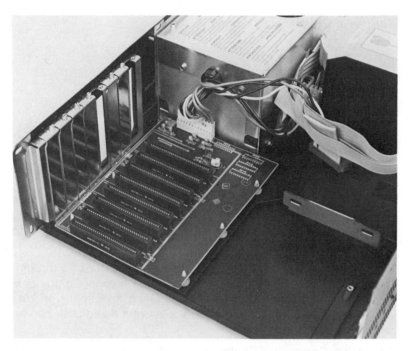

Pictured is the interior of the Expansion Unit, showing the Expansion Board with its eight slots and separate oscillator crystal (above the topmost slot), the power supply, and portions of the Fixed Disk and bay, used for mounting an additional Fixed Disk.

not available. The problem of "crosstalk," the electrical interference that is possible with long parallel lines, does not make advisable the mounting of additional mini-floppy drives in the Expansion Unit.

The Extender and the Receiver Cards of the Expansion Unit contain the necessary circuitry to *redrive* (enhance or recharge) the Expansion Unit's I/O Channels. The additional distance of the expansion lines causes electrical signal delays, which are rated between 27 and 133 ns. (nanoseconds, or billionths of a second). Additional circuitry in the cards assures that "slow" memory or input/output devices work properly in the Expansion Unit.

All RAM memory or multifunction RAM boards should be placed in the System Unit, not the Expansion Unit. The same is true for some non-IBM expansion boards. If the expansion board's function, or functions, fall into the category listed in the table as "System Unit only," then the board should be placed only in the System Unit.

A bank of switches on the Extender Card must be set, in addition to the proper System Board switches, to reflect the amount of RAM memory in the System Unit.

When the computer system is powered-up, the Expansion Unit must be turned on before the System Unit. This allows the RIOS, during its self-test, to determine whether an Expansion Unit is connected to the system.

In summary, the Expansion Unit is a valuable addition to the Personal Computer family. The unit provides the mechanism to add up to six expansion boards to the Personal Computer system. The Extender and Receiver Cards extend the bus of the Personal Computer to include the Expansion Unit. The Expansion Unit also provides the necessary mounting and power for a Fixed Disk drive, or drives.

The Power Supply

The power supply uses a "switching action" that literally "chops" the 120 volts a.c. (North American models) into the necessary four voltages (+5, -5, +12, and -12 volts d.c.). A grounded cord provides a.c. power on all System Units. The proper voltages are also provided for any disk drives. The power supplies are connected to their respective System or Expansion Boards (in the case of the Expansion Unit) by two 6-pin, "Mollex-type" connectors. The power supplies of all units, System and Expansion, use a nonstandard connector for the IBM Monochrome Monitor. The Monochrome Monitor contains its own power supply; this connector simply provides an outlet for a.c. power, thereby reducing the number of wall outlets required.

A comparison of the power supplies of the different models of the Personal Computer shows subtle, but major, differences between the Personal Computer and the Personal Computer XT or the Expansion Unit.

In the Personal Computer only, the power supply is rated at 63.5 watts, providing ample power for the System Board, most expansion cards, and the mini-floppy disk drives. Two of the four connectors from the supply are specifically for mini-floppy disk drives. The other two are for the System Board.

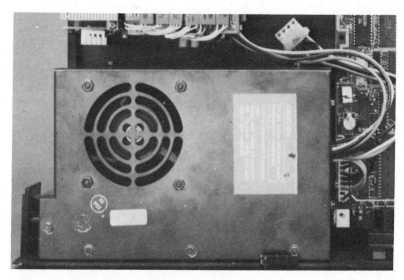

Closeup of the Personal Computer's Power Supply.

The power supplies of the Personal Computer XT and Expansion Unit are rated at more than twice the rate of the Personal Computer: 130 watts. Like the Personal Computer, the XT's power supply powers the System Board and disk drives, with two lines supplying power to the System or Expansion Board. However, only one connector is provided for a mini-floppy disk drive. The fourth power connector is used by the IBM Fixed Disk. The additional voltage of the XT's and Expansion Unit's power supply meets the higher power requirements of fixed disks and the increased number of expansion slots. The XT and Expansion Unit supply 11 amperes of power to the expansion slots as opposed to the 4 amps generated by the Personal Computer.

Two different ways of protecting the computer's circuitry are incorporated into the power supplies. To ensure that the proper a.c. voltage is present, a power-sensing device automatically shuts off the supply if too much or too little voltage is detected. If an overvoltage or overcurrent condition occurs because of a short circuit in the disk drives, System Board, or expansion boards, the supply shuts down until this situation is corrected.

The power supplies of the Personal Computer XT and Expansion Unit adequately meet the demands of the additional expansion

Power Supply at a Glance

Purpose:	To provide regulated power to the System Board or Expansion Board, expansion slots, and disk drives. Additionally, pass through a.c. power to Monochrome Display
Location:	Right-rear (all units)

Characteristics:

All units

1. Fuse and "power good sensing" protected, switching-type supply
2. Output (a.c.) for Monochrome Display
   120 volts @ .75 amps. (average)
   101 volts (min)-130 volts (max.)
3. Output for System and Board and disk drives
   Four d.c. voltages +5, −5, +12, −12
4. Two 6-pin connectors for providing power to System Board

Personal Computer

1. Input (ac)
   120 volts @ 50/60 Hz.
      (104 v min., 127 v max.)
   2.5 amps (63.5 watts) maximum
2. Output

d.c. volts	+5	−5	+12	−12
amps (max.)	7.0	0.3	2.0	0.25

3. Two power connectors for mini-floppy disk drives provided

Personal Computer XT and Expansion Unit

1. Input (a.c.)
   110 volts @ 50/60 Hz.
      (90 v min., 137 v max.)
   4.1 amps (130 watts) maximum
2. Output

d.c. volts	+5	−5	+12	−12
amps (max.)	15.0	0.3	4.2	0.25

3. One power connector for mini-floppy disk drives and one connector for hard disk drive provided.

boards and Fixed Disks. The lower power supply of the Personal Computer is also adequate for most configurations.

The Disk Drives

Since the introduction of the Personal Computer, the major hardware advance has been the increase in disk storage. Initially, the Personal Computer offered a mini-floppy disk drive that would store 160K. Today, the IBM mini-floppy drive holds more than 360K, and the IBM Fixed Disk has more than 20 times that capacity. In fact, the origins of both floppy and fixed disks can be traced to IBM.

Disk drives are called by many different names, including mass storage, disk storage, mechanical storage, and permanent storage. Disk storage has a dual purpose. First, it provides a "permanent" way of holding programs and data. Like ROM (read-only memory), when the power is withdrawn, the disk retains what has been recorded. Unlike ROM, disk storage can be altered. Disk space is not dedicated to holding only one program or set of data. Disks may be recorded, and the information on them may be retrieved or changed; then the disks may be erased and reused. Because of its "fixed" nature, ROM memory is not as versatile or cost effective as the magnetic disk.

The second feature of disk storage is its transportability. Programs and data may be moved from machine to machine with this removable memory. Programs or data developed with one computer can be used by another through mobile media (although several restrictions mentioned in chapters 4 and 5 apply). By merely inserting a different diskette in a drive, different tasks can be performed by the same computer system, a fact that distinguishes a general-purpose computer from a dedicated system. These are some of the reasons why floppy diskettes have become popular in the personal comuter industry.

The Floppy Disks

Floppy disks, originally designed by IBM for its "larger" systems almost 20 years ago, remain a leading vehicle for mass storage in smaller computers. Accordingly, the term "IBM format" for 8-inch diskettes dominates the entire computer industry.

A *floppy diskette* is a circular piece of Mylar or other plastic-like material that is coated with a metallic oxide. This flexible (hence, the term "floppy") diskette is housed in a protective jacket. When inserted into a drive, the diskette spins inside the jacket. A moving recording head mounted inside the floppy disk drive, commonly called the "read/write head," records on, and retrieves information from, the magnetic surface.

Originally, floppy diskettes were 8 inches in diameter and capable of recording 241K of information on one side of the diskette in a "single-density" format. This format is the basic IBM format, also known as 3740 format, the model number of the IBM disk drive. The common abbreviation for this format is ss/sd (single-sided, single-density).

As disk technology progressed, another 8-inch diskette format appeared, known as System/34™ (an IBM computer system), or double-sided, double-density (ds/dd). This method records information on both sides of the diskette and in less space. An 8-inch, System/34-formatted diskette holds 972K—almost four times the amount of an IBM-formatted diskette.

Although both methods are now considered "standards," the most common 8-inch diskettes are the single-sided, single-density (ss/sd) or IBM-formatted diskettes. Almost all computers that use 8-inch disk drives can be "coerced" into reading and writing diskettes in IBM format.

The Mini-Floppy Disk Drives

The IBM Personal Computers use a mini-floppy, or 5 1/4-inch diameter floppy diskette. (The flexible characteristics of both the 8-inch and 5 1/4-inch varieties have caused the computer industry to apply the term "floppy" to both sizes of diskette, although the term originally applied to the 8-inch variety only.)

The major supplier of mini-floppy disk drives to IBM is Tandon Magnetics, Inc. When it was first introduced, the IBM Personal Computer used the Tandon 100-1 drive, a single-sided, quad-density (quad, or four times the normal density) drive. It is normally used in double-density form, making it a single-sided, double-density, mini-floppy disk drive. Mini-floppy diskettes recorded on this drive originally held 163,840 bytes of information, or 160K.

In 1982, IBM began shipment of the Tandon 100-2 disk drive, a double-sided, double-density disk drive (although this drive is also rated for quad-density use). With this new drive, the capacity of a single disk nearly doubled from 160K to 320K, or 322,560 bytes.

The Mini-Floppy Disk Drive at a Glance

Purpose: To provide removable and transportable disk storage of programs and data for the Personal Computer Systems

Primary Manufacturer: Tandon Magnetics, Inc.

Model Numbers: 100-1 (single-sided)
100-2 (double-sided)

Capacity:

100-1   Unformatted   250K (double-density)
500K (quad-density)
Formatted   160K (PC DOS V1. x)
180K (PC DOS V2. x)

100-3   Unformatted   500K (double-density)
1,000K (quad-density)
Formatted   320K (PC DOS V1. x)
360K (PC DOS V2. x)

Both drives   Double-density (System/34) format used
48 TPI (tracks per inch) rated/40 tracks used
8 sectors per track (PC DOS V1. x)
9 sectors per track (PC DOS V2. x)
512 bytes per sector

Speeds: 6 ms. seek time (track-to-track)
25 ms. head stepping rate
500 ms. maximum start/stop time
250K bits/second transfer rate

Other information:
1. Mini-floppy adapter must be housed in System Unit.
2. Drives are optional on Personal Computer.
3. One 100-2 type drive standardly supplied with Personal Computer XT.
4. Mini-floppy drives are not to be placed ir. Expansion Unit.
5. System Unit houses maximum of two mini-floppy drives.
6. Two additional mini-floppy drives are possible.

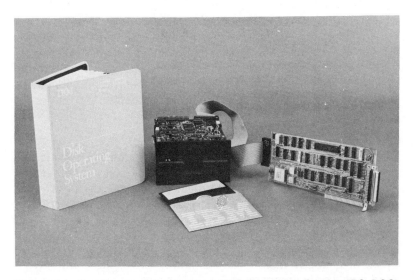

Pictured is the Personal Computers' Disk Operating System (PC DOS) manual and diskette, Tandon mini-floppy disk drive, and IBM Diskette Adapter.

The release of PC DOS V2.0 in early 1983 brought another increase in mini-floppy disk capacity.

Diskettes are divided into concentric circles called *tracks*. For mini-floppy drives, 40 tracks are recorded on each side of the diskette. Under previous versions of the IBM Disk Operating System (PC DOS V1.0 or V1.1), each track was subdivided into eight sections called *sectors*. Each sector held 512 bytes. In DOS V2.0, the tracks are divided differently, yielding nine sectors per track.

The difference in the number of sectors, accomplished by changes in software, increases the capacity of each drive. Single-sided drives, which previously held 160K, now hold 180K, an increase of 20,480 bytes, or 12.5 percent. Double-sided disk drives, which previously held 320K, now hold 360K, an increase of 40,960 bytes or 12.5 percent. These increases can be achieved only by Personal Computer owners who use operating systems that support 9 sectors per track, and who format their diskettes accordingly. (This is discussed further in chapter 4.)

All System and Expansion Units hold two disk drives. The two mini-floppy disk drives go in the System Unit of the Personal

Computer. The Personal Computer XT holds one mini-floppy in the leftmost bay. The master drive, on the left-hand side, is drive *A*. A second mini-floppy drive, if installed, is called drive *B*. Switches on the System Board are set according to the number of mini-floppy diskette drives in use with the system. The mini-floppy drives are controlled by the 5 1/4-inch Diskette Drive Adapter.

Hard Disks

With the announcement of the Personal Computer XT, IBM made a Fixed Disk available for the Personal Computer family. A *hard disk* is similar to a floppy diskette. The main differences begin with the media. The hard disk uses a rigid, metal ring (called a platter) that is coated with a metal oxide, thus giving it the name of "hard," or "rigid," disk drive. The hard disk spins at rates of thousands of rotations per minute, usually 3600 r.p.m. as compared to the 300 r.p.m. of a floppy disk. Unlike a floppy drive, the hard drive's recording heads do not touch the surface of the disk when in use. These heads "fly" thousandths of an inch above the surface on a cushion of air that is generated by the disk movement. Whereas a floppy disk drive uses only one diskette at a time, a hard disk drive may have several platters in the unit, stacked vertically. Each platter has two sets of recording heads, one for each side of the platter.

These factors—the type of media, the multiple platters, the speed of rotation, and the nature of the recording heads—lead to three observations about hard disks.

First, hard disks hold more than comparable floppy disks. Because recording is more dense (more information recorded per inch), hard disks are able to store more information in less space than floppy diskettes. Whereas 5 1/4-inch floppies hold between 90K and 1M of information, 5 1/4-inch hard disks, using one platter, can store 5M of information.

Second, hard disks store and retrieve information faster than floppy diskettes. Because of the faster platter rotation and compactness of the recorded information, hard disks usually take less time to "find" and transfer information to the computer system.

Third, some hard disks are vulnerable to "head crash." Because of the high rotation speed of the hard disk platters, the recording heads of a hard disk fly on a cushion of air. The distance between the recording head and the platter is only thousandths of an inch. Dust, dirt, cigarette smoke or ash, fingerprints, or a human hair are larger than the space between the platter and the recording head. If this type of contamination falls on the disk platter, the recording head will fly into the contamination, bounce, and fall into the hard disk platter. This falling into the platter's surface is called "head crash." It usually ruins the recording heads and the sections of the platters involved in the crash. From several thousand bytes to several megabytes of information may be lost. A hefty repair bill is another likely result.

Head crash is most common with removable hard disks. Removable hard disk platters are placed on spindles in a container. The entire package is called a *cartridge*. The recording head of the disk drive gains access to the platter through a door in the cartridge. When the cartridge is placed in the disk drive, filtered air is circulated around it, removing most contamination. The air filter keeps airborne contaminants such as dust and smoke from entering the chamber that contains the cartridge. Many medium-to-large computer installations do not permit smoking in rooms that house disk cartridges or drives because of the possibility of contamination.

How do contaminants get to the platter's surface and cause head crash? Lack of careful handling of the cartridges is the most common reason. Contaminants can enter through the door of the cartridge. The air purge of the disk drive is not adequate for removing heavy or oily particles, such as human hair or a fingerprint. Improper mounting of the air filters for the disk drive, allowing particles to enter the drive, is another reason.

Mishandling hard disk cartridges, such as dropping or bumping them against hard objects, is another cause of head crash. In these cases, the spindle is bent, or the platters get out of line. Dropping a cartridge as little as six inches onto a hard surface can be fatal to the cartridge, disk drive, or both. Bumping or moving an in-use disk drive can also cause the recording heads to crash into the platters.

Fortunately, head crash is an infrequent event. The term "disk crash" refers to any malfunction, electronic or mechanical, that causes the disk drive to fail. Disk crash occurs more frequently than head crash. To reduce significantly the possibility of head crash, the most serious of hard disk problems, the hard disk drive must be designed differently.

The solution to this design problem is simple. If the recording heads are placed in the same cartridge with the disk platters and the entire unit is sealed, outside contamination will be prevented from entering the drive. This type of drive is sturdier and less vulnerable to shock. It eliminates one cause of head crash and greatly reduces the effects of the other two.

Winchester is the code name IBM gave to one of its hard disk projects in the 1970s. The Winchester is a reliable, high-speed disk storage device that comes in two varieties: the Fixed Disk and the removable Winchester.

In the Fixed Disk, the disk drive and sealed recording heads/platters section are combined in one unit. This type of unit is installed in the Personal Computer XT.

The removable Winchester uses a "data pack," a sealed unit containing just the platters, the recording heads, and connections. The data pack is placed into a disk drive. The disk drive contains the motor to turn the platters and the necessary controlling and interfacing electronics.

The advantage of the fixed Winchester drive is that the drive and disk are in one unit. The advantage of the removable Winchester disk is the same as that of floppy disks. Changing the data pack allows more programs and information to be used without an additional disk drive.

A disadvantage of the fixed Winchester disk is in "backing up" the information stored on the hard disk. Although Winchester disks are almost immune to head crash, disk crashes in the form of electronic failures do occur. The average time between failures in a Winchester drive is about 8,000 to 10,000 hours of use, or about once every 2.7 to 3.4 years if the drive is used 8 hours a day every day of the week. However, this figure is only an "average," and disk failure can occur earlier. To ensure that data is not lost, the user should make and maintain separate copies of the information on the hard disk.

A disadvantage of the removable Winchester disk is that it can suffer some of the problems of the cartridge hard disks. The data packs do not tolerate harsh handling, such as dropping the data pack or bumping it into solid objects. This rough handling will ruin the data pack. Removable Winchester disks, however, do not suffer contamination problems. No dust or particles can enter the sealed chamber containing the recording heads and platters. Removable Winchester drives are more immune to physical shock than cartridge hard disks. Mounting the recording heads with the platters reduces this problem. The removable Winchester disk is more expensive and not as widely available as the fixed Winchester disk. For these reasons, IBM chose the fixed Winchester disk for the Personal Computer family.

The Fixed Disk

The Fixed Disk drives used by IBM in the Personal Computers are manufactured by Seagate Technology of California and Miniscribe Corporation of Colorado. The formatted capacity per drive is 10,653,696 bytes, or 10.4M of information. The actual usable storage capacity is about 10.37M because a small part of the disk is devoted to internal purposes. For descriptive ease, the 10.4 or 10.37 megabyte figure is rounded down to the more common notation of 10M.

The drives use two 5 1/4-inch platters, stacked vertically. Each platter has two recording surfaces, one on the top and one on the bottom of the platter. Each surface has its own recording head, and all four recording heads are mounted on a common arm. The arm moves back and forth in a straight line across the surfaces of the disk. All four surfaces are used to hold information. (Earlier drives devoted the bottom surface of the lowest platter for internal use by the disk drive; and, therefore, this surface was not available for storing programs and data.)

The Fixed Disk drive has 306 cylinders. A cylinder is actually based on the floppy diskette's track. Each surface of the hard disk is divided into 306 concentric circles called tracks, as on a floppy diskette. The 306 tracks of each surface are vertically aligned with the 306 of the other three surfaces. The four sets of 306 tracks form an imaginary three-dimensional figure called a *cylinder*. (Although the term is used less frequently, it also applies to all floppy diskettes, but more importantly to the double-sided variety.)

Multiplying the number of cylinders (306) on the IBM Fixed Disk by the number of surfaces (4) gives the drive's total number of tracks: 1224. Each track (or cylinder) is divided into 17 sectors, and each sector holds 512 bytes of formatted data. The total storage available to the fixed disk is calculated as

```
              306 cylinders
    x           4 surfaces
    ————————————————————————————
              1224 tracks per drive
    x          17 sectors per track
    x         512 bytes per track
    ————————————————————————————
         10,653,696 bytes per drive
```

This amount is the 10.4M figure mentioned earlier. However, one complete cylinder is used by the drive for diagnostic purposes. This means that the "real" usable storage capacity is

```
              1220 tracks (1224 -4 tracks or 1 cylinder's worth)
    x          17 sectors per track
    x         512 bytes per track
    ————————————————————————————
         10,618,880 bytes per drive
```

or 10.37M, a reduction of only 34,816 bytes. Because 10.37M is still an unwieldy term, 10M is used instead. It is important only to note that the real total is a fraction more than 10M. This is an approximate equivalent of having 64 single-sided, mini-floppy disk drives (at 160K per diskette), or 29 double-sided drives (at 354K per diskette) on-line at one time.

Fixed Disk drives operate at much higher rates of speed than floppy drives. Technically, the mini-floppy disk drive must load (move) the recording head, or heads (for a double-sided drive), to the surface of the diskette; start the motor; and wait until the motor reaches the proper speed. The Fixed Disk is always in motion (while the power is on), and its heads are always at the proper distance above the spinning platters. In other words, the Fixed Disk takes one-third of the time needed to start up a mini-floppy disk drive. (There is a one-time delay of several seconds while the Fixed Disk "comes up to speed" when it is first turned on.) Whereas the mini-floppy diskette takes 6 ms. (milliseconds) to move between each track, the Fixed Disk takes only 3 ms. The Fixed Disk has an access time of 90 ms. *Access time* refers to the amount of time taken to move the recording heads to the required section and begin reading information.

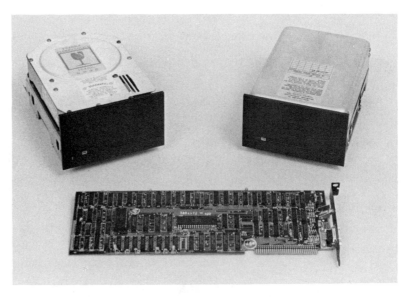

Pictured in the foreground is the Fixed Disk Adapter. The two hard disk drives currently used by IBM are the Seagate (left) and the Miniscribe (right).

The difference in transfer rate (how many bits of information can be transferred in one second) between the mini-floppy and hard disk drives is significant. The mini-floppy disk drive can transfer 250 Kbits (thousands of bits, not bytes) per second, but the Fixed Disk transfers 5 Mbits (millions of bits) per second, 20 times more than the mini-floppy disk drive. The direct memory addressing (DMA) circuitry of the 8088 CPU and the inherent speed of the Fixed Disk itself make this increased transfer rate possible.

The average actual performance improvement of the Fixed Disk over the mini-floppy is not 20 times, but more on the order of 50% to 1000% (1/2 to 10 times) faster. Some of the factors that influence this performance are operating systems, the type of disk operation (reading information versus writing), programming languages, and whether portions of the program or data files are scattered across the disk or adjacent.

A Personal Computer can have two IBM Fixed Disk drives, provided through the Expansion Unit. Personal Computer XTs can use two Fixed Disk drives, both located in the Expansion Unit.

The Fixed Disk at a Glance

Purpose: To provide high-speed, high-capacity disk
                            storage for Personal Computer systems.

Primary manufacturer: MiniScribe Corporation and Seagate Technol-
                            ogy, Inc.

Dimensions: 3.25 in. (82.55 mm) height
                            5.75 in. (146.05 mm) width
                            8.0 in. (203.2 mm) depth
                            4.6 lb. (2.08 kg)   weight

Type of technology: Winchester (environmentally sealed rigid
                            media/recording heads)

Characteristics: 2 rigid platters per unit
                            2 recording surfaces per platter
                                345 cylinders possible
                                306 cylinders (formatted)
                                  1 cylinder reserved for
                                     diagnostics
                                 17 sectors per cylinder
                                     (formatted)
                                512 bytes per sector
                                     (formatted)

                                1,220 total tracks[1]
                                20,740 total sectors[1]
                            10,618,880
                            or   10. 3M total bytes[1]

                            Access time — 3 ms track-to-track
                            Average latency — 8.33 ms
                            Transfer rate — 5M bits/second

                            Shock — 10G (while operating)
                                  — 20G (while not operating)

Notes: [1] based on true user capacity (306 cylinders
                                — 1 reserved cylinder)

When two Fixed Disk drives are used, a power cable and a data
cable connect the first drive to the second.

Unlike mini-floppy drives, the System Board does not have switches to set for the Fixed Disk. The RIOS (ROM BIOS) of the Personal Computer XT and the updated Personal Computer contains the basic subroutines for using the Fixed Disk, and will automatically attempt to boot (load) the operating system from the Fixed Disk if it cannot boot the system from the mini-floppy drive A. This will occur when the diskette in drive A does not have a copy of the operating system, or when the drive door is left open. This desirable feature allows the system to boot itself without keeping a mini-floppy diskette in the drive. For more efficient operation, the Fixed Disk should contain a "bootable" copy of the operating system.

The Fixed Disk uses its own controller board. The board contains a special microprocessor that makes the Fixed Disk an "intelligent subsystem." The drive performs a sophisticated self-check and correction of the data it stores and retrieves. This is called error checking and correction, or *ECC*. The ECC circuitry of the disk drive will automatically detect and correct improper storage of information. Although this slows performance slightly, the increased storage reliability that ECC provides is worth the decrease in speed.

Fixed media can create additional problems. The operating system used with the hard disk stores special tracking information with the data on the disk. The tracking information is placed on the disk when it is formatted. If the tracking information is lost, this part of the disk becomes unusable. It is inconvenient to reformat the entire disk just to restore the timing information for one section of it. For the completion of this process, all information must be backed up, the formatting performed, and the information restored. Another possibility is to "hide" that portion of the disk from the operating system to prevent further use. The same problem can also occur when a hard disk platter develops a flaw.

ECC plays an important role in these cases. It can detect and correct minor flaws in data stored on the Fixed Disk. Hard disks have been using this concept for more than 10 years. ECC is also used with RAM memory in larger systems, where the contents of the RAM memory must be absolutely correct, and resetting the system is impractical.

As mentioned earlier, all Winchester disks withstand physical abuse better than the cartridge-type hard disk. However, no matter how hardy a disk is, it is not built to survive great shock. The Fixed Disk is rated to withstand 10 Gs (10 times the force of the Earth's gravity) when in use, 20 Gs when turned off. It is reasonably safe to move a Personal Computer across a desk when the unit is on. The desk holding the system can also receive a substantial jar without causing any damage to the Fixed Disk.

When a unit with the Fixed Disk drives is moved across an office or to another building, common safety procedures dictate that the unit be turned off and that the Winchester cease spinning before the machine is moved. Medium- to long-distance moving requires more precautions. A special program is provided on the Diagnostics Diskette of the Personal Computer. This program should be run before a Personal Computer is moved any long distance, or before any traveling takes place that might excessively jar the Personal Computer's hard disk drives, such as in a car. It is a good idea to run this program before turning off the Personal Computer whenever the Personal Computer travels and whatever the distance. This program forces the disk drive recording heads into a safe position, preventing them from "crashing" into the platters' surfaces. (The program is automatically canceled the next time the Personal Computer is turned on.) If any bumpy traveling is anticipated, especially shipping the Personal Computer by commercial carrier, the unit should be placed in its original box for greater safety.

The Fixed Disk may be used with several different operating systems. A utility provided by IBM with its disk operating system allows the disk to be divided into different "logical" volumes. Each operating system may use *one* and *only one* volume.

The Fixed Disk represents IBM's intent to satisfy the serious Personal Computer user. It offers many times the storage space of mini-floppy diskettes and also realizes a significant improvement in speed. Although the Fixed Disk has obvious advantages, the issue of backing it up has not been fully resolved. Like most other pieces of hardware, the Fixed Disk's full capability lies in the software written for it. However, IBM recognized the need for faster, high-capacity, disk drives. The Fixed Disk satisfies most of these requirements.

The Keyboard Unit

One of the joys (and occasional frustrations) of using the IBM Personal Computer stems from the Keyboard Unit, another major part of all Personal Computer systems. Its unique nature means that many of its important features are dependent on the software used.

The Keyboard Unit of the Personal Computer. The 10° or 15° tilt to the keyboard's face is through the two pivotal legs (one shown on the upper left of the unit).

The keyboard of the Personal Computers is virtually identical to the keyboards used on the Displaywriter and the Datamaster/23. Economy, in both numbers and ergonomics, may have dictated this decision, but the Personal Computer operator benefits greatly.

The Keyboard Unit's mobility and pivotal legs allow an operator to type with the unit on a desk or lap. Capacitance technology, coupled with the "feel" of the keys, gives operators the impression of using an IBM Selectric II™ typewriter. The Keyboard Unit is an effective product of applied ergonomics.

For convenience, the keys are arranged into three groups: standard QWERTY keys in the center; a cluster of 15 numeric/cursor-control keys to the right; and 10 special-function keys to the left.

The term QWERTY comes from the top left-hand row of letters. International symbols are used on the backspace, tab, shift, and enter (or return) key caps, which can cause some initial confusion.

A group of 15 keys on the right side of the Keyboard Unit serves double-duty as a numeric keypad and cursor-control/editing keys. When used as a numeric keypad, the numbers 0 through 9 and the period (.) are entered. Plus (+) and minus (-) keys are conveniently located on the right edge of this pad. However, only one enter (return) key is available on the entire keyboard, located in the normal

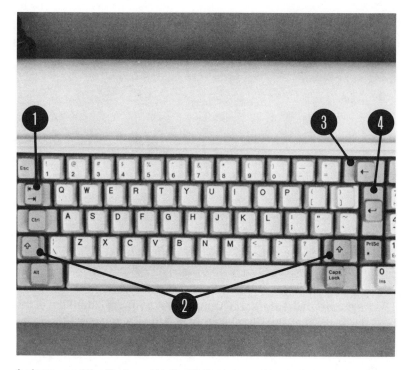

A close-up of the Keyboard Unit with the international symbols used for the tab key (1); the shift keys (2); the backspace key (3); and the enter, or return, key (4).

position. An operator can easily adjust to this arrangement after a short period of time.

The cursor-control/editing keys are also housed on the 0 through 9 and period (.) keys. The 2, 4, 6, and 8 keys move the cursor in four different directions (down, left, right, and up, respectively) one character at a time. The 7 key is the Home key, used for reaching the upper-left position of the current video page. The 0 key is used to insert characters, and the period key deletes the character under the cursor. The other keys function as: 1, End; 3, Page Down; and 9, Page Up.

The use of these keys depends on the operating system and applications program. For example, in PC DOS, the Home key has no special purpose. In IBM BASIC, however, the Home key moves the cursor to the upper left-hand corner of the screen, the "home" position. When the Ctrl key (control key, one of the two "supershift" keys) and the Home key are pressed together, the video screen is cleared and the cursor is moved to the home position. Different programs may use all, some, or none of these cursor-control/editing keys. The use of the keys may even be changed between programs. The intended uses of these keys are indicated in IBM's different PC DOS manuals.

The *default state* (condition on power-up or reset) of these keys is the cursor-control/editing mode. To use the keys as a numeric keypad, the operator may either shift a single key (with the Shift key) or shift the entire keypad by depressing the Num(ber) Lock key located above the pad. In cursor-control/editing mode, a shift of the 7/Home key types a 7. In numeric mode, a shift of the same key would 'home' the cursor if the operating system or program accommodates this. To restore the keypad to cursor-control/editing mode, the operator depresses the Num Lock key again.

The 10 special-function keys (two vertical rows of five keys each) are located to the left of the standard keyboard. The default of the special-function keys for PC DOS is to edit lines before the enter key is pressed. IBM BASIC, CP/M-86 (another operating system for the Personal Computer), and other programs use the special-function keys for a variety of operations, such as striking one special-function key to enter strings of commonly typed characters or to execute programs or commands.

Several additional keys complete the unit: the Alt key (alternative character key, the second supershift key), the */PrtSc (asterisk/-print screen) key, the Caps Lock key, and the Scroll Lock key.

The Alt key is used to enter directly any ASCII character code from the keyboard. This key is held down while the three digits are typed on the numeric keypad (the keypad may be in number-lock or cursor-control/editing mode). The RIOS determines the corresponding ASCII character and enters it. This is one method of obtaining graphics characters. (The other uses of the Alt key are described later.)

Positioned below the enter key is the */PrtSc key. When depressed in the unshifted mode, this key enters an asterisk. When the key is shifted, the computer prints the characters that are on the video screen at that time. (PC DOS V2.0 and CP/M-86 with the GSX graphics also allow the printing of medium- or high-resolution graphics.)

The Caps Lock key affects only the A through Z keys, not the numeric keypad, the special-function keys, the topmost row (where the numbers and some punctuation symbols are located), the punctuation keys, or the print screen (PrtSc) key. This is standard for computers, but unusual for typewriters. Like the Caps Lock key, the shift keys are intelligent. As with a typewriter when Caps Lock is off, the shift key will produce the upper-case letters. Unlike a typewriter, shifting a letter while Caps Lock is on will produce a lower-case letter. The shift key always reverses the case of the letters A through Z, relative to the condition of the Caps Lock key.

The Scroll Lock key indicates that the display text, not the cursor, should be moved when a cursor-control key is pressed. This allows the cursor to stay at one spot while the text on the video screen moves up, down, left, or right. This function is not supported by the RIOS; therefore, special software must be written to obtain it.

Other keystroke combinations that are meaningful to the Personal Computers are listed below. These functions are not absolute because the "interpretation" of the key (what action should be taken when the key is depressed) depends on the operating system and programs used. In all of the cases listed below, the Ctrl (control) key must be held down while the second and third keys are depressed.

Ctrl-Scroll Lock: halts the program in progress (a break key).

Ctrl-Num Lock: Pauses printing (either to the video screen, the printer, or both). Depressing any key restarts printing.

Ctrl →:Moves the cursor back one word

Ctrl ←:Moves the cursor forward one word

Ctrl-End:Erases the display from the current cursor position to the end of the line

Ctrl-PgDn:Erases the display from the current cursor position to the end of the screen

Ctrl-PrtSc:Directs all video output to the printer also

Ctrl-Alt-Del: Causes a system reset (identical to turning the machine off, then on again, except the system's self-test is not performed)

The keyboard has several negative aspects. The placement of the shift keys is unusual. These keys are located on the second row from the bottom, rather than the customary bottom row. This location

A close-up of the cursor control/editing and numeric keypad on the right side of the keyboard. The Num Lock key (1) shifts the pad between editing and numeric uses.

forces readjustment on the part of the operator, and some confusion for touch-typists.

The Caps Lock, Num Lock, and Scroll Lock keys do not have indicators to show if they are active. Operators frequently begin typing and then find that the keyboard is in the wrong state. (Having cursor controls rather than numbers on the right-hand keypad is the most common mistake.)

The location and use of the Esc (escape) key with IBM's BASIC is a disadvantage. The escape key (a key unique to computers) functions as the "clear line" key under PC DOS. Striking this key erases the entire line that the cursor is on. Inadvertently striking this key erases the current line being entered and the prompting question as well. Neither the program nor the computer is damaged, but the operator can easily be confused when this happens.

Pictured is the left side of the keyboard showing the 10 special-function keys.

Part of the keyboard's power comes from its non-ASCII form of "speech" with the Personal Computers. *ASCII* (pronounced ASS-key) is the standard method of representing a character in a byte. A byte holding the value of 65 is equivalent to the ASCII value of the letter *A*. The ASCII value of the number 5 is 53. Each letter, number, punctuation mark, and special computer character has a unique ASCII value. By using the ASCII character set, microcomputers and minicomputers can "talk" to each other. (IBM's other systems use a different character coding method called EBCDIC, pronounced ebb-SEE-dick.)

The Keyboard Unit's "intelligence" comes from the Intel 8048 microprocessor. The 8048 is a relative of the 8080 CPU with 2K of on-chip ROM. By using an inexpensive microprocessor in the Keyboard Unit, the Personal Computers' keyboard can perform more functions that are more sophisticated than those of a standard

Keyboard Diagram

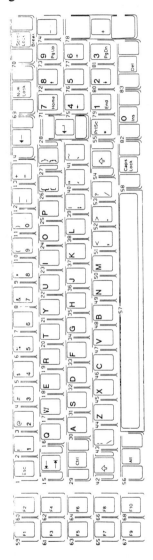

The Keyboard Diagram (above) and Keyboard Scan Codes (next page) from the Technical Reference Manual. The 8048 of the Keyboard Unit sends out a unique code as each key is depressed. (Reprinted with permission from International Business Machines Corporation.)

Table 1. **Keyboard Scan Codes**

Key Position	Scan Code in Hex	Key Position	Scan Code in Hex
1	01	43	2B
2	02	44	2C
3	03	45	2D
4	04	46	2E
5	05	47	2F
6	06	48	30
7	07	49	31
8	08	50	32
9	09	51	33
10	0A	52	34
11	0B	53	35
12	0C	54	36
13	0D	55	37
14	0E	56	38
15	0F	57	39
16	10	58	3A
17	11	59	3B
18	12	60	3C
19	13	61	3D
20	14	62	3E
21	15	63	3F
22	16	64	40
23	17	65	41
24	18	66	42
25	19	67	43
26	1A	68	44
27	1B	69	45
28	1C	70	46
29	1D	71	47
30	1E	72	48
31	1F	73	49
32	20	74	4A
33	21	75	4B
34	22	76	4C
35	23	77	4D
36	24	78	4E
37	25	79	4F
38	26	80	50
39	27	81	51
40	28	82	52
41	29	83	53
42	2A		

The Keyboard Unit at a Glance

Purpose:	To provide typed standard input to Personal Computers
Dimensions:	20 in. (500.0 mm) width
	2.5 in. (57.0 mm) height
	8 in. (200.0 mm) depth
	6 lbs. (2.8 kg) weight
Connector:	5-pin DIN
Location:	Back center of the System Unit
Cable:	6-foot (1.83 m), 4-wire, coiled and shielded cord
Characteristics:	1. 5°, 10°, or 15° tilt to face (using pivotal legs in unit)
	2. 83 keys, including 10 special-function keys and 10 numeric/cursor-control keys
	3. Capacitance technology keys
	4. Auto-repeating at rate of 10/second after key is depressed .5 seconds
	5. 15 keystroke buffer
	6. Intel 8048 microprocessor controlled, including self-test
	7. Non-ASCII code generation

keyboard. The system's power-up test includes the Keyboard Unit, which reports if any key is stuck, or if its ROM is faulty. The self-test even determines whether the Keyboard Unit is plugged in. If any test fails, the Personal Computer beeps, and an error code is displayed on the video screen.

A subprogram in the RIOS supports the keyboard's additional functions. This program captures each keystroke (both depressing *and* releasing a key sends a signal to the Personal Computer) and translates it into the appropriate ASCII code. The special-function keys, cursor-control/editing keys, and other special-purpose keys are interpreted by this subprogram. To control the "meaning" of each keystroke, it is easier to change the translation values for each keystroke than to change how the keyboard "speaks." Most operating systems for the Personal Computers offer utility programs to redefine the meanings of the various keys. The non-ASCII-speaking keyboard is an enhancement to the Personal Computer systems, not a detriment.

The Keyboard Unit contains a 15-character, type-ahead buffer. It allows experienced operators to enter the answer to a program's question before the question is asked.

The Keyboard Unit is the most visibly used component of the Personal Computer systems. The construction of the keyboard makes it a light, mobile, and comfortable unit. The cursor-control/editing and special-function keys, both of which are programmable, make the Keyboard Unit invaluable to frequent users.

CHAPTER 3
The IBM Peripherals

Peripherals are devices that are connected to a computer system to increase its functionality. They are not part of the computer itself. Peripherals can be vital pieces of the computer's hardware. Technically, the disk storage and its adapters, the Expansion Unit and its cards, and the Keyboard Unit are peripherals. (They were discussed in the previous chapter because of their close relationship with the System Unit.)

The peripherals discussed here include the Monochrome and Color Displays, the display adapters, printers, and adapters for communications and games.

Although there are several differences between the Personal Computer and the Personal Computer XT, there is only one difference between adapters for the two systems: the width of the cards. Because the expansion slots on the XT are mounted closer together than the ones on the Personal Computer, there are two versions of almost every adapter card sold by IBM. The XT's and Expansion Unit's cards are narrower, so they don't overlap a second expansion slot. There is no functional difference. In rare cases, such as the Asynchronous Communications Adapters, some additional features have been added. Any differences between the original card and the current version will be clearly stated.

The Monochrome Display, Printer, and Adapter

Since 1976, the computer video display, or *CRT* (cathode-ray tube), has dominated the industry. The display permits rapid communication between computer and operator as well as visual editing for entering data or text into a computer system. The alternative was a noisy, paper-creasing Teletype machine, which offered far fewer advantages than a CRT. As local computing power has found its way into more homes and offices, the Teletype's telephone-communications ability has become less useful. Although many of these machines are still in service, the standard for the terminal (the operator's display and keyboard) is the CRT.

The Monochrome Display

The IBM Monochrome Display is like a black and white television set, but with several improvements. The Display's picture tube uses green phosphor (number P-39 for a black and green display) to minimize eye fatigue and also has a much higher resolution (more dots per square inch) than regular televisions for a crisper character image.

The physical dimensions of the Monochrome Display are similar to those of a 12-inch portable television. The Display has two 3-foot (914 mm.) cables, a power cable, and a signal cable. The power cable has a unique three-prong connector that plugs into the back of the System Unit or Expansion Unit to receive a.c. power. The on/off switch of these Units also controls a.c. power to the Mono-chrome Display. This arrangement of using one one wall receptacle

Pictured is the Monochrome Monitor, the IBM 80 CPS Dot-Matrix Printer, and the combination Monochrome Display/Printer Adapter.

for the Display/System Unit or Display/Expansion Unit allows the Personal Computer to be used in rooms with few wall outlets.

The Display's signal cable plugs ino the Monochrome Display/ Printer Adapter (described later in this chapter). The display fits on either the System Unit or the Expansion Unit. Because the display's cables are short, any other arrangement is difficult.

The Monochrome Display has a bandwidth of 16.27 MHz. and high vertical and horizontal resolution. Its characters are made up of dots in a 7- (horizontal) by 9-dot (vertical) format in a 9- by 14-dot box. Appropriate lower-case letters have *descenders*, which give letters such as *y* or *p* their proper appearance in a line. The Display supports 80-character columns by 25 lines.

The Monochrome Display at a Glance

Purpose:	To provide monochrome (two color) video output for the Personal Computers
Cables:	AC power cable — integral three-prong, non-standard plug, 3 ft. (.914 m) cord
	signal cable — integral 9-connector, 4 ft. (1.22m) cable, 9-pin "0" connector for adapter
Power:	AC power supplied from System or Expansion Unit
Characteristics:	1. 80 x 25 display
	2. 7 x 9 characters with descenders in a 9- x 14-character box
	3. Direct drive video
	4. 16.27 MHz bandwidth (max.)
	5. Screen refreshed at 50 Hz, 720 horizontal resolution, 350 vertical lines
	6. Contrast and brightness controls located on front of unit.
	7. Incapable of light-pen use

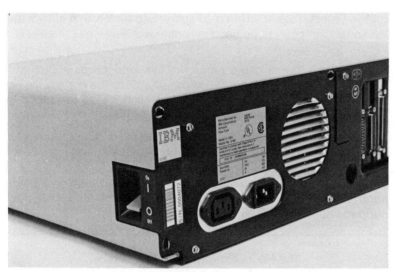

*A close-up of the left, back corner of the System Unit. The on/off switch
controls power to the Monochrome Display. The leftmost, three-prong
outlet is used to supply the Monochrome Monitor with power. The right
outlet is used to connect the a.c. power cord to the System Unit.*

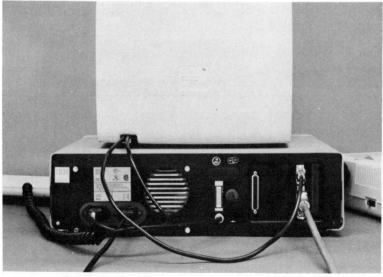

*The back of a Personal Computer with the various cables shown for each
major unit (Keyboard, Monochrome Display, and Printer).*

One convenient feature of the Monochrome Display is the placement of the brightness and contrast controls on the front of the unit. This arrangement facilitates screen adjustment for an operator's preference or room lighting.

The features of the Monochrome Display combine to yield crisp, flicker-free, easily discernible characters for eye comfort during long working sessions. This benefit is largely due to the slow-changing (highly retentive) P-39 phosphor of the display's cathode-ray tube. The only disadvantage of P-39 phosphor is that it negates the use of graphics or a light pen on the Monochrome Display.

The IBM Printers

When the Personal Computer was first introduced, IBM offered the 80 CPS Printer. In the latter half of 1982, IBM introduced a second, improved version of this printer with graphics capabilities, understandably called the Graphics Printer. This section discusses both printers, although the original 80 CPS Printer has been discontinued.

The IBM Printers are manufactured by Epson America, Inc., and have the same two-tone buff color of the Personal Computers. The Matrix 80 CPS printer is Epson's MX-80 printer, a very popular dot-matrix printer. In early 1983 Epson incorporated the popular and low-cost Graftrax™ ROM into the MX-80 and called it the FX-80. This is the IBM Graphics Printer. When the FX-80 was announced, the MX-80 model was discontinued.

Both printers, Matrix and Graphics, operate at a speed of 80 characters per second (cps). They are *bidirectional* printers, which means that printing can occur as the printhead moves in either direction. This type of printing yields more continuous characters per second than printers with unidirectional printing.

IBM printers accept forms between 4 (101.6 mm.) and 10 inches (254 mm.) wide and 3 plies thick, with sprocket holes on the side for tractor feeding. The paper is fed from the back of the unit. The printers use a removable cartridge containing a black ribbon with a capacity of three million characters for 10.4 hours of nonstop use. Typical ribbon life, depending on use, is between 3 and 12 weeks. Frequent graphics printing rapidly reduces this figure. Blue ribbons are available from Epson, and companies other than Epson and IBM sell different colors.

The IBM Printers at a Glance

Purpose:	To provide printed copy
Manufacturer:	Epson America, Inc.

Types of printers
and manufacturer's
model numbers:

Matrix 80 CPS Printer (original)	MX-80
Graphics 80 CPS Printer	FX-80

Date of introduction: 1979 (MX-80),   1983 (FX-80)

Dimensions:
  Matrix Printer:

    4.2 in. (107 mm) height
    14.7 in. (374 mm) width
    12.0 in. (305 mm) depth
    12 lb.   (5.5 kg)   weight

  Graphics Printer:

    4.3 in. (110 mm) height
    15.7 in. (400 mm) width
    14.5 in. (depth)   depth
    12.9 lb. (5.9 kg)   weight

Printer cable: 6 ft (1.8 m) length
                 1.25 lb. (0.57 kg) weight

Power cable: 6 ft (1.8 m) length (three-prong)

Output speed: 80 CPS (characters per second)

Interface type: Parallel (Centronics-standard)

Forms handling: Sprocket (tractor) feed paper
                 min. width —   4 in. (102 mm)
                 max. width — 10 in. (254 mm)
                 max. thickness — 3-ply, 0.012 in. (0.3 mm)

Power: 120 vac, 60 Hz (104 vac min., 127 vac max.)
        1 amp. max., 100 VA max. power consumption

Characteristics:
1. 9-pin, dot-matrix printing head (replace-able)
2. Bi-directional printing with logic seeking
3. 9 by 9 dot characters, with full 96 character ASCII set, 9 international symbols/characters.
4. Removable black ribbon cartridge (3 million character life)
5. Software control of all printing functions and features.

Print sizes[1]:

Normal	10	80
Enlarged	5	40
Condensed	16.5	132
Condensed-enlarged	8.25	66
Superscript[2]	10	80
Subscript[2]	10	80

Print fonts:

Normal	single-strike of character
Double	double-strike of character
Emphasized	shadow print (single strike, step sideways by $\frac{1}{216}$ in. (0.118 mm) and strike again)
Underline[2]	underline character

Vertical spacing: Matrix Printer adjustable to 6, 8, 10 lines per inch (25.4 mm)
Graphics Printer also adjustable in $\frac{1}{216}$ inch (0.099 mm) increments.

Horizontal and Vertical tabs: at any line or character position.

Major differences between Matrix and Graphics Printer: Matrix has one additional set of 64 block characters.
Graphics has two additional sets of symbols, signs, characters, and block characters (95 and 132, respectively). Selection of sets or graphics is software controllable.

Dot-by-dot addressing (graphics): Matrix — no;   Graphics — yes

Printing modes: Matrix — 5 modes
Graphics — 8 modes

Graphics printer can also skip line perforations, print unidirectionally, move the print head to home (leftmost) position, use 480, 960, 1920 bit graphics modes; print enlarged characters without affecting entire line.

Notes: [1] Not all combinations of features (print sizes with certain fonts) are simultaneously usable.
[2] Available only on Graphics Printer.

The printers use a replaceable, 9-wire printhead. A new printhead can be installed in less than 15 minutes by a nontechnical person. The printhead has an average life of 30 million characters, or an average real lifetime of five months to five years. Graphics printing, because of its heavy use of the printhead, reduces the life span of the printhead.

With the 9-wire printhead, a basic 9- x 9-dot pattern is used to form the characters. Horizontal character sizes of 5 to 16.5 characters per inch (CPI) are available. On an 8-inch line, the printer produces a maximum of 40, 66, 80, or 132 characters. Characters may be emphasized by using different effects or fonts, bold or shadow printing, and/or double strike (printing the same character twice in the same spot). Some combinations yield near letter-quality printing.

Vertical formats include 5, 6, 8, or 10 lines per inch (LPI). The printers allow horizontal and vertical tabbing for rapid indexing through preprinted forms. All features are controlled through software.

The printers have a self-test pattern and "paper-out" sensing. Paper-out sensing is detected by the RIOS of the Personal Computers. This sensing and "time-out" (the printer is turned off) can be returned to programs as errors.

The Matrix Printer cannot print most of the graphics character set that is available to the display. The Graphics Printers, on the other hand, can print the entire graphics set. In addition, the Graphics Printer can print graphics. These statements may seem redundant, but they are not. A brief explanation of graphics characters and graphics is necessary.

Graphics characters are the special symbols used by the Personal Computer's display. They include Greek and math symbols, playing-card symbols, block symbols, and others. Basically, any characters not found in the standard ASCII character set but produced by the IBM displays are graphics characters. (The *BASIC Reference Manual* has a complete list of these characters.)

The standard definition of *graphics* is dot-by-dot control of the video screen. The proper program can also control the printhead of the Graphics Printer and allow the printing of high-resolution graphs, charts, and even pictures. (Graphics is discussed further in the sections on the Color Display and adapter.)

Through this enhanced ability to control its printhead, the Graphics Printer can fully reproduce the image from any IBM display, whether

This is Normal printing.
This is a line of printing from the IBM 80 CPS Printer.

This is Condensed printing.
This is a line of printing from the IBM 80 CPS Printer.

This is Enlarged printing.
This is a line of printing from the

This is Emphasized printing.
This is a line of printing from the IBM 80 CPS Printer.

This is Double printing (bold).
This is a line of printing from the IBM 80 CPS Printer.

This is Condensed-Enlarged printing.
This is a line of printing from the IBM 80 CPS Printer.

This is Emphasized with Normal and Enlarged.
This is a line of print from the IBM 80 CPS Printer.

This is Condensed-Double printing.
This is a line of printing from the IBM 80 CPS Printer.

This is Emphasized-Double printing.
This is a line of printing from the IBM 80 CPS Printer.

This is Condensed-Enlarged-Double printing.
This is a line of printing from the IBM 80 CPS Printer.

Some of the various printing styles available on the 80 CPS printer.

it is composed of graphics characters or graphics. The Matrix Printer cannot. By installing the Graftrax ROM, not available through IBM, owners of the original 80 CPS Printer can obtain most of this capability. (Certain graphics symbols are not in the Graftrax ROM.)

The IBM printers, light and transportable like the computer itself, are suitable choices for most users of the Personal Computers. However, the limited paper width (maximum of 10 inches, or 254 mm.) makes this printer unsuited for some types of work. Tasks that demand 14-inch wide paper, for example, need a different printer. It should be remembered that, through software, the IBM printers can print 132 characters per line on 8-inch paper.

These printers do not produce letter quality output. If letter quality is desired, other printers, or a combination of IBM and non-IBM printers, may be necessary.

The Monochrome Display/Printer Adapter

The Monochrome Display/Printer Adapter (D/P) serves the dual purpose of linking the Personal Computers to the display and the printer. The printer functions of this card are identical to those of the separate IBM Printer Adapter.

Serving as the computer's pathway to the printer, the printer interface uses *parallel* communication, in which the 8 bits that represent a character are simultaneously sent down eight separate lines. *Serial* is the other principal form of communication, in which the 8 bits are sent down one line, one bit after the other, to the listening device (printer, display, modem, etc.).

The printer interface conforms to the electrical standard established by Centronics Data Products Corporation. Centronics™, a major printer manufacturer, established an electronic and physical connection that is used by most manufacturers of parallel printers today.

Although the electrical connections and the physical connector (36-pin) of the IBM Printers are Centronics-standard, the printer adapter's connector is not. The printer interface uses a DB-25 (25-pin) female connector mainly for serial devices. To connect the adapter to the Centronics-style connector, the IBM Printer Cable must be used. This cable will attach almost any printer that uses the Centronics parallel interface with the Personal Computers.

The Monochrome Display/Printer Adapter

Purpose:	To provide an interface between the Monochrome Display and Centronics-compatable printer.
Location:	Any full-length System Unit expansion slot
Dimensions:	14 in. (357 mm) width 4 in. (102 mm) height 0.25 in. (6.3 mm) depth
Display Adapter contents:	1. Motorola 6845 CRT Controller 2. 4K static RAM for display buffer 3. 8K ROM for 256 character codes 4. Support circuitry 5. 6-pin connector for light pen 6. 4-pin connector for RF modulator 7. 9-pin "D" connector for monitor
Display Adapter Characteristics:	1. 80 or 40 by 25 text display 2. Normal, reverse (black on white), and underline character modes with independent flashing and high-intensity modes 3. Software compatible with Color/Graphics Adapter (some combinations restricted) 4. DMA addressing of on-board memory, effective transfer rate 1.8M bytes/second 5. Light pen not usable with P-39 phosphor displays
Printer Adapter contents and characteristics:	1. Centronics-compatible, bidirectional 8-bit parallel port 2. Handles Acknowledge, Busy, Paper Out, and Select signals. 3. Uses any Centronics-compatible device 4. Has 12 TTL, buffered output lines writable software control 5. Has 5 "steady-state" input lines readable under software control 6. Use female 25-pin "D" connector

There are two reasons for this unusual connection at the adapter end. The Centronics interface does not require all 36 lines; therefore, a 25-line Printer Cable may be used. In addition, long cables can suffer a problem called *crosstalk*, in which the parallel wires interfere with each other. This can occur in both serial and parallel cables. Serial cables have several parallel lines, but only one line transmits the 8 bits in one direction. The number of lines in a serial cable is usually less than in a parallel cable. The greater the number of lines, the greater the probability of crosstalk.

To combat crosstalk, additional lines that ground (absorb) these signals are added. The IBM Printer Cable has several of these ground lines and a strong cover to resist wear.

Because the Centronics standard is preserved by the Printer Cable, almost any printer using this standard can be connected, including most dot-matrix and several letter-quality printers. However, unless the printer responds and appears like an IBM Printer, some features can be lost. This problem does not affect the screen-printing ability of the Personal Computer, but does apply to software commands such as changing fonts, character and line spacing, and the printing of graphics and graphics characters. Physical differences in the character sets available, differences in the commands that control features, and the lack of graphics capabilities can affect printer performance. Prospective purchasers of non-IBM printers should review each printer's capabilities and select the appropriate printer based on anticipated applications.

The printer interface contains the necessary "intelligence" for hardware *handshaking*, the monitoring of the printer's ability to accept more characters in its buffer. Without handshaking, the printer would lose characters, and its output would be unreliable.

A little-publicized feature of the printer interface is its function as a general-purpose, input/output parallel port. Any parallel device that uses TTL (Transistor to Transistor Logic) levels of electricity can be connected and used. The RIOS handles the exchange of information to and from the parallel port. However, only one device, such as a printer, can be used at a time. If the interface is used as a general-purpose I/O port, the user must also choose the necessary software to obtain data from the port.

The only difference between the combination Monochrome Display/Printer Adapter and the Printer Adapter is *memory location* (where the computer "sees" and communicates with the adapters). The base (starting) addresses for the printer portions of the D/P Adapter and Printer Adapter are 68 locations apart. Otherwise, the cards function identically.

Pictured is the Printer Adapter. The Printer portion of the Display/Printer Adapter is functionally equivalent to this card.

The Printer Adapter may be placed in the Expansion Unit, if desired. However, the Monochrome Display/Printer Adapter must reside in the System Unit for proper use.

The Monochrome Display portion of the D/P Adapter controls the communications between the Personal Computers and the display.

The adapter contains all the necessary circuitry to support the various modes of the display.

The 6845 CRT Controller

The D/P Adapter (and the Color/Graphics Adapter) uses the Motorola 6845 CRT Controller chip. This controller is very versatile. It offers a variety of character widths on a line (80 and 40 characters per line are the two standard modes), a variety of display modes (blinking and intensity, for example), and great flexibility with graphics characters. The 6845 is software controlled; a program can "talk" directly to the chip and control its operation of the video display.

Data entry is one example of how the Controller is used. A program can direct the chip to control the window (the area of the screen where text may be placed) on the video display. By restricting this window, the program can place a form on the screen and prompt the operator to fill in the blanks, without erasing any of the text. Other programs that require high-speed updating of the screen, such as spreadsheet programs, use the 6845 for this purpose.

The Monochrome Display/Printer Adapter contains 8K of ROM and 4K of RAM. The ROM holds the 256 different character formats (codes), and the RAM holds one 80-character by 25-line screen of information. The display is updated (refreshed) every 1/50th of a second, and the adapter can scroll text without flickering.

The D/P Adapter and Color/Graphics Adapter are compatible. Each uses two bytes of memory for every displayed character. The first byte contains the ASCII code for the character. The second contains the *attribute code.* The attribute byte controls four different video features: the darkness of the background, the darkness of the foreground (the character), the brightness (intensity) of the characters, and whether the character will blink on and off. (The Color/Graphics Adapter is discussed later.)

There are six possible combinations for the attribute byte on the monochrome screen:
1. Light characters on a dark background (normal video)
2. Dark characters on a light background (reverse video)
3. Flashing bright characters on a dark background
4. Flashing dark characters on a light background
5. Light characters on a light background (invisible character)
6. Dark characters on a dark background (also invisible)

Because a programmer can directly access the memory used to display characters, better entertainment and educational programs

---

The 6845 CRT Controller at a Glance

Purpose: To provide the necessary interface to drive a raster scan CRT

Primary manufacturer: Motorola Semiconductors, Inc.

Date of introduction: 1978

Location: Used on Monochrome Display/Printer and Color/Graphics Monitor Adapter

Characteristics: 1. 19 internal registers (between 4 and 6 bits wide)
                        2. Address register loaded with index to other registers
                        3. Other registers control
                            a. Number of characters on line
                            b. Number of scan iines
                            c. Cursor start and end
                            d. Horizontal and vertical sync. positions and adjustments
                            e. Reading of Light pen position

---

can be created. This direct access, coupled with the programmer's control of the 6845 controller chip, makes many ultrafast visual effects possible.

The 25th line on the display (with both adapters) is used primarily as a *status line*. The status line shows the time and date with CP/M-86, and the settings of the special-function keys with IBM BASIC. It can be used to issue prompts to the operator, such as to change diskettes, or to report the status of the program's work in progress. The 25th line represents a "safe" place for information because programs do not normally use this area of the display.

The Monochrome Display/Printer Adapter is also capable of using a *light pen*. With this device, the computer can "read" and tell the locations pointed at on the video screen. However, a light pen cannot be used with the IBM Monochrome Display or any other slow-phosphor display because the phosphors cannot be turned on and off fast enough.

The Monochrome Display/Printer Adapter's dual purpose of handling the display and parallel printer makes it a powerful multifunction card. This card, the Monochrome Display, and the Printer are found on many Personal Computer systems because of their low cost. The Monochrome Display is a logical choice for those seeking a nonglare, high-resolution display without graphics or color. The IBM Printers, although not the fastest or most versatile printers, fit their roles well, particularly the current Graphics Printer. All three pieces make an outstanding contribution to the overall performance and use of the Personal Computer systems.

The Color Display
and
Color/Graphics Monitor Adapter

An alternative to the Monochrome Display and adapter is now available to Personal Computer owners: the Color Display and the Color/Graphics Adapter. Many of the Color Display's capabilities are linked to the Color/Graphics Adapter (described in a separate section).

The Color Display

The two-tone, buff-colored Color Display, introduced in March of 1983, is a 13-inch (34 cm.) RGB monitor. *RGB* stands for red, green, and blue—the three primary colors of the visible spectrum. The Color Display is different from other color video monitors in that it has a greater resolution and can display 80-column lines without blurring the characters.

The Color Display has a bandwidth of 14 MHz. Four different, independent lines are used to drive the display—a red, a blue, a green, and an intensity (brightness) line. The screen can hold 200 dots vertically and more than 640 dots horizontally, although the Color/Graphics Adapter supports only 640 dots in monochrome mode.

When the Color Display is used with the Color/Graphics Adapter, 16 different colors are possible. Characters are formed in an 8-dot by 8-dot matrix. The characters shown on the Color Display are not as clearly delineated as they are on the Monochrome Display. Because the Monochrome Display and Adapter use a 7- x 9-dot format in a 9- x 14-dot box, there is more space between characters on the

The Color Display at a Glance

Purpose:
To provide colored and monochrome video output for the Personal Computers.

Dimensions:
11.7 in. (297 mm) height
15.4 in. (392 mm) length
15.6 in. (407 mm) depth
26 lb.   (11.8 kg)   weight

Video screen:
13 in. (340 mm) diagonal screen
High-contrast (black) screen
Red, Green, and Blue phospher

Cables:
AC power cable — three-prong, 6 ft. (1.83 m), detachable cord
signal cable — Integral 9-conductor, 5 ft. (1.5 m) cable; 9-pin "D" connector for adapter

Power:
120 vac @ 60 Hz or 220 vac @ 50 (standard a.c. wall current)
Unit self-senses and self-switches to supplied power

Characteristics:
1. 80 x 25 display
2. 7 by 7 characters with 1 dot descenders in 8 by 8 character box
3. Direct-drive video; independent signals to red, green, blue, and intensity
4. Capable of displaying up to 16 colors (when used with Color/Graphics Adapter)
5. 14 MHz bandwidth (maximum)
6. Screen refreshed at 60 Hz with 200 lines of vertical resolution
7. 15.75 KHz horizontal drive
8. On/off indicator, on/off power switch, brightness and contrast controls on front of unit.
9. Capable of light pen use.

Monochrome Display than on the Color Display. On the Color Display, lower-case letters with descenders appear almost to merge with characters on the next line. Because characters are easier to discern on the Monochrome Display, it is preferred for text work.

Pictured at the top is the IBM Color Display. The front of the RGB monitor contains (from top to bottom) the power indicator, the on/off knob, and the brightness and contrast controls. At the bottom is the back of the Color Display with its vertical size and hold controls.

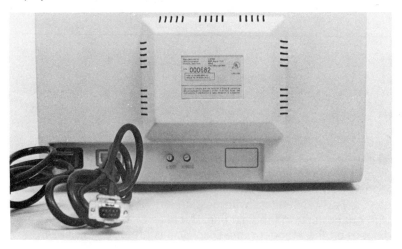

The Color/Graphics Adapter at a Glance

Purpose: To provide video signals for display on a monitor or television set with RF modulator

Location: Any expansion slot if Monochrome Display/Printer Adapter is used. Only System Unit's expansion slot if this is the only display adapter.

Dimensions:
4.25 in. (108 mm) height
13.25 in. (337 mm) length
0.5 in. (12.7 mm) depth

Contents:
1. 6845 CRT Controller chip
2. 16K RAM for display buffer
3. 8K ROM for character codes
4. Supporting circuitry
5. Connectors
   a. 9-pin "D" connector for RGB monitor (back of board)
   b. RCA-phono for composite video monitors (back of board)
   c. 4-pin connector for user-supplied RF modulator (rear of board)
   d. 6-pin connector to user-supplied light pen (rear of board)

Characteristics:
1. Privides RGBI (red, green, blue, intensity) signals for high-resolution monitors (RGB).
2. Provides composite video signals for monitors (monochrome or color) or RF modulators.
3. Program control of video characteristics.
4. Has two display modes (A/N and APA)
5. Color burst (characteristics) killed on composite video outputs when in A/N mode.

Display Modes:
A/N (alphanumeric or text primary mode)

7 by 7 dot or 5 by 7 dot characters with 1 dot descenders (jumper-selectable) on a 8 by 8 dot character box

Two sets of secondary modes

Characters per line secondary mode (25 lines per screen)

	80 characters per line — 4 different screens available
	40 characters per line — 8 different screens available
	Color or Monochrome secondary modes
	Color mode — independent intensity supported with 16 possible colors[1]
	Monochrome mode — blink, reverse, and intensity available.
	Background, foreground, and boards independently selectable in either color or monochrome mode.
	Sets of secondary modes work independently.
APA (all-points addressable) graphics primary mode	Three secondary modes available, only one secondary mode available at a time.
	Low-resolution mode[2] 160 pixels by 100 pixels 2 by 2 dots per pixel 16 colors available
	Medium-resolution mode 320 dots by 200 dots 4 colors available at one time
	High-resolution 640 dots by 200 dots monochrome colors only
Notes:	[1] dependent upon the type of display used. [2] not supported by RIOS of Personal Computers

In other areas, ease of use has guided the construction of the Color Monitor. The display has two cables: one for power and one for the video signals. Each cable is about 5 feet (1.5 m.) long. This cable length allows the display to be placed on top of, or next to, the Personal Computers and is helpful for systems that use both the Monochrome and the Color Displays.

The Color Display has its own power supply, which requires that the cord be plugged into an a.c. wall outlet. The power supply is constructed to sense and adjust to 120-volt, 60-Hz. or 220-volt, 50-Hz. power, allowing the display to be used in North America or overseas. The second cable, the signal cable, plugs into the Color/Graphics Adapter.

Three controls are located on the front of the unit: brightness and contrast, which allow screen adjustment to suit the operator's preference or room lighting, and an on/off switch with an indicator for power control. Controls for vertical size and hold are on the back of the unit.

The IBM Color Monitor is a valuable addition to the Personal Computer family. (A further review of its capabilities appears in the next section.)

The Color/Graphics Monitor Adapter

The Color/Graphics Monitor Adapter is conceivably a misnomer because of the two possible misconceptions that can be derived from its name. The first is that the adapter can be used with only a monitor. In fact, the adapter can be used with a monitor, or with a user-supplied RF modulator and a television. The second misconception comes from the term "color/graphics." The adapter has the same graphics characters as the Monochrome Display/Printer Adapter. Color characters and individually addressable dots (graphics) are also provided.

The Color/Graphics Monitor Adapter (C/G) is the computers' pathway to either a video monitor or a television set. Like the D/P Adapter, the C/G Adapter uses the 6845 controller. The basic difference between the boards is that the C/G provides color and graphics, whereas the D/P provides neither. In addition, the C/G Adapter contains 16K of RAM, whereas the D/P Adapter has only 4K.

The C/G Adapter comes in two versions: the original (for the Personal Computer), and a trimline version for the Personal Computer XT and the Expansion Unit. If two monitors, one Monochrome and one Color, are used, the C/G card may be placed in any slot. If the

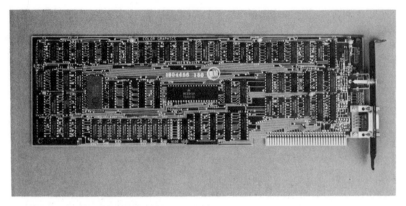

A close-up of the Color/Graphics Adapter.

C/G Adapter is the only display adapter used, it must reside in the System Unit. (This applies to systems that use the Expansion Unit.)

The C/G Adapter has two primary modes of operation:

1. Alphanumeric (text) mode (abbreviated A/N)
2. All points addressable (controllable dot-by-dot graphics) mode (abbreviated APA)

Each primary mode contains several secondary display modes. The secondary modes for A/N are 40-or 80-character lines, in color or monochrome. All A/N secondary modes have 25 lines. The 40-character per line mode is used by televisions and low-or medium-resolution monitors. The 80-character per line mode is used by high-resolution monitors (including the IBM Color Display) that can legibly display an 80-character line.

The monochrome A/N mode can display characters in reverse (inverse), high-intensity, and blinking video. The A/N color mode supports 16 different foreground (character) colors and one of eight background colors at a time. Blinking characters are also available.

The A/N characters, including graphics characters, can be displayed in two formats: 5-x 7-dot or 7-x 7-dot in an 8 x 8 box. The 7 x 7 format is the default. Changing a jumper on the adapter allows the use of the 5-x 7-dot characters. These are not as crisp looking as those on the Monochrome Display. Only one row is provided for descenders, giving some lower-case letters in the 7 x 7 format the appearance of almost merging with the characters on the next line.

Like the D/P Adapter, the C/G Adapter's RAM memory is used for the video display. Each character uses two bytes: one for the ASCII character and one for the attribute code. The D/P Adapter holds 4K of RAM. The C/G Adapter uses the additional 12K of RAM to hold eight 40-by 25-character or four 80-by 25-character screens of data. The memory and the 6845 controller chip are directly accessible. Some ingenious programs use this feature to write information to a nonactive "screen," then flip the display to the just-updated screen. This multiple-screen capability allows information to be displayed "instantly."

The colors available to the Color/Graphics Monitor Adapters and the Color Display are listed in Table 3.1. The numbers used to denote the colors are identical to the numbers used in IBM's BASIC.

TABLE 3.1
Available Colors for Color/Graphics Monitor Adapter

#	Color	R	G	B	I	#	Color	R	G	B	I
0.	Black		none			8.	Dark Gray				X
1.	Blue			X		9.	Light Blue			X	X
2.	Green		X			10.	Light Green		X		X
3.	Cyan		X	X		11.	Light Cyan		X	X	X
4.	Red	X				12.	Light Red	X			X
5.	Magenta	X		X		13.	Light Magenta	X		X	X
6.	Brown	X	X			14.	Yellow	X	X		X
7.	Light Gray	X	X	X		15.	White	X	X	X	X

Medium Resolution Graphics foreground colors

Set 1		Set 2	
1.	Cyan	1.	Green
2.	Magenta	2.	Red
3.	White	3.	Brown

R = Red   G = Green   B = Blue   I = Intensity

Note: Colors 8 through 15 may not be available on some TVs or monitors.

The 16 possible colors are variations of the three primary colors (red, green, and blue) and the intensity (brightness or drive) signal. (In electronic and photographic color mixing, green, not yellow, is the third primary color.) The three primary colors produce eight different colors (including black, the absence of color). The intensity signal produces an additional set of eight lighter tints. Some monitors and television sets cannot detect the intensity signal; therefore, the eight additional colors may not be available on these displays. This makes the proper choice of a display important if all 16 colors are desired.

The APA (graphics) mode has three secondary modes: low-, medium-, and high-resolution.

In *low resolution*, the screen is formed into 160 by 100 pels; each pel is 2 dots by 2 dots. All 16 foreground and background colors are possible. However, the RIOS (ROMed Basic Input/Output System) and other system software do not support low-resolution graphics.

Medium-resolution graphics divide the video display into 320 by 200 points. The color scheme for medium-resolution graphics is somewhat complex. Two sets of colors are available for each dot: (1) cyan, magenta, and white; or (2) green, red, and brown. Only one set of colors can be used at a time. However, any dot may have the same color as the background, where all 16 colors are available. This means that four colors can be used with medium-resolution graphics.

For example, if the background color is blue and the first set of colors is selected, a program can draw a cyan, magenta, white, or blue dot. If the second set of colors is chosen, the program can draw a green, red, brown, or blue dot.

Colors from the two different sets cannot be intermingled on the screen. The only exception is the background color, which may be chosen freely without this restriction. If green is used with the first set of colors, green must be chosen as the background color. This allows cyan, magenta, white, or green dots to be drawn. Similarly, if cyan is used with the second set of colors, cyan must be selected as the background color, thereby making green, red, brown, and cyan the available colors.

This limitation on color use in medium-resolution mode is related to the RAM memory on the adapter. Each dot uses two bits, giving four possible combinations. The 320- by 200-point format requires 128,000 bits of memory, or 16,000 bytes. Only four colors are available in the medium-resolution mode because the adapter's 16K (16,384 bytes) of memory can work with only four colors at a time.

```
60 LOCATE 7,12,0:PRINT "Personal Computer"
70 COLOR 10,5,0:LOCATE 10,5,0:PRINT CHR$(213)+STRING$(21,205)+CHR$(184)
80 LOCATE 11,9,0:PRINT CHR$(179)+"       SAMPLES       "+CHR$(179)
90 LOCATE 12,9,0:PRINT CHR$(179)+STRING$(21,32)+CHR$(179)
100 LOCATE 13,9,0:PRINT CHR$(179)+"    Version 1.00     "+CHR$(179)
110 LOCATE 14,9,0:PRINT CHR$(212)+STRING$(21,205)+CHR$(190)
120 COLOR 15,0:LOCATE 17,7,0:PRINT "(C) Copyright IBM Corp 1981"
130 COLOR 14,0:LOCATE 23,7,0:PRINT "Press space bar to continue"
140 POKE 106,0 'CLEAR KYBD BUFFER
150 CMD$ = INKEY$
160 IF CMD$="" THEN GOTO 150
170 IF CMD$ = CHR$(27) THEN GOTO 360
180 IF CMD$ = " " THEN GOTO 200
190 GOTO 140
200 SCREEN 0,1:COLOR 15,0,0:CLS:LOCATE 5,3:PRINT "SAMPLE PROGRAMS"
210 LOCATE 7,3,0:PRINT "A - MUSIC    (32k)"
220 LOCATE 8,3,0:PRINT "B - ART     (32k-Color/Graphics)"
230 LOCATE 9,3,0:PRINT "C - MORTGAGE (48k)"
240 LOCATE 10,3,0:PRINT "D - CIRCLE  (BASICA-Color/Graphics)"
250 LOCATE 11,3,0:PRINT "E - DONKEY  (BASICA-Color/Graphics)"

Ok

1LIST  2RUN  3LOAD  4SAVE  5CONT  6        7TRON  8TROFF  9KEY      0SCREEN
```

A picture of text (above) and medium-resolution graphics (below) from the Color/Graphics Monitor Adapter and Amdek Color-II monitor. An RGB monitor is necessary to obtain a full 80-character display with legibility. (Monitor courtesy of Amdek, Inc.)

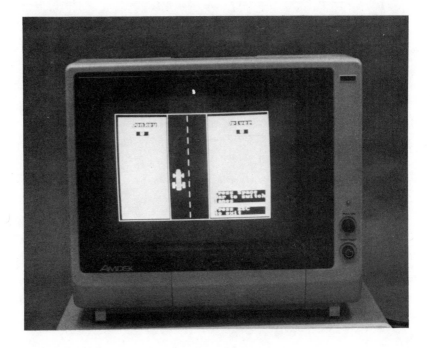

Color/Graphics Monitor Adapter Auxiliary Video Connectors

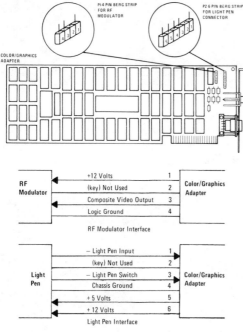

Color/Graphics Monitor Adapter Direct Drive, and Composite Interface Pin Assignment

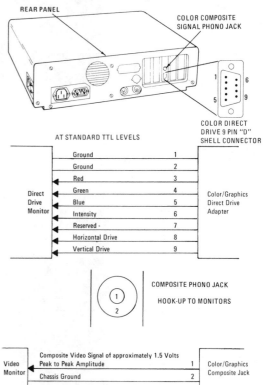

Information on connections for the Color/Graphics Adapter from the Technical Reference Manual. (Reprinted with permission from International Business Machines Corporation.)

The 384 bytes of memory on the adapter are used for other purposes.

The *high-resolution* APA mode divides the screen into 640 by 200 dots. This arrangement has twice the resolution of the medium-resolution mode. Each dot requires one bit of memory and also uses 16,000 bytes of on-board memory. Only black and white colors are available at this resolution because not enough RAM memory is available to support other colors. In addition, few monitors and no televisions can support colors at this resolution. Therefore, most monitors displaying this high-resolution mode can do so only in black and white.

Monitors, Televisions, and the Adapter

Three basic display devices may be used with the Color/Graphics Monitor Adapter: a television, a medium- or high-resolution monitor, and an RBG monitor.

A television with an *RF modulator,* a device that converts composite video signals into television-channel frequencies, can be used with the C/G Adapter. A 4-pin jack is provided on the C/G Adapter for most RF modulators. Because of the television's limited bandwidth (5 MHz. versus the typical 7 to 14 MHz. of video monitors), the 40 by 25 A/N mode must be used. Televisions simply cannot support the 80-column alphanumeric mode. Like other computers that use RF modulators, some television sets perform better than others. Some sets do not perform at all, and the display will be illegible. In the United States, RF modulators should be FCC (Federal Communications Commission) approved so that they do not interfere with other television sets.

Most black and white (or monochrome) video monitors can handle the 80 by 25 A/N mode. An RCA™ "phono" jack on the back of the adapter provides the necessary composite video signals. These signals may be used with color and monochrome monitors. The RCA-type connector is common, and many prefabricated cables and connectors are available.

The second connector on the back of the C/G Adapter is a 9-pin "D" connector. It is identical to the Monochrome Display's connector. This connector, however, is used with color or RGB monitors, not with the Monochrome Display. Very few monitors use the 9-pin connector (the 8-pin connector is more common), and, until recently, connection cables were not readily available. The 9-pin "D" connector is important because it makes available to RGB monitors the four necessary color signals (red, green, blue, and intensity).

Most standard color monitors do not have the resolution necessary for displaying the 80 by 25 A/N mode. As a result, the characters are smeared and illegible. Most monitors with this limitation can successfully use the 40 by 25 mode.

If a standard color monitor is unsuitable, an RGB monitor will be required. The IBM Color Display can be used for all modes of display, text, and graphics. However, most RGB monitors are three to ten times more expensive than standard color monitors. (The IBM Color Display is in the lower price range.) If a non-IBM color monitor is considered, the prospective purchaser should ensure that the monitor is compatible with the C/G Adapter. The non-IBM display (television with RF modulator; or monochrome, color, or RGB monitor) should be tested on the Personal Computer in the various video modes before purchase.

When the Personal Computer and Color/Graphics Monitor Adapter were announced, the prospects of high-quality software using these components were good. Many outstanding business graphics and engineering, entertainment, and educational programs have now been developed for the Personal Computer. The C/G Adapter and Color Monitor make a valuable contribution to the usefulness of the Personal Computer Systems.

The Communications Adapters

There are two types of communications adapters: the *Asynchronous Communications Adapter*, and the *Synchronous Data Link Adapter*. The Asynchronous Communications Adapter was introduced at the same time as the Personal Computer. This adapter is a vital part of computer-to-computer communication. An additional piece of equipment was missing at that time: a bisynchronous adapter to permit Personal Computer-to-IBM mainframe communication. IBM stated its intent to sell such an adapter and, late in 1982, announced the SDLC Adapter.

The Asynchronous Communications Adapter

The Asynchronous Communications Adapter is used for computer-to-computer communication and Personal Computer-to-peripheral (for example, printer or plotter) communication. This adapter is standard equipment with the Personal Computer XT and optional with the Personal Computer. There are two versions of the card: the original version, and the current version. Unlike most other adapter cards, the current version can be used by both the Personal Computer and the Personal Computer XT.

Asynchronous is the method of sending information, one bit at a time, with additional information that tells the listener (receiving device or computer) where the starting and stopping points of each character lie. The start bit and the stop bit, or bits, "frame" the character. In short, asynchronous communications send serialized data (characters) between devices on an irregular timing basis. (Asynchronous communications for computers is discussed in chapter 7. The use of the Personal Computers with serial devices, printers, plotters, and others, is discussed further in chapter 4.)

The Asynchronous Adapter can be placed in any expansion slot in the System Unit or Expansion Unit. Because it is a short board, the adapter fits the short expansion slots well. As supplied by IBM in the Personal Computer XT, the adapter is located in the eighth slot. More than one Asynchronous Communications Adapter may be placed in the system. This is true for only this adapter. No two other identical IBM adapters for the Personal Computers may be placed in the same computer system because they have no way of changing the memory locations that the system uses to communicate with the device. If a second adapter (other than the Asynchronous) is placed in the system, both will attempt to interpret commands and communicate with the CPU, a situation that will produce undesirable results.

The current Asynchronous Communications Adapter differs from the old one in that the new adapter has a jumper block in the upper right-hand corner. If the adapter is the second Asynchronous Communications Adapter in the system, the jumper is reversed. The old and current cards are compatible in all other ways. To add a second asynchronous adapter to the system, the owner simply reverses the jumper block and plugs the adapter into any available slot.

The adapter has an industry-standard DB-25 connector that extends through the back of the unit. A jumper block near the lower left

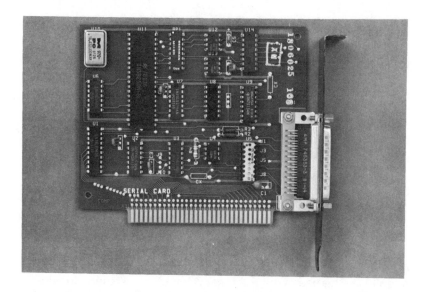

Pictured are the two Asynchronous Communications Adapters. At the top is the original adapter, and at the bottom is the recent model. The addressing block (highlighted in the bottom picture) allows two of these adapters to be used in the same Personal Computer or Personal Computer XT.

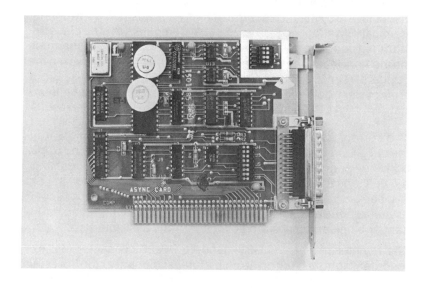

The Asynchronous Communications Adapter at a Glance

Purpose: To provide asynchronous serial communica-
                    tions between the Personal Computers and
                    other devices, including modems and printers.

Location: Any expansion slot

Number: Two maximum

Dimensions: 4 in.   (102 mm) height
                    5 in.   (127 mm) width
                    0.25 in. (6.35 mm) depth

Contents: 1. INS 8250 Asynchronous Communications
                       Element (ACE)
                    2. Support circuitry for ACE
                    3. Male 25-pin "D" connector (back of board)
                    4. Jumper block for RS-232-C or 25 .ma cur-
                       rent-loop (TTY-compatible)
                    5. Jumper block for addressing board as first
                       or second Asynchronous Adapter[1]

Speed: 50-9600 baud, software programmable

Characteristics: 1. Asynchronous communications only.
                    2. Communications information handled by
                       RIOS.
                    3. Fully software controllable.
                    4. Handles all necessary communications
                       without additional software to add/strip tim-
                       ing bits.
                    5. Can handle all necessary hardware signals
                       for handshaking with modems or printers.

Notes: [1] Addressing block not available on earlier
                       versions.

---

side of the card allows either RS-232-C (standard computer electrical signal levels) or 25 ma. current loop (type-level signals). The card
is capable of 50- to 9600-baud (approximately 0.5 to 960 bytes per
second) transmission rates. The INS 8250 chip on the board adds or
deletes the necessary additional communication bits (start, stop,
and parity bits), leaving the CPU free to handle other tasks. This chip

The INS 8250 ACE at a Glance

Purpose: To provide programmable asynchronous com-
                            munications hardware support.

Primary manufacturer: National Semiconductor, Inc.

Date of introduction: 1978

Characteristics: 1. 40-pin LSI chip
                            2. All features software selectable
                            3. Supports
                                 5-, 6-, 7-, or 8-bit data characters
                                 Even, odd, or no parity
                                 1-, 1½-, or 2-stop bits
                                 50-19,200 baud rates[1]
                            4. Adds/deletes start, stop, and parity bits
                               from characters
                            5. Double-buffered for inprecise variations in
                               baud rates
                            6. Independent transmit, receive, line status,
                               and data set interrupts.
                            7. Three-level, prioritized interrupt-system
                               controls available.
                            8. Line-break signal generation and detec-
                               tion
                            9. 12 user-designated output registers avail-
                               able
                           10. Supports EIA-standard I/O signals

                               Transmit Data (TD)
                               Clear-To-Send (CTS)
                               Data Set Ready (DSR)
                               Ring Indicator (RI)
                               Receive Data (RD)
                               Request-To-Send (RTS)
                               Data Terminal Ready (DTR)
                               Carrier Detect (CD)
                               Received Line Signal Detect (RLSD)

allows character lengths of 5 to 8 bits; even, odd, or no parity; and 1-,
1 1/2-, or 2-stop bits. It controls all necessary auxiliary lines for a
modem (telephone communications device) or serial printer.

The Asynchronous Communications Adapter is highly flexible; it
allows software control of all of its features. It can also handle most

asynchronous communications needs. A BASIC program, provided with the Adapter, allows a modem or acoustic coupler to be used for some fundamental computer-to-computer communications.

More work may be required to use the adapter with serial printers or plotters. A suitable cable may be necessary to connect the adapter and the printer. Changes to the system's software must also be made. Version 1.10 of PC DOS accommodated the use of hardware handshaking with serial printers, the standard method used with most dot-matrix printers. Most serial, letter-quality printers use a series of software signals to control communications. PC DOS V2.0 can accommodate these software signals (called software protocols), but the additional software is not generally available.

The Asynchronous Communications Adapter represents half the communications ability of the Personal Computer. The other half is the Synchronous Data Link Communications Adapter.

The Synchronous Data Link Communications Adapter

The Synchronous Data Link Communications Adapter (abbreviated SDLC), along with the appropriate software, allows the Personal Computer to communicate with IBM mainframe computers. It can be mounted in any expansion slot, in either the System Unit or the Expansion Unit. An optional cable for a modem may be purchased and used with the 25-pin "D" connector that protrudes from the back of the board.

Like asynchronous communication, synchronous communication requires that the two units involved use the same baud rate. In addition, a coordinating timing signal, called a clock, is used to synchronize the sender and the receiver. This clock signal may be generated by both devices, by only one device and transmitted to the other, or by an intermediate device such as a modem. In asynchronous communication, information does not have to be sent continuously, but in synchronous communication characters are sent within a strict time frame based on the coordinating clock's signal. Because a common timing clock is used, start and stop bits to inform the receiving system where data starts and ends are unnecessary and not used.

The true effect of synchronous communication is in its potential for higher efficiency. The SDLC Adapter can operate at rates of up to

The IBM SNA 3270 software package and the SDLC Adapter.

9600 baud. The Asynchronous Communications Adapter can also operate at this rate, but typically it must insert two or three additional bits per character transmitted. The SDLC usually does not. This means that at 9600 baud, the Asynchronous Adapter transmits 960 characters per second, whereas the Synchronous Adapter can transmit up to 1,200 characters per second.

Because synchronous communication requires very strict handshaking between devices, the SDLC Adapter is more complex and uses more integrated circuits than the Asynchronous Adapter. With the SDLC Adapter, the Personal Computer can talk with other synchronous computers, such as the largest members of the IBM computer family.

The core of the SDLC Adapter is three chips: the Intel 8273, the Intel 8255A-5, and the Intel 8253. The Intel 8273 is an SDLC protocol controller that provides the same functions as the INS 8250 for the Asynchronous Adapter, but for synchronous communications. An Intel 8255A-5 provides the necessary controls for a modem or other direct hardwired connection between the SDLC Adapter and a suitable communications controller. The Intel 8253 provides the necessary timing and interrupt signals for the synchronous data link control. Most of the features of these chips are controlled through programming (software). The adapter has sufficient versatility to handle these tasks.

A close-up of the Synchronous Data Link Communications (SDLC) Adapter.

Synchronous Communications Adapter at a Glance

Purpose: To provide a synchronous communications link
                            between the Personal Computer and other de-
                            vices, such as a modem or communications
                            controller.

Location: Any expansion slot

Contents: 1. Intel 8273 SDLC Protocol Controller chip
                            2. Intel 8255A-5 programmable peripheral in-
                               terface
                            3. Intel 8253 programmable interrupt timer
                            4. 25-pin "D" connector (rear of board)
                            5. Additional support circuitry

Speed: 9600 baud maximum

Characteristics: 1. Synchronous communications only.
                            2. External clocking signal provided by mod-
                               em or communications controller necessary
                               for operation
                            3. Fully software controllable
                            4. Uses DMA (direct memory addressing) for
                               transfer of information to and from system
                               to adapter.

Three facts should be noted about the SDLC Adapter. First, the
SDLC Adapter is a half-duplex device. It cannot simultaneously
receive and transmit information. Second, the SDLC Adapter does
not supply the clock signal for synchronous transmission. This
signal must be supplied by an outside device, such as an appropriate modem or communications controller. Finally, neither the
SDLC Adapter nor the Asynchronous Adapter affects the character
set used. The natural (built-in) character set for microcomputers is
ASCII. EBCDIC is the character set for most IBM computers, except
the Personal Computers, which use the ASCII set. The SDLC and
Asynchronous Adapters do not convert ASCII characters into
EBCDIC or the reverse. This transformation of ASCII and EBCDIC
must be handled elsewhere, such as through software in the Personal Computer. (These aspects are discussed in chapter 7.)

In summary, the SDLC Adapter is the second major communications adapter for the Personal Computer systems. With this adapter, IBM's SDLC and System Network Architecture (SNA) protocols can be handled and used to communicate with larger computers, both IBM and non-IBM.

Other Equipment

Several other IBM-marketed pieces of equipment are available for the Personal Computer. They include a printer stand; a Game Adapter; a Prototyping Card; communications cables; and a set of advanced diagnostics, one for the Personal Computer, and another for the Personal Computer XT. Only the boards are reviewed in this section.

The Game Adapter is IBM's acknowledgment that the personal computing field is not "all work and no play." The Game Adapter is a short board that fits in any slot of the System Unit or Expansion Unit. It also fits well into the short expansion slots of the Personal Computer XT or the Expansion Unit. IBM does not manufacture game paddles, joysticks, or cables for this adapter. The adapter does accommodate fairly standard parts, however: a 15-pin "D" connector, pots with ranges of 0 to 100K ohms, and "normally open" buttons. The BASIC language has extensive commands to handle the game controls.

The Prototyping Card is a long unpopulated (blank) board that is ideally suited for building interface or expansion circuits for the Personal Computer Systems. The card has provisions for on-board circuits that use any or all of the 62 I/O channel lines. Holes are drilled on 0.1-inch (.254 mm.) spacing for most integrated circuits or IC sockets. Provisions have been made on the card for a 9- to 37-pin "D" connector, mounting holes, and other circuitry. The *Technical Reference* manual points out that the components should be installed on only one side (the component side) of the card, and that the total width of the card should not exceed 0.5 inches (1.27 cm.). These limitations are imposed because of the more restrictive center-to-center space of the expansion slots in the Personal Computer XT and the Expansion Unit.

This paragraph applies only to those who wish to construct their own adapters. The Prototyping Card may be placed in any long slot in the System or in the Expansion Unit. However, the same restrictions apply to the Prototyping Card as to any other IBM-marketed adapter. If the owner has "homebrewed" (constructed) a board similar to one of IBM's adapters, it must be mounted in accordance with the expansion board table (as shown in chapter 2).

Observations and Speculation about the Personal Computers

In the first edition of this book, we speculated about the future of the Personal Computer hardware and peripherals. This speculation was based on material presented in the *Technical Reference* manual, past history, observation, and plain guessing.

Of the twelve speculations made, ten were fulfilled, the major ones being the ROM change for the new RIOS; the use of 8-inch drives with the 5 1/4-inch Diskette Drive Adapter (although this wasn't done by IBM), the use of double-sided disk drives, the fixed Winchester disk, the Expansion Unit with fixed disk, the use of 64K RAM memory chips, and the new version of the operating system to accommodate the new disk drives. The two major speculations that totally missed were the possibility of IBM marketing a letter-quality printer and the use of the cassette port for recording and using speech. (The response to the cassette port was so small that IBM removed it in favor of three additional expansion slots in the Personal Computer XT.)

Based on the facts above, the reader is reminded of three things. First, IBM does not announce a product until it is near completion (typically, less than two months away from the dealer's shelves). Second, IBM is very cautious about providing information on a new product before it is announced and does not reveal this information to outsiders. Finally, the author is not omniscient. The following set of speculations, therefore, may or may not be realized.

On CPUs

The Personal Computer systems use the 8088 CPU, the 8-bit version of the 16-bit Intel 8086. The 8086, from the iAPX 86 family, is the first in a line of 16- and 32-bit CPUs. The 8088, called the iAPX88, is an offshoot of the iAPX 86 family. The next family group is the iAPX 186 with the 80186 CPU, basically a faster 8086 CPU with many of the additional support circuits moved into the iAPX 186 chip. Systems that use the iAPX 186 can be made smaller, are less expensive to build by 30 to 40 dollars, and operate faster.

The iAPX 286 family is spearheaded by the 80286 CPU, a faster 80186 (which is a faster 8086 with additional support circuitry on the chip) with a memory management unit and a virtual memory management unit available. Briefly, a *memory management unit* greatly aids multitasking operations, where the computer does more than one task at a time. The unit also increases the feasibility of having multiple users on a computer system. A *virtual memory management unit* allows users to believe that they have more memory (virtual or apparent memory) than the actual amount of physical, real memory. The 286 can address 16M of real memory, and any user can have 1G (gigabyte, or a billion bytes) of virtual memory.

The iAPX 386, headed by the 32-bit 80386, is a family of 32-bit chips. With 32-bit processing, faster and even more powerful computer systems are possible.

The iAPX 186 is available. Intel announced that the iAPX 88, the 8088 version of the 186, will be in production in the summer of 1983. The iAPX 286 family is slated for production in late 1983, and the iAPX 386 in 1984.

When the current and future capabilities of the Intel family of microprocessors are considered, the iAPX families offer many advantages. The iAPX 186 and 188 are fully software compatible with the 8086/8088 family. Of the two, the iAPX 188 is more attractive, considering the Personal Computers' 8-bit data bus.

The iAPX 286 is compatible with the 8086/8088 family; however, the advantages offered by the memory management unit and virtual memory management are new concepts for the 8086 family. Rewriting the operating system software to take advantage of the iAPX 286's additional features (especially the memory management unit) will be required before this CPU can be used fully. This rewrite would take between four and twelve months to complete, from first draft to customer delivery. Many applications programs could be used immediately. Others, using the new features of the operating system, would take from one to many months to "switch over" to the new microprocessor.

The expected delivery date of the iAPX 386 is too far in the future to have any impact on the current Personal Computer user.

Should IBM have used a different CPU in the Personal Computers? Would the iAPX 186 or the iAPX 188 have been a better choice? The answer to the first question is no. When the Personal Computer was introduced, the 8088 was the logical choice. The 8088's price (less than the 8086 CPU), availability, and performance made it the proper choice. At the time, the iAPX 186 and the 188 were not available.

Furthermore, if IBM had chosen a member of the iAPX families (186, 188, 286, 386) the Personal Computers' System Board would have needed redesigning. If a 16-bit processor had been chosen, such as the 186 or 286, the redesigning of the System Board would have been more complex because the 8-bit data bus to the expansion slots needed to be preserved. If it were not, this design could make unusable most existing expansion cards for the Personal Computers. A significant part of the attractiveness and power of the Personal Computers is derived from the vast number of IBM and non-IBM products available. A sudden move to the iAPX 186 or 286 families without preserving the expansion slot characteristics could destroy this advantage.

Redesigning the Personal Computer with the iAPX 188 would not require any changes to the expansion bus, which means that current boards for the Personal Computer would be guaranteed to work. The iAPX 188, with its summer, 1983, delivery, may become the logical successor to the current 8088. After the iAPX 188, the 286 would be the next logical successor.

On Memory

IBM has already made the transition from 16K RAMs to 64K RAMs. The next step would be 256K RAMs. This means that if the current 4 rows of RAM were maintained on the System Board, 1M of RAM memory would be available. However, either no room would be available for the necessary ROM memory or some multiplexing scheme would be used. This scheme would not be practical for the 8086, 8088, iAPX 186, or iAPX 188, which only address 1M of memory. That, coupled with the fact that the 256K RAM chip will not be as cost-effective as the current 64K RAM chip until 1984, makes it doubtful that IBM will incorporate these chips in the near future.

More plausible is the use of 256K chips with the iAPX 286. The 286 can address 16M of RAM memory. A unit using this processor would benefit from 256K RAM chips.

On Disk Storage

The computerist's definition of mass (disk) storage is that it is "not massive enough." The IBM Personal Computers have approached the point where, for the intended uses of the machine, disk storage is adequate.

The prospects for new mini-floppy disk storage appear to be limited. Although the IBM drives are rated for quad-density (twice the current storage capacity is possible), the diskette manufacturers are just now producing quad-density rated diskettes. Use of these diskettes in quad-density drives does not have the proven track record of reliability that double-density recording now enjoys.

The major innovations in mini-floppy disk drives are in the half-width or trimline™ drives. Two half-width floppy drives can fit in the space of one full-width drive. The capacity of mini-floppy drives is increasing, but not as quickly as that of Winchester disk drives. The half-width drive is also lighter. The current adapter is fully compatible with these drives. This seems to be one of the several possible areas of change for the Personal Computer systems.

The new generation of *microfloppies*—disk drives that use 3-, 3 1/4-, or 3 1/2-inch diskette packages—is another possibility. These microfloppy disk drives have a storage capacity of up to 1M. Because of their heavier weight and lack of standardization, however, these drives are not yet attractive.

The highest ratio of bytes stored to dollar invested is the Winchester disk drive. Currently, both suppliers of the fixed drives for IBM make a 15M and 30M drive. The 5 1/4-inch fixed Winchester disks have already been designed to yield more than 100M per drive. Unfortunately, the supporting interface circuitry makes these drives too expensive for consumer use. As the price of this support circuitry decreases, larger Winchester drives will be practical.

Because high-capacity Winchester disk drives increase the problems of backing up vital data, cartridge 1/4-inch tape or the traditional 9-track open-reel tape drives are required. This additional equipment makes the Personal Computer less portable and less "personal."

The logical next step may be the removable Winchester disk, in which the data pack can be removed like a floppy diskette. Removable Winchester disk drives do not have the same backup problems as fixed Winchester disks. The removable Winchester drives have not reached high-quantity, cost-effective production levels. This rules out the removable Winchester drive during most of 1983, but leaves it as a strong contender in 1984.

On Printers

A letter-quality printer is a likely development in the near future. However, prices of letter-quality printers have plummeted in the past two years, and it may be difficult for IBM to find a "winning" letter-quality printer that is still cost-effective to both IBM and its customers.

On Other Equipment

The impact that IBM has made on the personal computer industry is tremendous. The number of expansion boards and devices available for the Personal Computer is staggering.

Que's *The IBM PC Expansion and Software Guide* lists more than 2,200 products, one-third of which are hardware products. By far, the largest single area of growth has been in multifunction RAM boards. This was a response to the perceived limited number of expansion slots. More unusual areas, such as voice processing and networking, are also growing rapidly. The prospects for more unusual expansion boards and hardware products are excellent.

The "hottest" areas for expansion growth appear to be in very high-resolution graphics boards (used mainly in engineering or computer-assisted design), local area networking boards, and disk and printer servers. The latter two are not expansion boards, but do complete the scheme for local area networks.

IBM has announced plans for local area networks, but has not implemented them. A future expansion board for IBM networking is probable once other IBM-manufactured computers establish this network.

Summary

Given effective software, the Personal Computer systems' capacity lies in the System Unit and the peripherals that surround it.

The most important peripheral is the video display and adapter. The choices available are (1) the Monochrome Display and Monochrome

Display/Printer Adapter; (2) a television with RF modulator, monochrome or color monitor, or RGB monitor (including the IBM Color Display) and the Color/Graphics Adapter; or (3) both. The adapters and associated display, or displays, vary in price, nature or use (monochrome versus color, no graphics versus graphics), and quality of output (number of characters in a line, legibility of characters, and resolution of the graphics). The outstanding feature of the adapters is that any program can use the special text (A/N) mode regardless of which adapter is chosen.

The IBM Matrix 80 CPS Printer and its successor, the Graphics 80 CPS Printer, cannot handle all printing tasks. However, these printers have many basic and enhanced features. The Graphics Printer has the ability to print graphics. Both printers are attractive to many Personal Computer users.

Communications has a heavy emphasis in the Personal Computer. The Asynchronous Communications Adapter can serve as the vital link to other computers or as the adapter to a serial printer or plotter. The SDLC Adapter serves as the Personal Computers' link to the larger IBM mainframe computers.

Because a computer's purpose is not just "all work and no play," IBM makes a Game Adapter, without joysticks, for entertainment enthusiasts and a Prototyping Card for hardware buffs.

The identifiable impact that a specific item has on a marketplace is related to the number of manufacturers that produce auxiliary equipment for it. IBM's impact is substantial: more than 400 companies manufacture equipment for the Personal Computers.

The future of the Personal Computers is bright. IBM has improved the capability of the machine by adding the Color Display and the SDLC Adapter, and by increasing its disk storage and RAM capacity. Further developments from IBM will most likely come in the form of high-capacity Winchester disk and a new CPU, but these two factors are still many months away. The most exciting single expansion prospect is local area networking.

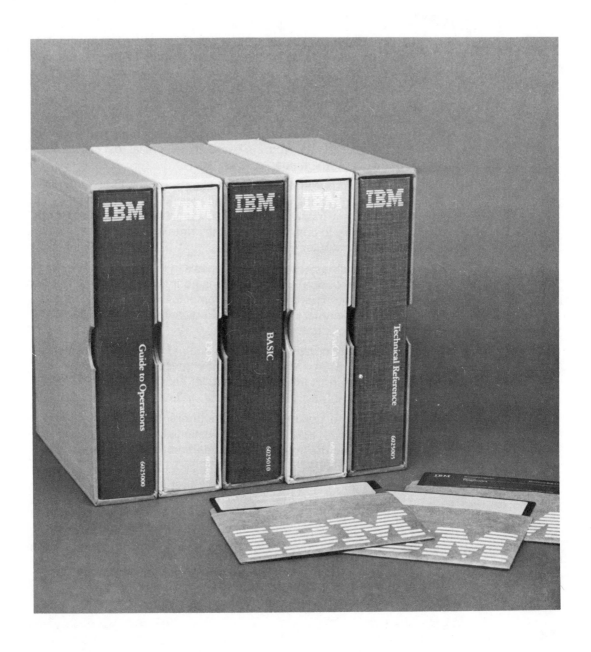

CHAPTER 4

Operating Systems

A computer system consists of the hardware and software that enable it to perform a task. *Software* is the set of commands that directs the computer to do specific work. Just as there are many types of hardware (CPUs, memory, peripherals), there are also many types of software.

There are three levels of software: operating systems, programming languages, and application programs. Each level builds upon the preceding one.

An *operating system* is the set of programs and subprograms that directs the fundamental operations of a computer. The IBM Personal Computers can use five different operating systems: PC DOS; CP/M-86; the UCSD p-System; OASIS-16; and the UNIX, Xenix, and UNIX-like family of operating systems. Because IBM markets only the first three operating systems listed, only these three systems will be covered in this chapter. Since two versions of the CP/M-86 operating system are available, both will be discussed.

Most operating systems for the Personal Computers are *disk operating systems*. A disk operating system (DOS) is a group of programs that controls the computer and its disk storage. For the Personal Computers, only the Cassette BASIC operating system does not fulfill this requirement.

Ultimately, all of these operating systems accomplish the same task: they give the user control of the computer. However, each operating system has its own way of interacting with the hardware, other software, and the user of the computer. The operating system gives the computer a "personality." Many of the Personal Computer features discussed in this book are a function of the operating system.

PC DOS

The IBM Personal Computer's Disk Operating System, commonly abbreviated as PC DOS, is a collection of programs that helps manage the Personal Computer's resources (the System Board, disk storage, printers, keyboard, display, etc.).

History of PC DOS

PC DOS has evolved through several generations. Tim Paterson of Seattle Computer Products is the original author of the operating system, which was first marketed as SCP 86-DOS™ (the 86 referring to the 8086 microprocessor). Microsoft later bought the exclusive rights to market 86-DOS. They then obtained semi-exclusive rights for the software and named it *MS-DOS*. (Seattle Computer Products also markets MS-DOS, but only for its own products.) This system was known as version 1.00 of MS-DOS. Paterson continued with Microsoft where he helped complete the revisions of MS-DOS through version 2.0 before he returned to Seattle Computer. During this time, many computer manufacturers licensed MS-DOS from Microsoft for use on their systems. One of these companies was IBM. IBM obtained the right to market MS-DOS for its system as Microsoft was completing version 1.00 of MS-DOS.

Since IBM acquired MS-DOS, it has released three versions of the system under the name PC DOS. The first version, V1.00 (Microsoft's V1.10), was released with the first Personal Computers. The second IBM version, V1.10 (Microsoft V1.25), was released simultaneously with double-sided (320K) disk drives. The most current version is PC DOS V2.00 (Microsoft's 2.00), released in March, 1983.

The latter two versions of PC DOS, noted as V1.1 and V2.0, will be discussed here, along with some brief comments about the differences between V1.0 and V1.1. Most, but not all, of this discussion, may be applied to MS DOS V1.25 and V2.0.

Inside PC DOS

The major sections of PC DOS can be functionally divided into four areas: the disk handlers, the nondisk peripheral handler, the command interpreter, and utility programs.

MS-DOS Structure and Characteristics

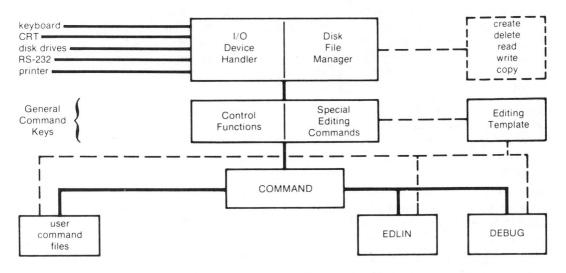

Diagram of MS-DOS structure and characteristics. (Illustration courtesy of Microsoft)

Disk file handlers are programs that transfer information to and from the disk drives. These programs, stored in the file IBMDOS.COM, maintain the directory (list of files on the disk); locate, place, or retrieve information on the disk; and perform several other built-in functions.

The *nondisk peripheral handler* is the complicated name for the software that handles the keyboard, display, communications, and similar devices. This set of software is located in the file called IBMBIO.COM. It significantly extends the capabilities of the RIOS (covered in chapter 2) and handles error reports for the covered devices, e.g., when the printer runs out of paper, or the communications adapters do not function properly.

The *command interpreter* (formally, the command processor) resides in the COMMAND.COM file. Of the three files discussed so far, COMMAND.COM is the only one that may be directly examined and modified. The other two files are *system files*, which require special handling for accessing and examining.

The last area of PC DOS is composed of a set of *utility programs* for housekeeping tasks. These programs format diskettes and hard disks, give statistics on the disk and memory, and compare diskettes and files. The utility programs reside on the disk and are loaded into memory for use.

Although all versions of PC DOS have the four areas outlined above, there are major differences in the program sets between V1.0 and V1.1, and V1.1 and V2.0. The major functional differences between V1.0 and V1.1 are

1. the addition of routines to handle double-sided diskettes.

2. additional commands that handle the serial (asynchronous) port, particularly for use with printers.

3. the incorporation of the set/display time and date commands into COMMAND.COM rather than separate utility programs.

The differences between PC DOS V1.1 and V2.0 are discussed in the next section.

COMMAND.COM

COMMAND.COM has four functions in V1.0 and V1.1. (See the section on PC DOS 2.0 for additional functions.) First, COMMAND

This is a summary of the DOS editing keys and their functions.

DEL   Skip over one character in the retained line. (The cursor does not move.)

ESC   Cancel the line currently displayed. (The retained line remains unchanged.)

F1 or ⟶   Copy one character from the retained line and display it.

F2   Copy all characters up to a specified character.

F3   Copy all remaining characters from the retained line to the screen.

F4   Skip over all characters up to a specified character (the opposite of F2).

F5   Accept edited line for continued editing— the currently displayed line becomes the retained line, but it is not sent to the requesting program.

INS   Insert characters.

Summary of the editing keys for PC DOS from the DOS Manual. (Reprinted with permission from International Business Machines Corporation.)

(an abbreviated form for COMMAND.COM) handles device inter-rupts (devices "demanding" attention), the Ctrl-Break (stop pro-cessing) function, critical error handling (disk error or divide by zero problems, for example), and end-of-program housekeeping. With end-of-program housekeeping, if the copy of COMMAND in me-mory is destroyed by the preceding program, COMMAND will reload itself from the disk.

The second responsibility of COMMAND is batch file handling. *Batch files* are text files that contain commands for the operating system. When executed, batch files appear to the computer as typed commands from the keyboard.

One example of a batch file is the AUTOEXEC.BAT. When PC DOS is loaded (booted) initially, COMMAND searches for a file on the disk with the name AUTOEXEC.BAT. If the computer does not find the file, it asks for the date and time. If the file is located, the computer automatically executes the commands in the file. Computerists use the term *turnkey* to describe the computer's ability to run a program automatically when it is first turned on.

Many of the IBM-marketed software products use the AUTOEXEC.-BAT feature. For example, VisiCalc uses this file to run a single command, "VC80." This command executes the 80-column display version of VisiCalc. When the VisiCalc diskette is booted, PC DOS automatically loads and executes the VisiCalc program, freeing busy executives from the necessity of learning typed commands to start the program.

The third major function of COMMAND is to execute the housekeep-ing commands it contains. Housekeeping commands are called internal commands because they are actually subprograms of COMMAND. Tables 4.1 and 4.2 list the internal commands that are directly available from COMMAND.

The final function of COMMAND is to load and execute programs from the disk, as directed, e.g., program files with names that end in the suffix .COM or .EXE. If the file is one of the housekeeping programs provided with PC DOS, the program is called an external command. By definition, these files must be on a disk (a diskette in a drive or a Fixed Disk in use) for the command to be used. Table 4.3 lists the external commands of PC DOS.

Table 4.1

List of PC DOS 2.0 Internal (resident) Subprograms/Commands

batch—Batch processing (see next table).

BREAK[3]—Off or on function. BREAK ON causes PC DOS to check for a Ctrl-Break on every system (function) call. BREAK OFF causes PC DOS to check for Ctrl-Break on input/output to screen, keyboard, or printers only. Default setting is OFF.

CD[3] or CHDIR[3]—Displays or changes the default (current) directory or subdirectory.

CLS[3]—Clears the active video display.

COPY[2]—Copies information or files from one device to another. Devices may be the video screen, keyboard, printers, communication adapters, or disk drives.

DIR[2]—Displays the disk's directory (list of files) with the exact size in bytes of each file and the date and time of file's creation or last change.

DATE[1]—Displays/sets the date. Date is in the form of mm/dd/yy for United States versions.[5]

DEL[1] or ERASE[2]—Erases disk file(s). PC DOS V2.0 versions will verify if all files are to be deleted (ERASE *.* command).

MD[3] or MKDIR[3]—Creates a new subdirectory on the disk.

PATH[3]—Tells PC DOS to search for commands or batch files in specified directory if this command/file is not found in current directory. A list (chain) of directories directing PC DOS from the current directory through many directories may be specified, but PC DOS will only search for the files in the last directory in the list.

RD[3] or RMDIR[3]—Removes (erases) a subdirectory from the disk. The current or root (system) directories cannot be erased. Also, a directory must be empty of all files (except the "." and ".." files) before it may be erased.

REN[2] or RENAME[2]—Changes the disk file's name(s).

SET[3]—Displays or sets additional strings for use by commands or programs. This command may be used to inform programs where to look for files (in other subdirectories).

TIME[1]—Displays or sets the time of day clock in the form of hh:mm:ss:tt.[5]

TYPE[2]—Displays on the video screen the contents of a file.

VER[3]—Displays on the video screen the version number of DOS.

VERIFY[3]—Off or on command. VERIFY ON causes PC DOS to re-read information after it is placed on the disk to assure its accuracy. VERIFY OFF does not verify the information on the disk. Default setting is OFF.

VOL[3]—Displays the disk label/i.d. of the specified drive.

Table 4.2

List of PC DOS 2.0 Internal (resident) Batch Processing Commands

ECHO[3]—Off or on command. ECHO ON displays each command or comment from a batch file as the command is executed. ECHO OFF causes PC DOS not to display any command or comment. ECHO *message* is used to display a comment regardless of ECHO's setting. Default setting is ON.

FOR..IN..DO..[3]—Repeats the batch command(s) for the specified file(s). Allows one batch command to be used for a series of files.

GOTO[3]—Causes PC DOS to jump to the specified location and continue processing the batch commands after the specified location.

IF/IF NOT[3]—Allows conditional execution of a batch file command, including GOTOs. Works like BASIC's GOTO.

SHIFT[3]—Moves batch file parameters one to the left, allowing the use of more than ten batch file parameters (batch file arguments). Leftmost paramater is disregarded.

PAUSE—Causes the Personal Computer to display a message and wait until a key is struck to continue batch file work. If ECHO OFF is given, no message is displayed.

REM—Displays a remark on the video screen from the batch file. If ECHO OFF is given, no message is displayed.

Table 4.3

**List of PC DOS 2.0 External (transient)
Programs/Commands**

ASSIGN[3]—Informs PC DOS to look for programs or information on a different disk drive than specified by the program. Used for compatibility with programs that only use the A and B drives (the Fixed Disk is C and D).

BACKUP[3]—Archives files from the Fixed Disk upon one or more floppy diskettes. Portions of the Fixed Disk or all of the disk may be backed up. Additionally the date stamp (date of creation/last alteration) of a file may be used to select files for back-up.

CHKDSK[2]—Displays the statistics on the used and free space for a disk, can check and optionally mend the disk directory or File Allocation Table, and reports used and free memory statistics.

COMP[2]—Compares a set of files and reports where they differ (if at all).

DEBUG[2]—Assembly language program debugger. Assemble command added in PC DOS V2.0.

DISKCOMP[2]—Compares two diskettes and reports where they differ (if at all). Useful after the DISKCOPY, but not after the COPY command. DISKCOPY makes an exact copy of the disk, COPY transfers files between diskettes, but may not place the files in the exact same location as the first disk. This command is not usable for comparing the Fixed Disk to a floppy disk. COMP must be used for that purpose.

DISKCOPY[2]—Makes an exact copy of the entire diskette. This command is not usable for the Fixed Disk.

EDLIN[2]—Line editor. Some improved editing commands are available in V2.0.

EXE2BIN[1]—Converts suitable formatted .EXE (relocatable program) files into .COM (directly executable program) files. Used principally by programmers.

FIND[4]—Displays all lines from a file(s) containing, or not containing, the specified string. Line numbers may also be printed.

FORMAT[2]—Formats mini-floppy diskettes or the Fixed Disks. A copy of the operating system may be placed on the diskette (/S), or a space for a copy of the operating system (/B). Will also produce single-sided diskette (/1) or PC DOS V1.0 and PC DOS V2.0 compatible diskettes (/8 for eight sectors per track).

GRAPHICS[3]—Off or On command. GRAPHICS ON allows suitable printers to "dump" (reproduce) the graphics display (graphics characters or medium- or high-resolution graphics). GRAPHICS OFF does not allow a dump of the graphics screen. Default setting is OFF.

LINK[2]—The program linker used principally by programmers, including those using the BASIC Compiler.

MODE— 1. Sets the number of characters on a line and the vertical spacing for the printer.

2. Sets the number of characters (80 or 40) per line, shifts the lines left or right, and displays a test pattern for a monitor or television. (Last part only effects displays connected to the Color/Graphics Adapter, not Monochrome Display.)

3. Sets the baud rate; parity; number of start, stop, and data bits; and type of hardware handshaking on the Asynchronous Communications Adapter.[1]

4. Redirects printer output from the line printer (parallel system printer) to a serial printer attached to Asynchronous Adapter.[1]

5. Switches the video display between the Monochrome Display and display using Color/Graphics Adapter if both exist on the computer.[3]

MORE[4]—Displays one screenful of data and pauses for keystroke before continuing.

PRINT[3]—Used to queue (line up) disk files to be printed during free CPU time (background). Also used to abort one or all files that are printing, or are about to printed, in the background.

PROMPT[3]—Used to change the customary A> prompt that PC DOS gives the operator when working at the operating system level. The prompt can include the date, time, working directory, complete path of directory, disk drive, other system information, and user-provided text. Helpful in providing a more friendly or more informative prompt than A>.

RECOVER[3]—Recovers file(s), diskettes, or disks that contain bad disk sectors or bad directory sectors which would otherwise prevent any use of the file/disks.

RESTORE[3]—Restores file(s) that were archived using the BACKUP command. Files are transferred from the diskette(s) to the Fixed Disk.

SORT[4]—Sorts data in ascending or descending order. The operator can specify which column on a line to use for the sort.

SYS[2]—Places the PC DOS operating system on the diskette or disk. Can only be used on specially formatted diskettes that have the proper space reserved for the PC DOS operating system, such as diskettes formatted with the /B option of V2.0's FORMAT.

TREE[3]—Displays all directories and paths on a disk and optionally displays the files in each path (the subdirectory).

Notes

[1]=Functions/features changed in V1.1.
[2]=Functions/features changed in V2.2.
[3]=New commands/additions to commands in V2.0
[4]=New filters (programs) in V2.0.

Other Utilities

In addition to two levels of IBM BASIC and demonstration programs, PC DOS provides an editor, a linker, and a debugger.

EDLIN is the line editor for creating and editing text files. It allows the insertion, deletion, changing, and displaying of lines of text. EDLIN also allows the operator to search for text and optionally delete or replace it. EDLIN can be used to create and edit batch files, program text (the humanly readable source code), data files, and any other file that involves text characters rather than commands (object code).

EDLIN is not a powerful text editor or word processor; it is merely a line-oriented editor. With EDLIN, the operator can edit only one line of text at a time. Better screen-oriented editing programs that allow an operator to manipulate any text on the video screen, (e.g., the IBM Personal or Professional Editor) also are available. However, EDLIN is a useful line editor that is included with PC DOS at no additional charge.

LINK.EXE and DEBUG.COM are programming tools that most IBM Personal Computer owners may never use. The LINK.EXE program converts (links) specially formatted program portions and joins them together. After this linking, the new program may be altered to execute from a specific starting point in memory (a .COM file, for example). Several useful options for the linking process and finally joined programs are available. LINK can be used with the IBM programming languages, the BASIC Compiler, FORTRAN, Pascal, Macro Assembler, and other programming languages and assemblers. For those who use only "canned" software programs or IBM BASIC, LINK is not necessary.

DEBUG.COM is an interactive machine-language program debugger. It allows a user to load a program and examine, alter, and reexamine the instructions. Any disk file or memory location may be examined or altered, with the exception of ROM memory which cannot be changed. (Although DEBUG is an extensive programming tool, a more complete explanation is not provided here.)

One program missing from PC DOS is an *assembler*. An assembler converts English-like instructions for the CPU into the native language of the computer. This program, provided with most operating systems, is optional for PC DOS. DEBUG in version V2.0, however, contains an ASSEMBLE command for short assembly language programs.

PC DOS 2.0

In March of 1983, IBM unveiled PC DOS V2.0, the IBM implementation of Microsoft's MS-DOS V2.0. Several new functions and features were added in this version.

One change involves the number of commands. PC DOS V2.0 has 45 commands, a large increase compared to V1.0's 17 commands and V1.1's 18 commands. Many of the new commands have been incorporated into COMMAND, the command processor, as shown in Table 4.3.

The increase in commands is one of the reasons why PC DOS V2.0 occupies more RAM memory. PC DOS V1.0 occupies 12,143 bytes

Table 4.4

List of PC DOS 2.0 Configuration (CONFIG.SYS) Commands

BREAK—Same as internal BREAK command.

BUFFERS—Sets the number of disk buffers.

DEVICE—Loads the specified device driver software.

FILES—Sets the maximum number of open disk files at one time.

SHELL—Loads/uses different command processor than COM-MAND.COM.

Notes

[1]=Functions/features changed in V1.1.
[2]=Functions/features changed in V2.2.
[3]=New commands/additions to commands in V2.0
[4]=New filters (programs) in V2.0.
[5]=

Special Characters to PC DOS

Ctrl-PrtSc—Toggles the printer (prints on both the video display and system printer.)

(Shift)-PrtSc—Prints the contents of the video display on the system printer. If GRAPHICS ON command has been given, will print medium-or high-resolution screen on suitable printers.

>[1]—I/O redirection character to tell PC DOS to read information from this file or device rather than receiving information from the keyboard.

<[1]—I/O redirection character to tell PC DOS to put information to this file or device rather than display the information on the video screen.

|[1]—Piping symbol. Tells PC DOS to write the information produced by the program (on the left of the symbol) into a temporary file and have the program on the right of the symbol use this information as input.

\[1]—Used to specify the following name as a directory rather than a file name.

of RAM, whereas PC DOS V1.1 occupies 12,400 (the movement of the TIME and DATE commands into COMMAND accounts for most of this increase). V2.0 typically occupies 24,576 bytes for floppy disk-based systems and 24,800 bytes for systems that use the Fixed Disk, twice as much as V1.1.

Floppy disk-based Personal Computer systems require an absolute minimum of 64K of RAM memory; 128K or more is practical. Fixed Disk Personal Computer systems, including the XT, require at least 128K. IBM includes 128K in the Personal Computer XT as standard equipment. More than 24K may be required for PC DOS itself, depending on the options used.

In addition to the increased number of commands, many new features have been added to PC DOS 2.0. They are

1. extended support for serial devices, graphics printers, and systems that use two displays (one monochrome and one color).
2. an increase in minifloppy disk storage.
3. support for hard disk drives.
4. more batch processing commands.
5. background printing.
6. extended control for the disk, display, and keyboard.
7. provisions for installable device drivers and extended control for PC DOS operations.
8. incorporation of hierarchical (tree) disk directories and support programs.
9. redirection of input/output and piping.
10. new utility programs (filters).

Because the last two functions are new concepts for many microcomputer users, these functions will be discussed in detail below.

Extended Support

PC DOS has become more versatile for existing equipment. In PC DOS V1.1, further control of the Asynchronous Adapter was added to the MODE command.

MODE

Options for setting the baud rate, parity, type of hardware handshaking, and number of start and stop bits for each character were also added. These new options facilitated the use of serial printers with the Personal Computers. Another option added to the MODE command allowed a serial printer to be used as the system printer, thereby using the print-screen function.

With PC DOS 2.0, the MODE command can switch the video output between the Monochrome Display/Printer Adapter and the Color/Graphics Adapter. This useful feature for systems with both displays allows the operator to switch between monitors without having to disconnect adapter cards.

GRAPHICS

The new V2.0 command, GRAPHICS, gives the operator the ability to dump (print) the graphics screen (graphics characters and medium- or high-resolution graphics) on a suitably equipped printer, such as the IBM Graphics Printer. Although colors cannot be printed, four shades of gray are used to represent the four primary colors when medium-resolution graphics are dumped. Text or high-resolution graphics are printed in black and white. The GRAPHICS command option occupies 688 additional bytes in memory and, therefore, increases the amount of memory taken by PC DOS. While the GRAPHICS command is on, however, the operator or a program can dump the contents of the graphics screen at any time.

Increase in Mini-floppy Disk Storage

PC DOS V2.0 extends the storage capacity of mini-floppy disk drives. As mentioned in chapter 2, the terms "160K" and "320K" are no longer applicable to mini-floppy disk drives. Under PC DOS V1.1, a single-sided disk drive could record 160K of information, and the double-sided drives 320K. PC DOS V2.0 records one additional sector per track, allowing nine sectors rather than eight. This increase gives single-sided drives a 180K capacity per diskette and double-sided drives 360K per diskette.

No changes in the mini-floppy drive or adapter are required. The 12.5% increase in storage capacity is performed only in the PC DOS V2.0 operating system. To use this extended capacity, diskettes must be formatted with PC DOS V2.0's FORMAT program.

The FORMAT program can also produce single-sided and 8-sector (V1.0- and V1.1-compatible) diskettes. PC DOS V2.0 automatically recognizes the diskette format (single- or double-sided, 8 or 9 sectors per track) used. The recognition of the four diskette formats is another reason for V2.0's increased size. The return in convenient operations, however, justifies the increase.

PC DOS V1.0 does not automatically recognize varying diskette formats. It recognizes only single-sided, 8-sector-per-track diskettes. Verson 1.1 can use PC DOS-formatted, single- or double-sided diskettes, but does not recognize 9-sector diskettes. Only PC DOS V2.0 recognizes the four diskette formats.

Hard Disk Drive Support

Another new function of PC DOS V2.0 is its support of the IBM Fixed Disk V2.0 supports two Fixed Disks. The additional or changed utility programs allow the Fixed Disk to be subdivided for use with multiple operating systems, formatted for use with PC DOS and efficiently backed up and restored.

The BACKUP command is versatile. It allows the operator to back up all or selected portions of the hard disk to mini-floppy diskettes. The selection of the files to back up may be based on: paths or subdirectories (an important new concept discussed later); the date of creation/last update of the files; whether the file has already been archived (backed up); or filename(s). The RESTORE program complements BACKUP; it recovers files from backed up diskettes to the Fixed Disk. Because BACKUP and RESTORE can handle files that are larger than the mini-floppy diskettes, backed up files are used only for archiving purposes, not during normal operations.

Batch Processing Commands

Several new commands have been added to the COMMAND batch capabilities of PC DOS. These commands apply only to batch files. The ECHO command, for example, can turn on or off the display of each command as it is executed, including comments that use the REM (remark) batch command. All versions of PC DOS start with this display of commands turned on. ECHO can also unconditionally display a message, regardless of whether the display of commands is inhibited (turned off).

The FOR..IN..DO command allows one command to be used with a set of files. (A full explanation of this command is not provided in this book.)

The batch command GOTO lets the operating system "jump" to another part of the batch file and execute the commands there. A label, composed of a word without spaces where only the first eight characters are recognized, followed by a colon, is typed on a line in the file. The line "GOTO labelname" is also typed into the file. When the GOTO command is encountered, COMMAND jumps and executes the commands that follow the label. By itself, the GOTO command is not very useful. When combined with other commands, however, it provides powerful batch processing capabilities.

The IF command is simple. If the condition tested is true, then the statement on the line with the IF is executed. If the IF condition is not true, the statement is ignored. IF NOT works the opposite way. IF may test whether two strings (sets of alphanumeric characters) are identical, if a file exists, or whether a special flag has been set by a program (called ERRORLEVEL; now only the BACKUP and RESTORE commands use this flag).

SHIFT is the final new command. When a batch file name is typed, a set of strings, separated by spaces, may also be typed. These strings can be used by the batch command. The strings are called *command line arguments* or *command line parameters*. Typically, the arguments are names of files to be handled by the batch file. PC DOS recognizes a maximum of ten command line arguments. The SHIFT command is used to trick PC DOS into using more than ten. When given in the batch file, SHIFT shifts the arguments left, making the second argument the first, the third argument the second, etc. When SHIFT is used, the previous first argument is discarded.

The complete set of batch commands, including REM (remark) and PAUSE, can perform extensive file manipulation. Experimenting with these commands will help the user become familiar with their power.

Background Printing

Background printing is controlled by the PRINT command. The PRINT command can start or stop printing that takes place while no other CPU-based activity is happening. This does not mean that printing cannot take place while a program is running. Background printing steals (uses) the CPU when it is idle. The CPU may be available many times during a program, such as when the program is waiting for operator input.

The information to be background printed must be in a disk-based file. More than one file can be queued (placed in line). Background printing is not the same as print spoolers, which buffer the information into the RAM memory. Almost any program can use a RAM printer spooler (really a printer buffer). Not all programs, however, produce files that can be background printed.

Installable Device Drivers

PC DOS V2.0 provides another new feature in installable device drivers. A *device driver* is the software that allows the operating system to use the device. The device may be a printer, a plotter, a disk drive, a voice input/output board, a terminal, or any other peripheral. Installable disk drivers give the operating system the intimacy and control required for effective use of devices.

With PC DOS V2.0, the driver becomes part of the operating system when PC DOS is booted. The driver is written to the specification published in the PC DOS V2.0 manual. Then a text editor (e.g., EDLIN) is used to create or change a special file called CONFIG.-SYS. The line

    DEVICE = filename

is added to the file (*filename* is the name of the disk file that contains the device driver software). After the computer is turned on or the system is reset, PC DOS is booted. IBMBIO.COM is loaded. IBMBIO.-COM searches for the CONFIG.SYS file in the primary directory of the disk. If it finds the file, PC DOS installs the driver into the operating system and loads IBMDOS.COM and COMMMAND.-COM. If CONFIG.SYS is not found, IBMDOS.COM and COMMAND.-COM are loaded. Although device drivers increase the size of PC DOS accordingly, the lost memory is a small price to pay for the advantages provided.

Device drivers also allow the proper use of serial printers that use software protocols for handshaking. A device driver is written by the hardware manufacturer and distributed with the product. The operator simply creates or edits the CONFIG.SYS with the driver's name and copies the driver software to the boot diskette. When PC DOS is booted, it will load and use the new driving software.

A clear line of responsibility has not been established for device drivers. Writing a device driver is a complex task that should be performed by a person skilled in assembly language programming and PC DOS, and familiar with the physical aspects of the device. Once the driver is written and functioning correctly, it is easier to install and use. (This explains why hardware manufacturers should make the appropriate software available with the device.)

ANSI Codes

One example of a supplied device driver is the American National Standard Institute's (ANSI) standardized terminal codes, which are provided by IBM for use with the IBM displays. This supplied software is a major feature.

A file called ANSI.SYS is provided with PC DOS. When ANSI.SYS is added to the CONFIG.SYS file and PC DOS is booted, the displays and the keyboard respond to the ANSI-standard control codes. A *control code* is a sequence of characters that is interpreted by the device. IBM Printers use control codes to set character fonts, line space, character sizes, vertical and horizontal tabs, and other control features. When used with the display and the terminal, the ANSI driver offers standard control codes that move the cursor (up, down, left, right, or to any part of the screen), erase part or all of a line, display graphics (not just graphics characters), and redefine keys (the special-function keys, cursor-control/editing keys, or alphanumeric keys).

The ANSI-standard control codes give the IBM Personal Computer owner two new advantages: the ability to redefine keys, and the ability to use standardized cursor controls and graphics from any language. IBM BASIC always had the ability to redefine the special-function keys, but when the operator left the BASIC language, the special-function keys reverted to PC DOS editing keys. IBM BASIC also had commands for cursor control and graphics. However, no other language—including IBM FORTRAN, Pascal, and Macro Assembler—had the same abilities.

With the ANSI terminal code, the software programmer who does not use BASIC has the ability to use cursor controls and graphics. The ANSI standard codes will further increase the base of high-performance software, word processors, spreadsheets, and accounting programs for the IBM Personal Computer. Programmers can write programs in compiler languages other than BASIC, while retaining the cursor control and graphics features of IBM's BASIC.

Performance Control

Another feature of CONFIG.SYS for PC DOS V2.0 is that it gives the Personal Computer owner more performance control.

The number of *disk buffers* (areas of RAM that hold information going to or coming from the disk) can be set. If many files are used in a program, increasing the number of disk buffers will generally increase the program's performance. Programs, particularly for accounting and data management, will benefit from more disk buffers (usually between 10 and 20). If the program reads or records a complete file at one time, increasing the buffers will yield little performance improvement. The operator will have to experiment to find the optimum number of disk buffers to use (the optimum varies with different types of programs). Each additional buffer (PC DOS starts with two buffers) increases the size of PC DOS by 528 bytes.

The BREAK option is identical to the PC DOS BREAK command. The initial state for BREAK is off. PC DOS will look for the Ctrl-Break key only during screen, keyboard, printer, or communications operations. BREAK ON makes PC DOS check for the Ctrl-Break any time it is called (during a function call).

The FILE and SHELL commands will not be discussed here because they are more technical and programmer-oriented. (See the IBM *Disk Operating System Manual* for a complete discussion.)

The combined capabilities of device drivers, the ability to tailor the operating environment, and the ANSI terminal control codes make PC DOS V2.0 a more powerful, adaptable operating system. V2.0 adopts a friendlier stance toward using non-IBM peripherals. The ANSI terminal control code provided gives any programming language the ability to perform cursor control and graphics with one set of commands. PC DOS allows Personal Computer owners to adjust the operating environment of PC DOS. All of these features are significant improvements over V1.1.

Hierarchical Directories

The hierarchical directories of PC DOS V2.0 are a new concept for most microcomputers. The directory is typically a reserved section of the disk (not available for storing user programs and data) where a list of files and their locations on the disk is maintained. Each disk has one directory. When a file is created, deleted, updated, or accessed, the operating system travels down the directory looking for the file name. When the name is found in the directory, the operating system can begin manipulating the file.

This approach to housekeeping, storing the information about the files on disk, works well for floppy diskettes. Most floppy and mini-floppy diskettes hold between 32 and 256 files in the directory. The number of files varies based on the operating system and the storage capacity of the disk. When the DIR command (to display a list of the disk's files) is invoked, a legible and easy-to-manage list of the files is displayed. Each time the operating system uses a file, little time is needed to move the directory by examining one entry at a time.

Large capacity disks, particularly hard disks, do not work as well with this scheme. When the number of possible files increases from 256 to 1,024 or more, the operating system needs more time to examine the directory. This longer directory search occurs almost every time the file is accessed or updated. The most search time is required when a file is first opened for use. Lengthy directory search time can significantly slow disk performance. The directory listing of files can become unmanageable as hundreds of files are presented when the DIR command is invoked.

To combat this long directory search, several schemes may be used. One method subdivides the hard disk into smaller, apparent ("logical") drives. Instead of seeing one large disk drive, the operating system now works with two or more smaller, logical drives. This scheme increases disk performance, but prohibits the creation of very large data files (no file can be larger than the logical disk that holds it).

In another scheme, the entire directory is read when the disk is first used. Each file name found is then converted into a code. The code, which is more compact to store, is held in memory with the location of the file's entry in the directory. When the operating system searches for a file, it uses the same technique and converts the file name into a code. The file's code and the codes from the disk's directory are compared. If a match is found, the real, noncoded file name is retrieved from the disk. If the real names match, the directed disk operation begins. If the names do not match, the process continues. This scheme, called a *hashed directory*, decreases the time required for directory searches.

A third approach, that of hierarchical or tree-like directories, is the method used by the UNIX/Xenix operating systems and PC DOS V2.0. A *hierarchical directory* is similar to a family tree. Each parent has one or more children. Each child may become a parent and have one or more children. This process continues until the end of the tree is reached. To locate a relative, a person maneuvers through the tree's structure, moving up, down, left, and right, until the relative is located.

The same is true of hierarchical directories. There is one starting parent, called the *root* or *system directory*. This root can hold a program or data file. The root directory in turn sires (owns) subdirectories. Stepping down into the subdirectory allows additional files or subdirectories to be stored. With the exception of the root or system directory, each subdirectory has one parent and may have several children. All directories can store program and data files.

When a file is used that is not in the current directory or subdirectory, the operator must specify the chain of directories to step through. In this case, each directory step becomes a *path*. The operator must direct PC DOS to move up, down, or across the directories to the location of the file.

By subdividing directories in this fashion, the problem of long directory searches is avoided. Although a small amount of time is needed to "step" through the directories, the speed of operations is not decreased significantly. An advantage to this approach is that files may be grouped together into one subdirectory (sometimes called a *bin* in UNIX and Xenix), making directory displays more manageable. By specifying the correct paths, an operator can use a file that is not located in the current directory.

Limitations

There are disadvantages to the hierarchical directory approach. Only programs located in the operator's current directory can be executed. This means that the operator cannot invoke a program in another directory. To remove this restriction, PC DOS V2.0 provides a new command called PATH. When invoking a program, PC DOS searches the current directory. If the program is not found, PC DOS follows the chain directed by the PATH command and searches for the program in the last directory in the path. If the program is found, it is executed. If the program is not found in either directory, an error message is displayed.

This problem does not occur with data files. To use a data file in another directory, the path is specified when the data file name is given. PC DOS V2.0 will use the specified path to locate the file.

Another problem with hierarchical directories involves maneuvering through the paths to a file. Because the root directory may not hold the desired file, the operator must learn how to move through the directories to the one desired. This is a new concept to most microcomputer users. Many will require time to experiment and learn this skill. Once learned, the advantages of hierarchical directories far outweigh the disadvantages.

A final problem is applications software. During the first months after the introduction of PC DOS V2.0, many programs and programming languages would not allow path names to be given with a file name. IBM BASIC, however, does have this ability. Many other programs will accommodate path names shortly. For programs that do not allow path names, the PATH command should be given before the program is executed if the program uses additional program files that are not kept in the same directory. If path names are not used, all data files must be in the current directory when the program is executed.

The number of files held in the root or system directory varies: up to 64 for mini-floppy diskettes and up to 112 for each Fixed Disk. Subdirectories do not have this limitation and may hold as many other directories and files as there is disk space available. This means that most mini-floppy diskettes do not need subdirectories; the root directory space is sufficient. The Fixed Disk, depending on how it is partitioned, will require only one subdirectory. This means that only hard disk owners are required to learn hierarchical directories, and that the number of subdirectories can be as extensive or limited as the owner desires.

Support Programs

The MKDIR command (the shorthand form is MD) is used to create a new subdirectory. When a directory is done for a newly created subdirectory, two entries are found. These entries are marked by a single dot (.) and a double dot (..). The single dot indicates the file that contains the information on the subdirectory (in reality, all directories are disk files). The double dot indicates the directory's parent (the directory that holds the subdirectory). The double dot is the shorthand notation for moving up one step.

The CHDIR (or CD) command changes the current directory, moving the operator up or down one level of directories. To move more than one directory at a time, the backslash (\) character is used to designate an additional directory. For example, if the root directory holds a subdirectory called WORDS, the command

    CD WORDS

would move the operator from the root directory to the WORDS subdirectory. To move back to the root directory, the operator would type:

    CD ..orCD\

While in the WORDS directory, the operator can get a directory of the root by typing:

    DIR ..orDIR\

To remove a subdirectory, the RMDIR (no shorthand form for this command) command is used. The subdirectory must be empty except for the single-dot and double-dot entries (the entries holding the current directory and the path to the parent directory). This command cannot be used on the root directory. PC DOS will not perform it on a subdirectory with other files in it or on the root directory.

To accommodate maneuvering through the directories, most PC DOS commands respect path names. Commands like COPY (copy files), RENAME (change file names), ERASE or DEL (delete files), and COMP (compare files) will accept and use path names in front of the file name.

The hierarchical directory system of PC DOS can be difficult to use for newcomers. Once the system has been learned, its power and advantages are welcomed.

Redirection of Input/Output

Redirection of input and output (I/O) is a feature of PC DOS 2.0 and of the UNIX/Xenix operating system. A brief explanation of standard input and output is necessary before the advantages of redirected I/O are examined.

When a program asks for input, the operator types the information on the keyboard. When the system displays information, it is usually directed to the video display. The keyboard (for input) and the video display (for output) are, therefore, the "standard I/O" devices.

If a program needs information from a disk file, the program must have specific instructions to open, read, and/or write, then close the disk file. If information is to be printed, the program must issue specific instructions for the system to send the information to the printer.

The redirection of I/O allows exceptions to these conditions. Two new characters, the *less than* sign (<) and the *greater than* sign (>), are used. The < tells the operating system to get information from a particular file or device rather than from the keyboard. The > tells the system to put information in a particular file or to a device rather than on the video display. When the program is run, its name and < and/or > (either, both, or neither) are typed with a file or device name. For example,

DIR > MYFILES

prints the disk's directory to a disk file called MYFILES. The line

DIR > LPT1:

would print the directory on the printer.

Piping

Piping is an extension of the redirected I/O concept. It occurs when the output from one program becomes the input to a second program. These programs may be chained together to form powerful combinations. The vertical bar (|) is used to designate a pipe. Information generated between programs is placed into a temporary disk file for use by the next invoked program.

PC DOS provides several utility programs for this purpose. FIND locates a *string* (series of alphanumeric characters) and optionally displays lines with or without the string, and prints the specified lines with line numbers. SORT sorts in either ascending or descending order. MORE displays 23 lines of input and the message "MORE," then waits for a keystroke. These programs are called *filters* or *black boxes*. Each filter accepts information from the standard input (keyboard), works on that information, then sends the information to the standard output (the video display).

By combining filters with pipes and redirection, some very useful tasks can be performed. For example, to get a sorted directory of a disk, the command

   DIR | SORT

is typed. A sorted directory will then appear on the video display. The command

   DIR | SORT | MORE

can be used to take the sorted directory and display only 23 lines at a time. The command

   DIR | SORT > LPT1:

would send the sorted list to the printer.

The redirection of I/O and piping are powerful tools. With these features, the writing of many short, one-shot, single-purpose programs can be avoided through the combination of filters and functions.

It is important to note that redirection and piping replace few applications programs. Regular applications programs, such as accounting, spreadsheets, and data management, cannot be replaced by redirection of I/O and piping. Many Personal Computer users may find that these advanced features are too difficult or have no bearing on their work, and, therefore will not need to learn anything about them.

Other Facets of PC DOS

Certain features are common to all versions of PC DOS. First, PC DOS file work is fast. A 16K program typically loads in less than two seconds. PC DOS usually does not need to reload COMMAND after a program is finished. The "warm booting" (reloading the command processor, COMMAND) required by other operating systems is usually unnecessary with PC DOS, thereby speeding up overall operation.

Second, PC DOS is a friendly operating system. Its understandable error messages and user prompts have set a standard for other operating systems on the Personal Computers.

On technical matters, PC DOS handles files as large as 16 gigabytes (billion bytes), although current floppy and hard disk technology cannot make cost-effective use of all of this capability. Increased file size means that large disk drives need not be subdivided for effective use. PC DOS can handle up to 63 different block devices (disk drives are the principal block device of a computer system). This amount is far greater than the 16-disk limitation of other operating systems. In most cases, device drivers must be written to accommodate the additional block devices. Currently, drives A and B (the two mini-floppy disks) and C and D (the Fixed Disk) are immediately recognized. As the device names start with A and travel up through the ASCII character set, some device names will be strange (names like [, }, and ~) and some unusable (lower-case letters are now automatically changed into upper-case letters). However, PC DOS has the capability to use all of these devices, even though 2 to 16 block devices (disk drives) are usually sufficient for most computer installations.

PC DOS also maintains three different classes of files: normal, system, and hidden. *Normal* files appear in the disk directory and are used in the conventional manner. *System* files, such as IBMBIO.-COM and IBMDOS.COM (PC DOS core), and *hidden* files, which have no predesignated purpose, do not appear in the directory and must be accessed through special programming. System and hidden files provide a safe, not normally accessible area on the disk for vital programs and data. COPY does not duplicate system or hidden files. In fact, these files elude copying in general. The FORMAT/S and SYS commands can copy the system files, but disks must be formatted with the PC DOS V2.0 FORMAT/B command for SYS to function properly.

There are many other aspects of PC DOS that cannot be covered in this book. For those who would like more operational or technical information about PC DOS, the *Disk Operating System Manual* is an excellent starting point. It is important to note that because of the increased complexity of the operating system, the V2.0 manual is not as easy to absorb as the manual for V1.1. The operator does not need to learn all of the PC DOS commands and operations, however. By experimenting with the necessary commands, the operator can gain the necessary confidence and proficiency with the operating system.

Overall, PC DOS operates efficiently. Version 2.0 has great flexibility, is difficult to "crash" (lock up into an endless loop of instructions), and is friendly to operate. PC DOS is an excellent foundation for the software of the Personal Computer.

CP/M-86

In the short history of microcomputing, two standards have withstood the test of time: Microsoft BASIC's programming language and the CP/M™ operating system. CP/M is the most universal operating system in the software world. More than 1,000,000 computer systems run on the CP/M family of operating systems. (Only a small portion of this number are IBM Personal Computers.)

CP/M-86 is the version of CP/M that is used by computers with 8086 or 8086-related microprocessors. CP/M for the 8080-related family of CPUs is the de facto standard for 8-bit (8080, 8085, Z80) microcomputers.

Two versions of CP/M-86 are available for the Personal Computer: one marketed by IBM; and one marketed by Digital Research, Incorporated (abbreviated DRI). Digital Research is the publisher of CP/M.

History of CP/M

CP/M first appeared in 1975 when a small company came before the Los Angeles Home Brew Computer Club, a group whose hobby was building microcomputers. The company, Digital Systems, provided a unique demonstration of a prototype floppy disk controller card for the then-popular Altair™ computer. The uniqueness of the demonstration was that the card actually worked, unusual for the state of the microcomputing arts at the time. Digital also demonstrated a crude, but working, disk operating system called Control Program/Microprocessor (abbreviated CP/M).

Later Digital Systems became Digital Microsystems, a subsidiary of Extel Group Systems, and the first commercial company to receive an OEM (Original Equipment Manufacturer) license for CP/M.

Table 4.5

List of CP/M-86 Resident (internal) Commands/Subprograms

DIR—Directory command.

ERA—Erase disk file(s).

REN—Rename disk file(s).

TYPE—Display contents of disk file on screen.

USER—Change user number.

Table 4.6

List of CP/M-86 Transient (external) Commands/Programs

ASM86—Machine-language Assembler.

ASSIGN—Changes logical device assignment.

CONFIG[1]—Configures CP/M-86 operating system.

COPYDISK[2]—Disk copy.

DDT86—Dynamic Debugging Tool.

DSKMAINT[1]—Formats and copies disks.

ED—Line-oriented editor.

FUNCTION—Assigns strings to special-function keys.

GENCMD—Command program generator.

HELP—Displays help files.

NEWDISK[2]—Formats diskette and places operating system on diskette.

PIP—Peripheral Interface Program.

PRINT[1]—Background printing.

PROTOCOL[2]—Sets communications protocol.

SETUP[1]—Configures/changes several CP/M-86 operating parameters.

SPEED[2]—Sets communications port's speed and attributes.

SDIR[1]—Special directory command to display system files (SYS) also.

STAT—Disk status and statistics.

SUBMIT—Batch processing program.

TOD—Displays/sets date/time of day clock.

Notes

[1]=Digital Research version only
[2]=IBM version only

The principal creator of this disk operating system, Dr. Gary Kildall, was an engineer at Intel where he worked on the development of the 8008 microprocessing chip. He also developed a high-level compiler for this chip (the PL/M programming language) and a rudimentary operating system to aid in development. As paper tape, the then popular but slow storage medium, was replaced by floppy disks, CP/M changed into a disk operating system. A line-oriented text editor, an assembler, and a debugger were added. Revised versions of these programs were provided with every CP/M package. Dr. Kildall later left Intel to form Digital Research, Incorporated.

By offering a standard operating system for nonstandard equipment, CP/M swept the 8-bit computer world. Computer companies such as Apple™, DEC™, Lanier™, Tandy™, Wang™, Xerox™, and Zenith™ now offer computers that use CP/M. In fact, more than 235 companies are licensed to offer CP/M for their systems.

CP/M-86 is similar in operation to the 8080 version of CP/M, except that it focuses on the expanded power of the 8086 CPU and can operate faster.

Inside CP/M-86

Like PC DOS, CP/M is divided into several parts. The four parts of CP/M-86 are the BIOS (Basic Input/Output System), the BDOS (Basic Disk Operating System), the CCP (Console Command Processor), and the TPA (Transient Program Area).

CP/M's BIOS is similar in function to the PC DOS IBMBIO.COM. Both CP/M-86 and PC DOS use the RIOS built into the Personal Computers' ROMs. The BDOS and the CCP are similar to PC DOS'

IBMDOS.COM and COMMAND.COM, respectively. The TPA, the area of RAM memory not used by the operating system, has no corresponding name in PC DOS.

Like PC DOS, CP/M-86 has built-in and disk-loaded commands. Commands built into the CCP are called *resident* commands. Disk-resident commands are called *transient* commands. CP/M-86's set of housekeeping utility programs are also similar to those provided by PC DOS. However, the similarity is greater between PC DOS V1.1 and CP/M-86 than PC DOS V2.0 because CP/M-86 does not use hierarchical directories, redirected I/O, or piping.

Limitations

The biggest liabilities of the IBM version of CP/M-86 are in its less friendly operations and slightly reduced performance.

Neither the IBM nor the DRI version can use disk drives larger than 8M. This means that the Fixed Disk must be subdivided into several "logical" smaller disks for use. Computerists often use the terms *physical* and *logical*. "Physical" means the actual properties of the device. The Fixed Disk can physically store 10M of information. When the Fixed Disk is divided through software into two 5M "apparent" areas, each 5M "drive" is a "logical" disk drive.

Technically, the FDISK program provided with PC DOS V2.0 does this division of the Fixed Disk. It divides the Fixed Disk into several sections, with each operating system owning and using only one of these sections. However, the concept of "logical" disk drives usually applies when one operating system must make this division, not when several operating systems share the same disk.

One limitation of both the IBM and DRI versions of CP/M-86 on the Personal Computer is in communications. With the implementation of a time-clock (based on the 50 or 60 cycles per second a.c. current), communication at rates over 1200 baud has become difficult. To communicate with other systems at a higher rate, the clock must be turned off. After the clock has been turned off, the mini-floppy disk drive continues to rotate rather than turning itself off. This is a minor annoyance.

Features

Some of the positive points for CP/M-86 include the continuous display of the date, time, and user number at the bottom of the screen; the incorporation of a HELP program that can be used to find the phrasing (syntax) for a command; and its versatility in using letter-quality printers.

Earlier it was stated that the system software accounts for some of the computer system's perceived features. The Keyboard Unit is an example. Whereas PC DOS normally sets the special-function keys for editing, CP/M-86 sets them to type commands (as does IBM BASIC). The FUNCTION program allows the user to change the commands typed by the special-function keys and the meanings of the cursor-control/editing keypad.

The DRI version of CP/M-86 offers more improvements. Many of the commands are more friendly. In the past, the operator had to supply all of the necessary information when invoking a command (CP/M calls this a *command line tail*, a different name for command line argument or parameter). Now, several DRI CP/M-86 commands will execute a menu if no arguments are typed when a command is invoked.

A SETUP program is provided with DRI's CP/M-86 to configure the operating system. Options such as error messages with tones (to alert the operator), built-in RAM disk (if sufficient memory is available), automatic execution of a program or batch file (similar to the AUTOEXEC.BAT facility), and permanent saving of the configuration (setup) are available through the SETUP program.

 The DRI version also incorporates the GSX graphics package. As CP/M and PC DOS are operating systems for computers, GSX is a *graphics suboperating system.* GSX provides programs with a standard method of invoking graphics. This method is superior to the ANSI-standard cursor controls because GSX has intimate knowledge of each graphics device, the video display, and printers and plotters. GSX performs the necessary conversions (transformations) for each device, the colors, the resolution (number of dots per inch), and other matters. With GSX, the programmer has a more efficient, friendly, and standardized way to use graphics than with the ANSI cursor controls. However, the features offered by standardized graphics are more beneficial to those writing software for a variety of computers rather than just for the Personal Computers. PC DOS' BASIC has the easiest to use graphics of all programming languages, but not the most efficient or standardized.

The DRI version of CP/M-86 also offers a background printing facility, identical in function to that provided with PC DOS V2.0.

Comparing PC DOS and CP/M

When PC DOS is compared to CP/M-86, there is little doubt that both have their origins in CP/M-80. The apparent differences in commands between PC DOS V1.0 and V1.1 and CP/M-86 are few, although the number increases when PC DOS V2.0 is compared with CP/M-86. Despite their dissimilar names, both sets of commands function similarly. Both operating systems copy files and diskettes, prepare disks and diskettes, display directories, and execute programs.

Although the commands seem the same, the ultimate effect of these commands and the basic "personality" of the Personal Computer differ. The advantages and disadvantages of both operating systems should be examined from two divergent points of view: the programmer's and the end user's.

For the Programmer

From the standpoint of the system programmer, both operating systems offer a line editor (not a word-processing editor), an assembly language debugging program, and a program for linking assembly language programs together. An 8086 assembler, however, is not provided with PC DOS. Both companies sell a more powerful assembler that is superior to the assembler provided with CP/M-86.

The full range of Microsoft languages is available only for PC DOS, whereas the Digital Research languages are now available for both systems. (The DRI languages are not marketed by IBM.)

If foreign (non-IBM) devices are considered, PC DOS V2.0 has a slight advantage over CP/M-86. The use of installable device drivers is more flexible and requires less work than CP/M-86's method of modifying its machine-language BIOS. Conversely, PC DOS V2.0's method of installing devices is convenient, but CP/M-86's is more permanent.

When booting, PC DOS V2.0 reads the CONFIG.SYS file and installs the new devices "on-the-fly." With CP/M-86, the machine-language Basic Input/Output System (BIOS) must be modified. Once the BIOS is modified and saved, CP/M-86 boots with the necessary software to handle the different devices. It does not require a series of device driver software files on the boot disk. This point applies to mini-floppy based systems, because once the necessary files are established, Fixed Disk users do not have to boot from a diskette and worry about maintaining all of the device driver files.

CP/M-86 is equipped to handle some of the serial printers that use software handshaking, whereas PC DOS is not. PC DOS V2.0, with the proper device driver software, however, will readily handle these printers. Both operating systems handle equally well the serial printers that do not require handshaking.

PC DOS V2.0 supports up to 63 disk-type devices; CP/M-86 supports 16. Although this makes PC DOS capable of using more disk drives, most Personal Computers do not have more than four disk drives. Therefore, the additional capacity is welcomed, but not utilized.

CP/M-86 cannot handle disk drives larger than 8M without subdividing them into smaller, "logical" drives. PC DOS handles drives up to 1G (gigabyte) in capacity. With the 10M Fixed Disk, CP/M-86's current inability to handle very large disk drives is not as important. Most Personal Computer owners using CP/M-86 will subdivide the Fixed Disk to accommodate both PC DOS and CP/M-86 anyway. However, if larger-capacity (greater than 10M) hard disks are used, this limitation becomes more important.

Other notable advantages of CP/M-86 include the protection of individual files from alteration or deletion (software write-protection, or *read-only* files), and the ability to group files into different disk "user" areas, making one set of files on a disk invisible to another set.

These advantages are also available to PC DOS. A hidden file is inaccessible to most programs and general use. This protects the file from accidental alteration or deletion. In PC DOS 2.0, read-only file-by-file protection (similar to CP/M-86) was added. However, no program is provided with PC DOS 2.0 to change a file into a read-only file or the reverse. CP/M-86's STAT command can be used to change a file's read-only status. Because PC DOS' hidden files cannot be accessed through normal programs and operations (such as copying the diskette), they are not as easy to use as the normal read-only protection scheme of CP/M-86.

Organizing files on disk through hierarchical directories performs the same function as "user numbers" in CP/M-86. CP/M-86 allows only 16 user numbers for file segregation, but PC DOS V2.0 can generate many more subdirectories for this purpose because the only limitation is the amount of available disk storage space.

The technically complex subject of memory management will not be fully addressed in this book. It will only be stated that CP/M-86 has better memory management techniques than PC DOS V1.1 and slight advantages over PC DOS V2.0.

From the standpoint of graphics, the Digital Research version of CP/M-86 is superior to IBM's CP/M-86 and PC DOS. The GSX graphics subsystem is very powerful in its capabilities to "scale" graphics between different devices. It also offers a more portable method of handling graphics. For those constructing programs for the Personal Computers, only GSX's ability to use the same "basic" program for a variety of devices is important.

For the program developer, the direction of input and output and piping are major advantages to PC DOS V2.0. These UNIX-like features assist in program testing and debugging, and in linking together a set of filters or black boxes into a powerful tool.

For the User

IBM's entire software library runs only on the PC DOS operating system—a fact of great importance to users of the IBM Personal Computer. Inasmuch as IBM sells its accounting, educational, entertainment, and word-processing software only for PC DOS, the owner must purchase PC DOS to use any of these programs.

PC DOS' orientation is toward the user. PC DOS is a friendly operating system. All error messages given by the operating system are in complete English statements that indicate the source of the error and the possible cause. Should a disk error cause a problem, most housekeeping commands or programs allow the operator to stop the command, repeat the operation, or ignore the problem and continue. Overall, IBM's interest in making the operations of a computer system nonintimidating for the first-time computer user or owner is clearly visible in PC DOS.

CP/M-86 has the HELP command, a positive step toward helping the operator remember the syntax (phrasing) and purpose of commands without referring back to a manual. However, this command cannot be used within a program (the operator cannot get HELP in the middle of issuing a command) and thereby loses some of its effectiveness. PC DOS does not have a HELP command. The Digital Research version of CP/M-86 offers menus with some of its utilities and is more friendly in some instances than PC DOS. Overall, however, PC DOS remains the most friendly of the two operating systems.

The documentation provided by both operating systems is, on the whole, equal. However, PC DOS' documentation has more examples of command usage than CP/M-86.

Users who want the ability to perform more than one task at a time or who want to grow into a more capable computer system have choices with CP/M-86 and PC DOS V2.0. The CP/M-86 family includes Concurrent CP/M-86 and MP/M-86. Concurrent CP/M-86, now in its second version, is available from Digital Research. It is a single-user, multitasking version of CP/M-86. MP/M-86 is the multiuser, multitasking version. Of the two, Concurrent CP/M-86 is the most attractive and better suited to the capabilities of the Personal Computer.

PC DOS does not handle multitasking operations. However, it does have a striking resemblence to UNIX/Xenix. Many of PC DOS V2.0's system calls and functions are similar. UNIX/Xenix is a multiuser, multitasking operating system that was originally developed by Bell Laboratories. Movement toward multitasking with Microsoft's version of UNIX/Xenix may be possible for the Personal Computer in the future.

If concurrent use of the Personal Computer is not important to a user, PC DOS has the definitive advantage with its friendliness. Most operating system housekeeping programs have friendly prompts and error messages that guide the user through such operations as copying and formatting diskettes, or directing the Personal Computer to use a different listing device (printer). The entire PC DOS system, through its ease of operation, displays a commitment to the novice or infrequent user.

In disk operations, PC DOS is faster than CP/M-86. PC DOS also maintains an exact count of the number of bytes in a disk file, displaying this information in the directory, along with the date of file creation or of the last addition to the file.

How a system handles errors is another test of system friendliness. PC DOS allows application programs to be tested for errors and gives the appropriate dialogue to the operator. PC DOS itself, through a clearly stated prompt, gives the operator the opportunity to retry, abort, or bypass a disk error. Some errors trapped by IBM's CP/M-86 force an abrupt termination of the program; however, the Digital Research version of CP/M-86 is more friendly in this respect.

With regard to both speed and friendliness, PC DOS allows the user to change diskettes on-the-fly. IBM's CP/M-86 does not offer this opportunity, whereas Digital Research's CP/M-86 does. The procedure of changing diskettes while a program is running can be disastrous because information yet to be written to a diskette may be destroyed. In any other case than the one just mentioned, PC DOS allows the user to make this change without consequence. This capability is partially found in the Digital Research version of CP/M-86. IBM's CP/M-86 judges a new diskette as "write-protected" and bars the placement of further information onto the diskette if the system is not informed of the change. Digital Research's CP/M-86 will permit the change if no information is waiting to be written to a diskette (i.e., the program has issued the appropriate system calls to close any used files on the diskette).

Another positive feature of PC DOS is its lack of distinction between disk and device files. Actually, the PC DOS operating system knows through its I/O System that a communications channel should be established with the serial port when a program opens and uses a file called "COM1:." CP/M-86, on the other hand, creates a disk file called "COM1:" if this procedure is used with one of its languages. This advantage of PC DOS is strengthened by the redirection of input/output and piping.

Upward compatibility is an issue that affects both technical and nontechnical users of the Personal Computer. Microsoft made the commitment that all versions of MSDOS (the predecessor of PC DOS) would be upward compatible. This means that programs running under PC DOS V1.00 (MS-DOS 1.0) should be able to run under PC DOS V1.10 (MS-DOS V1.25), or any later generation of PC DOS. In the movement from PC DOS V1.00 to V1.10, this upward compatibility applies. The same is true for programs making the transition between V1.1 and V2.0. However, this compatibility does not extend to programs that do not follow the conventions established for operating system calls, such as certain printer spooling programs. This incompatibility is not a fault of the operating system, but a failure of the program's author to use the operating system's standards. Nor does this compatibility extend to the need for increased RAM memory, a natural consequence of the additional functions developed for PC DOS V2.0.

Another reflection of IBM's commitment to upward compatibility is PC DOS V2.0's deliberate adoption of many UNIX/Xenix-like features. These features will give the Personal Computer owner the ability to use efficiently the UNIX/Xenix operating system as it becomes available.

CP/M-86 is generally upward compatible with its family of products, Concurrent CP/M-86 and MP/M-86. However, Concurrent CP/M-86 and MP/M-86 are multitasking operating systems. Additional system calls are provided by Concurrent CP/M-86 and MP/M-86 for record locking and other multitasking management functions. Most CP/M-86 software will function under Concurrent CP/M-86. However, programs that do not follow the conventions established for CP/M-86 system calls will not function properly with either Concurrent CP/M-86 or MP/M-86. In addition, CP/M-86 software must be rewritten to take full advantage of the facilities provided by Concurrent CP/M-86 and MP/M-86.

Summary

CP/M-86's greatest advantages are its versatility in the use of non-IBM marketed printers and similar devices, and in an upward path in Concurrent CP/M-86 and MP/M-86, with Concurrent CP/M-86 having the greatest potential for the Personal Computer.

PC DOS' advantages are its exceptional friendliness, faster disk speed, and the greater programmer and application program support provided by IBM. The guarantee of upward compatibility of PC DOS has also been given by Microsoft.

The "battle" of the operating systems is not finished. Both Microsoft, the original author of PC DOS, and Digital Research, the author of the CP/M family, are continually improving their products. The current advantage is in PC DOS' court; more application programs run on PC DOS than on CP/M-86. However, during the next few years, CP/M-86 will make an impact on more owners of the Personal Computer. As competition fosters new developments and better products, the competition between Microsoft and Digital Research can only improve the functions and features of the Personal Computers.

The UCSD p-System

The third operating system for the Personal Computer is the p-System from the University of California, San Diego campus. This system gives the Personal Computer a different personality.

History of the p-System

The p-System was largely developed at the Institute for Information Sciences at UCSD under the direction of Kenneth L. Bowes. It was first distributed in the late 1970s and licensed by the Regents of the University of California. Later, the California-based SofTech Microsystems, a subsidiary of SofTech, Inc., in Massachusetts, was awarded the sole distribution and maintenance responsibilities for the UCSD p-System.

The p-System was developed to offer programming students a friendly, menu-driven operating system for learning computer programming. It was also developed to maximize the small amount of RAM memory available in their microcomputers, which at the time were Digital Equipment Corporation's PDP-8s with 32K of RAM.

Inside the p-System

The *p* in p-System stands for the *pseudo*code produced by the various languages. Pseudocode means "not truly CPU-executable (machine-language) instructions."

PC DOS and CP/M-86 are machine-language programs that the CPU understands directly and executes swiftly. They occupy a relatively small amount of RAM memory.

Most of the p-System is written in UCSD Pascal. When the UCSD Pascal programs are compiled, they are not changed into the native instructions of the CPU, but rather are condensed into pseudocode. This pseudocode is either executed by a CPU that understands the code (Western Digital makes such a CPU), or it is translated into native instructions for the CPU by an interpreter, similar in concept to the IBM BASIC language (covered in the next chapter). This translation must be done for the Personal Computer system because its CPU, the 8088, does not directly understand the pseudocode (or P-code).

The Personal Computers, and many other systems, use the *P-machine emulator*. The P-machine is the name of the Western

Digital CPU set that understands the P-code. The P-machine emulator is the program that translates P-coded instructions into directly executable instructions for the varying CPUs. By changing the P-machine emulator (interpreter) for the native languages of the different CPUs, the entire p-System can be used on these different CPUs.

In short, the major impact of the p-System is that it runs on a variety of computers—not just on computers that use the same microprocessor, but on computer systems that use entirely different CPUs. This means that the p-System can run on machines like the Apple, Osborne, IBM, and DEC PDP-11 and LSI11 computers. The entire p-System remains basically unchanged; only the P-machine emulator is different. This universality allows the p-System to use a broader base of computer systems than the CP/M and MS/PC DOS families combined.

CP/M is a transportable operating system. There are versions of CP/M for the 8080, 8086, and Motorola 68000 (a 16/32-bit microprocessor in the way that the 8088 is an 8/16 CPU) families today, and work is underway for versions of CP/M for the 16-bit Zilog Z8000 and the 16/32-bit National Semiconductor 16000 families. However, most programs and programming languages written under this operating system can operate only on a specific CPU. They are not immediately transportable among members of the entire CP/M family.

The major difference between CP/M and the UCSD p-System is that programs written on any computer equipped with the p-System can run on any other p-System computer. No changes need to be made to the programs. The use of standard pseudocode gives programs written under the p-System the greatest transportability possible. One copy of a program may be developed on an Apple, IBM, or PDP-11 computer and used on any other computer equipped with the p-System. The P-machine emulator handles the differences between systems. This is the biggest reason for commercial software developers to use the p-System.

There is a price paid for the small, universal programs developed under the p-System, however: speed. Although p-System programs are small, their execution time is 10 to 40 times longer than comparable programs written in machine language. The constant interpretation of the operating system's programs allows them to be stored and executed in less disk and memory space, but the performance costs are great.

The UCSD p-System at a Glance

Purpose:	To provide a "processor-independent" operating system for the Personal Computer and others
Authors:	Institute for Information Sciences, University of California, San Diego Campus
Licensor:	Regents of the University of California, administered and maintained through SofTech Microsystems, subsidiary of SofTech, Inc.
Date of introduction:	1976
Current version:	IV.03
Central processing units supported:	Intel 8080, 8085, 8086, and 8088 Digital Equipment Corporation LSI-11™ and PDP-11™ MOS Technology 6502 Motorola's 6800, 6809, and 68000 Texas Instruments 9900 Zilog Z80
Contents:	Machine-dependent interpreter (P-machine emulator) Operating system and support programs (written in UCSD PASCAL)
Languages:	PASCAL, FORTRAN-77, BASIC, Assembler, and Cross-Assemblers
Major segments:	
Filer	Disk and peripheral file maintenance and transfer program
Assembler	Machine-language assembler program
Linker	Joins compiled or assembled programs
Debugger	PASCAL/FORTRAN/Assembly language symbolic debugger
Xecute	Run-time interpreter for programs

The UCSD p-System is composed of several distinct programs, often called *segments*. These segments are written in UCSD Pascal. The principal programs in the operating system are the filer, editor, compilers, assemblers, the linker, and the debugger. These programs perform the various housekeeping tasks for program development and execution.

The p-System Development package is a powerful program development system. Originally conceived as an environment for students, the p-System editor (a visual editor that is not line-oriented like CP/M-86's and PC DOS'), debugger, assembler, programming language, and compilers are excellent. In addition, the entire operating system is menu-driven.

For those who do not want to program in the p-System, the p-System Run-Time package is available for PC DOS. The Run-Time package is the core of the p-System without the filer, editor, debugger, or languages. It allows a Personal Computer owner to run programs developed under the p-System without having to purchase the entire "development" system. This reduces the purchase price of programs developed under the p-System. Before the Run-Time package was introduced, program publishers paid an additional royalty for including this package with each program. Now the Personal Computer owner can purchase the Run-Time package once and avoid the additional costs of buying several application programs.

The UCSD p-System gives the user the greatest opportunity to write one program for many dissimilar computer systems. However, Personal Computer owners who want the ultimate in program speed and do not want to write programs for dissimilar computers will find their mecca in PC DOS.

Some Speculation
about Operating Systems

Because they belong to an industry with tremendous dynamics, the operating systems for the Personal Computers have undergone many changes; and they will continue to change.

PC DOS has made a major transitional step with version 2.0. V2.0 allows greater freedom with non-IBM devices, a more open approach than before. It incorporates many features from the UNIX/Xenix worlds, such as redirection of I/O and piping. The incorporation of the ANSI terminal codes brings greater standardization for the use of graphics.

One of PC DOS' future enhancements will probably be graphics-oriented. Microsoft is currently working with the North American Presentation Level Protocols (NAPLP). In nontechnical terms (the ANSI NAPLP proposed standard is more than 140 pages), NAPLP is a method of expressing and transmitting graphics. It may be thought of as the ASCII of graphics. The incorporation of NAPLP drivers for graphics in the future is almost assured.

UNIX

UNIX, per se, has not reached the Personal Computers (a prediction made in the last edition). UNIX is the multiuser, multitasking operating system developed by Bell Laboratories. It is marketed by Western Electric and will also be available soon from American Bell.

Bell Laboratories has not developed a version of UNIX for the Personal Computer. Microsoft, the authors of PC DOS, have licensed the UNIX operating system, however, and sell it under their trademarked name of Xenix. One company in California has licensed Xenix from Microsoft and is selling it for the Personal Computer.

Venturecom, in Massachusetts, also sells Bell-licensed UNIX for the Personal Computers. Their Venix operating system has many features that are similar to Xenix.

Several other companies sell UNIX-like operating systems for the Personal Computer. The Mark Williams Company in Chicago, Illinois, for example, sells Coherent™. Quantum Software in San Jose, California, sells QNX™, another example of a UNIX-like system.

UNIX has reached the Personal Computer, but not on a large scale.

Part of the problem in implementing UNIX on the Personal Computers is the lack of hardware memory management. UNIX was developed on DEC PDP-8s and PDP-11s and extensively uses the memory management features of these machines. Briefly, hardware memory management protects programs from other executing programs and allows each program to believe that it "owns" (can use the entire resources of) the computer system. This memory management is vital to UNIX's operation. The Personal Computer's 8088 does not offer this feature. Therefore, either an expansion card, at additional cost, must be used for this purpose, or lower-performance software (programming) memory management.

The hardware memory management problem means that the current Personal Computer is not the ideal computer for UNIX. The UNIX-like operating systems available for the Personal Computer (e.g., Xenix and Venix), however, do allow it to take advantage of some of UNIX's features.

If IBM were to choose a processor that supports memory management, such as the iAPX 286, true UNIX or Xenix could be implemented. This path is possible because PC DOS V2.0 has many UNIX functions and features.

CP/M

Digital Research will continue to refine the CP/M-86 family. Concurrent CP/M-86 V2.0, the second version of their single-user, multitasking operating system, was released in June, 1983. Concurrent CP/M-86 offers many of the features of CP/M Plus™, the higher performance and friendlier version of CP/M-80. The next release of CP/M-86, date unknown, will also move to the Plus level, offering date and time stamps on files, built-in RAM disk, and other features.

The CCP (Console Command Interpreter or user interface) of CP/M-86 may change drastically in the next year. Menu operations of the entire operating system are possible. The Apple Lisa™ approach of using a "mouse"'' for cursor control is another possibility.

p-System

The p-System has moved from version IV.0 to IV.03, increasing its ability to handle concurrent processes, but not concurrent programs like Concurrent CP/M-86. The number of CPUs that run the p-System has also increased. The p-System now runs on more 16-bit microprocessors than before. Some improvements in performance were also gained in IV.1. The Run-Time package for the Personal Computers was an important step in reducing the cost of running programs written under the p-System. However, plans for the future evolution of the p-System, with the exception of running on more CPUs, are unclear.

OASIS-16

OASIS-16, another operating system, is not discussed in this book. It was developed and distributed by Phase One Systems in Oakland, California. This mature, multiuser, multitasking business operating system is used on Z80- and 8086-based computer systems. Although its features, similar to IBM's JCL, will be found on more Personal Computers in the future, it will obtain only a fraction of the popularity of PC DOS.

A multiuser, multitasking operating system other than OASIS-16 is unlikely for the Personal Computer systems. The Personal Computer simply does not have the ideal resources for effective multiuser use.

Local Area Networks

Local area networking is another area of concern for operating systems. The implementation of this system has several problems to overcome. First, several different standards have emerged for the local area networks, but no one standard dominates the field. Second, the cost of connection to the network must also decrease before networking will become popular. Third, the software for the local area network must be invisible to the operator. This problem applies to both larger machines in the network and to the operating systems for the Personal Computers.

To date, none of the authors of the operating systems for the Personal Computers has announced a solution to this last problem. This does not mean that the problem is being ignored. Such an announcement could come in late 1983 or early 1984. The problem is more complex because larger machines, minicomputers and mainframes, must be compatible with the chosen network. The lack of a popular standardized approach to local area networks has inhibited larger computer compatibility.

Conclusion

If the Personal Computers' future for hardware is bright, the prospects for the current and future operating systems are brilliant. The most likely future of operating systems is in the multitasking, not multiuser, use and incorporation of software for local area networks. Reliable predictions about the future limits of the Personal

Computers are difficult to make. Limits are based on software, and software is based on hardware. Changes in hardware bring new levels of software capabilities. The future scope of the Personal Computer systems is still too broad to predict accurately, and sometimes too large to imagine.

CHAPTER 5
The Language Series

Programming languages act as translators. They translate the operator's English-like instructions into the binary ones and zeros understood by the CPU and other resources of the computer system. Programming languages transform the programmer's instructions into word-processing, spreadsheet, accounting, communications, engineering, entertainment, and other applications programs.

The Personal Computer uses three different families of programming languages based on its three operating systems. Through IBM, the Personal Computers can use two BASIC programming languages, two different Pascal languages, three assemblers, two FORTRAN languages, and one COBOL. Microsoft and Digital Research add two C programming languages and one additional assembler, BASIC, Pascal, and COBOL. Different levels of capability in several programming language families (IBM BASIC has four levels) increase the number of languages available. If more outside language producers were added to the list, the total number and versions of languages available today for the Personal Computer would exceed fifty.

A programming language is like a tool. Each tool has one or more ideal uses, such as a saw for cutting or a drill for making holes. A tool can be forced into a task that it was not intended to handle, such as a screwdriver being used as a chisel. The result may or may not be as satisfying as having the right tool for the task.

Any programming language can create almost any type of program, including another programming language. Each programming language has one or more ideal uses. These uses are based on proficiency time, program development time, execution speed, size of the developed program, nature of commands and adaptability, and other factors. These factors should ultimately determine which tool (programming language) is best for the task.

BASIC and Programming Languages

BASIC is the most popular programming language. In comparison with other languages, BASIC runs on more computers, and more people in the world program in the BASIC language. BASIC has more versions and dialects than any other language. Specifically, IBM Personal Computer BASIC has more commands and statements than any other version of the BASIC language.

BASIC elicits two distinct reactions: people swear either "by it" or "at it." Most computerists simply groan. The original developers of BASIC are astounded at its growth and popularity.

BASIC is the acronym for "Beginner's All-purpose Symbolic Instruction Code." Developed at Dartmouth College in 1972, BASIC was meant to be a simple, number-oriented language for teaching students how to program computers. Bill Gates and Paul Allen wrote a version of this BASIC for the 8080 CPU in 1976. This version has become known as BASIC-80 and MBASIC. BASIC-80 represented the start of Microsoft, one of the two leaders in microcomputer language software (Digital Research is the other).

IBM BASIC is Microsoft's BASIC-86, the more-powerful version of BASIC-80 written for the 8086 CPU. Microsoft BASIC is the most popular programming language. It runs on more than one and a half million different computers.

Like any other tool, BASIC has many advantages. It is easy to use; its English-like commands and syntax are flexible and easy to remember. Programs can be constructed quickly. BASIC is a forgiving language. It allows new names for numbers or alphanumeric characters (called variables) to be introduced almost anywhere in the program. Its method of phrasing commands (syntax) is more tolerant than that of COBOL, FORTRAN, or Pascal. Each statement line has a number. The statments are executed in ascending order. BASIC can be told to GOTO another portion of the program and continue execution from that point. Program parts (subroutines) can be constructed and easily executed by telling BASIC to perform the subroutine (GOSUB) and RETURN control to the main portion of the program when finished.

PC DOS BASIC at a Glance

Purpose: To provide a high-level, English-like means of communicating commands to the Personal Computers

Location: In ROM on System Board, PC DOS master diskette, and BASIC Compiler diskette

Author: Microsoft

Date of introductions: 1981 V1.0
                     1982 V1.1 and BASIC Compiler
                     1983 V2.0

Levels: Cassette BASIC
                     Disk BASIC
                     Advanced BASIC
                     BASIC Compiler

Type of Language: Nonstructured (all levels)
                     Interpreter (Cassette, Disk, Advanced BASIC)
                     Compiler (BASIC Compiler)

Usable memory sizes:

	Minimum	Maximum
Cassette BASIC	32K	64K
Disk BASIC (V1.1)	32K	96K
Disk BASIC (V2.0)	48K	128K
Advanced BASIC (V1.1)	48K	96K
Advanced BASIC (V2.0)	64K	128K

Above memory sizes may vary due to communications and disk buffers for BASIC and disk buffers and other options with PC DOS V2.0.

BASIC also has its weaknesses. Computerists groan at its many semicompatible versions. Beginning programmers whose first language is BASIC have difficulty learning most other computer languages because BASIC encourages "sloppy" programming habits. It can be difficult to maintain and change BASIC programs. Additions may have undesirable side effects.

The comment that best describes BASIC is that it is "the quick and dirty way to get things done."

Types of Programming Languages

Programming languages are classified by two different sets of criteria: those concerning the structure of the language, and those for the interpretation of commands into executable instructions for the computer. Each set, in turn, has two categories.

Structured languages demand that certain information be presented at particular points in a program. This information includes: the name of a variable and what it will contain before it is used; a statement about whether the variable is valid for the entire program or for only a section of it; some indication that a subroutine will, or will not, request information (input) or display information (output); and the information that the subroutine (usually called a function or procedure) will produce. The particular information that must be presented "up front" varies among languages. Programs in structured languages use a building block approach to writing. Subroutines, functions, procedures, or blocks are usually developed to handle one purpose. The blocks are combined to build most of the program.

Nonstructured programs are less rigorous. New names for variables, their type, and size can occur anywhere in the program, provided that these statements are executed in the proper order. This approach involves less "up front" work for the programmer than with structured languages. Nonstructured languages make extensive use of GOTO and GOSUB statements, casually transferring the flow of the program among its various parts.

The second set of languages is divided into compilers and interpreters. This classification is based on how programming statements are handled by the language.

In most Pascal, C, FORTRAN, and COBOL languages, programs go through a step called *compiling*. The English-like program statements (source code) are transformed into instructions (machine-language object code) that the computer's CPU can directly execute, although a process called linking is usually required to finish the program.

Interpreters

In most versions of BASIC, the BASIC program acts as an *interpreter*. It translates each program statement as it is encountered into the appropriate instructions for the computer.

The best analogy is that compilers are like the Berlitz™ School of Languages. They "teach" (change) the program to speak the native language of the CPU. Interpreters, however, are like United Nations interpreters. They act as a go-between, on a line-by-line basis, for the program and the CPU.

The third category in this set is the *pseudocompiler* or *interpreted compiler*. With the interpreted compiler, the English-like command statements are translated into pseudocode. This pseudocode is then translated by a separate program. Digital Research's CBASIC (Commercial BASIC) is one example of an interpreted compiler. Technically, the UCSD p-System languages on the IBM Personal Computers also fall into this category because they use the P-machine interpreter.

Interpreted languages make programs easy to develop. A programmer can write a section of the program, try it out, then change it at any time. The programmer can easily stop the program; examine its progress; and, in most cases, continue the program. In addition, interpreted programs are more compact and require less disk space for storage.

Compilers

Compiled programs are more difficult to develop. One mistake in a statement requires that the programmer correct the source code, using a separate text editor; recompile the source code; relink it; and retest the program. Compiled programs generally use more disk space for storage.

An advantage to compiled programs is that they execute many times faster than interpreted programs. Compiled programs are faster because the CPU executes just the program, not the interpreter and the program. With programs written under pseudocompilers or interpreted compilers, however, the CPU must run both the interpreter and the program. Therefore, these programs take much longer to execute.

A second advantage to compilers or pseudocompilers is that the source code is protected. Once a program has been transformed by the compiler into object or pseudocode, reconstructing the programming statements is difficult. This protects the author of the program from the theft of any ingenious methods constructed for the program. (The technical term for this kind of safety is *source code protection.*)

Structured programming languages force the programmer to follow certain procedures when programming. They usually enforce good programming techniques, such as making variable names understandable (as MONTH.TO.PAY rather than MONTHTOPAY or MTP) by using one program statement on a line rather than several, and by avoiding the use of GOTOs and GOSUBs. These techniques increase program legibility and clarity.

The addition or alteration of a program's features or functions, or program maintenance, which is the bane of many programmers and computer installations, can be a nightmare to anyone (other than the program's original author) who attempts to understand how the original program worked. Even the author, returning to a program several days or weeks later, may have the same problem.

Structured languages, by virtue of the legibility of the program's variables and procedures, can actually reduce program maintenance costs. Other programmers, or the original author, can quickly examine, understand, and change the necessary parts of programs if they are written in a clear, structured style. Some programs written in structured languages are totally incomprehensible. A structured language alone does not guarantee legible programming. There are many other factors that affect program maintenance costs, but writing in a nonstructured or illegible style almost guarantees increased maintenance costs.

Once one structured programming language has been learned, it is usually easier to learn another one. The skills developed in one structured language are generally transportable to the second or third structured language. Those who learn a nonstructured language first have more difficulty learning the new concepts and procedures for their first structured language than a person who has already learned one structured language and is learning a second one. Chances for finding employment with companies that use a structured language like COBOL are greater if the applicant has already learned a similar, structured language.

It is easier to create a program with a nonstructured programming language. The programmer needs less forethought and planning when using these languages because variables and subroutines can be created "on the fly" as the program is written. This approach discourages good programming techniques and increases the difficulty in maintaining programs.

In summary, BASIC is a nonstructured language. It has two versions: interpreted and compiled. Because a programming language is a tool with an ideal set of purposes, different languages using different methods (structured, nonstructured, interpreted, and compiled) have been developed. BASIC is a friendly language that allows fast program development and is ideal for those who want to learn only one programming language.

The IBM BASIC Programming Language

The Personal Computer systems have four levels of BASIC. Three levels are interpreted BASIC: Cassette, Disk, and Advanced. The fourth level is compiled: the IBM (Microsoft) BASIC-86 Compiler. Cassette BASIC is supplied with every Personal Computer system, including the XT. Disk and Advanced BASIC are supplied with PC DOS. The BASIC Compiler is an optional program. All versions are similar to Microsoft's BASIC-80. A programmer who is familiar with BASIC-80 can make the transition swiftly.

Each new version of PC DOS has brought new versions of Disk and Advanced BASIC and the BASIC Compiler. Cassette BASIC, however, has remained virtually unchanged. There are three versions of Disk and Advanced BASIC (V1.0, V1.1, and V2.0) and one version of the BASIC Compiler (for PC DOS V1.1 and V2.0). The BASIC Compiler was not released by IBM until PC DOS V1.1 was released.

Interpreted BASIC

Cassette BASIC resides in ROM on the System Board. It is the basis for Disk and Advanced BASIC. Both Disk and Advanced BASIC extend the commands found in Cassette BASIC. This relationship explains why the Cassette BASIC ROM is included with the Personal Computer XT, which does not have a cassette port. The XT needs this ROM to use Disk or Advanced BASIC.

Both Disk and Advanced BASIC are included on the PC DOS master diskette(s). Each brings additional commands and capabilites to IBM's BASIC. Disk BASIC allows the use of disk storage. Advanced

BASIC has all of Disk BASIC's functions and adds further capabilities.

The BASIC Compiler is different from Cassette, Disk, or Advanced BASIC. It has many of the commands of Advanced BASIC, but does not use the ROMed Cassette BASIC. Programs produced by the compiler are mostly independent and free standing. (The BASIC Compiler is discussed later.)

Cassette BASIC

Cassette BASIC has 135 different commands and functions. It offers full numeric functions: addition, subtraction, multiplication, division, power (x^0), square root, exponential notation ($X * 10y$), sine, cosine, tangent, and others. Cassette BASIC also features extensive string (alphanumerics) handing functions: LEFT$, RIGHT$, MID$, INKEY$, INSTR, etc. It has program control statements (GOTO, GOSUB..RETURN, FOR..NEXT, etc.), cassette storage statements for programs and data (these statements cannot be used on the Personal Computer XT), several text and color graphics statements, and several uses for the special-function keys. Cassette BASIC is a fully functional BASIC.

Disk and Advanced BASIC

Since the Personal Computers were introduced, IBM Disk and Advanced BASIC have undergone some changes. Programs written under previous versions of BASIC can be used with the updated versions, typically without any change in the original program. However, older versions of BASIC may not function with some programs written in the newer versions because some new commands or functions have been added that do not exist in the older versions.

The major V1.1 (second release of BASIC) changes incorporated additional support for the communications adapter (the setting of baud rates, parity, and type of hardware handshaking; and the use of PUT and GET commands); the recognition of two more joysticks and buttons (the STRIG command in Advanced BASIC); and the VARPTR$ function, which is useful with the DRAW and PLAY commands. Almost an equal number of changes were made to both Disk and Advanced BASIC.

The major V2.0 changes include double-precision transcendentals (sine, cosine, arctangent, etc.), the necessary changes for paths (hierarchical directories), extended graphics commands, extended music commands (two notes can now be played directly in BASIC), the ability to test more events (ON event) and use more special-function keys, and the TIMER (seconds elapsed since last power-up or system reset) function. In this version, more new commands were added to Advanced BASIC than to Disk BASIC.

Disk BASIC

Disk BASIC V1.1 adds 15 commands to Cassette BASIC, and Disk BASIC V2.0 adds 26 commands. These new commands handle disk storage, the day-of-year/time-of-day clock, the communications adapter, and additional printers. Most V2.0 changes enhance disk file and communications operations.

Disk BASIC is loaded from the disk. The disk file's name for Disk BASIC is BASIC.COM.

The optional "switches" may be specified when Disk BASIC is invoked. These switches may decrease or, most often, increase the space taken by Disk BASIC. The options include the size of the communication buffer(s); the maximum number of open files; BASIC's (not PC DOS') disk buffer size; the amount of reserved workspace, such as for machine-language programs; and the use of single- or double-precision transcendentals. The last switch, double-precision transcendentals, applies to only BASIC V2.0.

Advanced BASIC

Advanced BASIC is also loaded from the disk file with the name BASICA.COM (commonly called BASICA in non-IBM literature). Advanced BASIC V1.1 adds 12 commands to Disk BASIC, and Advanced BASIC V2.0 adds 33 commands. This brings the respective command, function, and statement totals to 164 and 195. Advanced BASIC has more commands than any other microcomputer BASIC.

The actual RAM memory space taken by Disk or Advanced BASIC is deceiving. Both BASICs use the 32K Cassette BASIC as their core and are much larger and more functional than their RAM size indicates.

Advanced BASIC is a programmer's delight. Using the Cassette and Disk BASICs as its foundation, Advanced BASIC features extended color graphics commands; event trapping for the communications adapter, joystick, light pen, and special-function keys; and music support. The V2.0 additions for graphics, transcendentals, hierarchical directories, and other features make Advanced BASIC a highly functional programming language.

Table 5.1 lists some of the statements that are unique to Advanced BASIC. The ON.. event statements, for example, once they are given in the program, cause an unconditional jump to a subroutine based on the following devices: the communication adapter(s), special-function keys, joystick, or light pen. With Advanced BASIC, these event statements can be selectively enabled, disabled, or stopped. When disabled (device OFF), the respective program jumps are ignored. When stopped (device STOP), BASIC remembers the activity on the device and executes the proper subroutine when the device is reenabled (device ON).

The PLAY command gives the Personal Computers' speaker the ability to play music. The information to be played is stored in a string variable that can contain sharps and flats, octaves, tempo, key of the note, and the length of the note: normal (7/8), legato (4/4, or full period), or staccato (3/4). Although two simultaneous notes are possible in V1.1, this capability is fully supported by only Advanced BASIC V2.0.

Forethought is demonstrated in all levels of the BASIC interpreter, particularly in Advanced BASIC. Advanced BASIC allows only one level of GOSUBing for the event commands (ON..) at one time, thus preventing imaginative, but disastrous loops when two or more special-function keys—with or without the joystick button—are hit. In addition, the command to return from a subroutine (RETURN) can have an optional line number in Advanced and Compiler BASIC. Many programmers understand this ability to leave a subroutine and perform a different portion of the program, without returning to the invoking portion of the program.

Screen editing of program lines is featured in all interpreted levels of BASIC. It allows the cursor to be moved anywhere on the program line; characters inserted, deleted, or changed; and program lines added or replaced. This visual editing feature is identical to that of the Commodore™ computer family, except that 255 characters are allowed per program line for the Personal Computers (vs. 80 characters for some Commodore computers).

Table 5.1
Some Commands Unique to Advanced BASIC

Unique Color Graphics commands

CIRCLE	Draws part of or a complete circle with size, color, and placement options
DRAW	Draws a shape on the screen based on an alphanumeric string
GET	Reads the colors from the graphics screen and places the information in a numeric array
PAINT	Fills an area of the screen with color
PUT	Transfers a numeric array into colors on the graphics screen
WINDOW	Allows redefining of the physical graphics screen into a larger "logical" screen

Unique Event Trapping

ON COM	For asynchronous communications adapter activity
ON KEY	For recognition of the 10 or 15 special-function keys
ON PEN	For light-pen activity
ON STRIG	For the joysticks
ON TIMER	Based on the seconds timer (seconds since last power-up/system reset or midnight)

Music

PLAY	Plays a series of notes on the speaker based on a alphanumeric string. Supports polyphonic play

Program Control

RETURN linenumber	Allows the exit for a GOSUB to another section of the program

---

The Alt key has a new meaning in the interpreted BASICs. When Alt and an appropriate letter are pressed, 22 BASIC keywords (commands) are "typed" into the line. Command words like PRINT, INPUT, or OPEN are entered with just two keystrokes. The 10 special-function keys (15 in V2.0) can be redefined with up to 15 characters each to supplement the Alt key.

The implementation of BASIC on the IBM Personal Computers is a model of human and microcomputer interaction. Although BASIC rapidly consumes memory space and interpreting its large number of commands deteriorates processing speed, these inconveniences still allow the Personal Computers to operate faster and offer more memory than most 8-bit microcomputers.

BASIC Compiler

The optional BASIC Compiler greatly improves the execution speed of BASIC programs. The BASIC Compiler transforms programs normally executed by the BASIC interpreter into directly executable machine language. The program must be stored in an ASCII format. If the program was developed with the BASIC interpreters (Disk or Advanced BASIC), it must be saved with the ,A (ASCII) option.

The BASIC Compiler has many of the features found in Disk and Advanced BASIC, although BASIC V2.0 features have not been incorporated. Some commands of Disk and Advanced BASIC do not work with the compiler, such as LIST the program or RENUMber the program lines. These commands are applicable only to program development with an interpretive programming language and do not need to be included with a compiler.

This compiler can be used to produce high-speed programs in BASIC. The improvement in speed attained from compiling programs varies. Programs that extensively use string and real numbers can operate two to four times faster, whereas programs that make extensive use of integer numbers can operate as much as ten times faster. The average improvement in speed is between 200 and 600 percent. When a program is compiled, the source code and any trade secrets in the program are protected.

Options

The BASIC Compiler is actually a set of programs and libraries. BASCOM.COM is the BASIC Compiler itself. A library of BASIC subroutines (BASCOM.LIB), a run-time support library (BASRUN. LIB), and a run-time package (BASRUN.EXE) are also provided. The library is a set of proven subroutines. The run-time support and run-time package are additional library sets. The run-time support and run-time package are joined with the program and the BASIC subroutine library to create the finished program.

The BASIC program is changed into a specially formatted file by BASCOM.COM (the BASIC Compiler itself). When BASCOM is invoked, many options become available for using or controlling certain features of the BASIC language or the compiler. One of these options is ON ERROR and RESUME statements. Other capabilities include the ability to determine when event trapping should take place (ON COM, ON KEY, ON PEN, or ON STRIG) and when Microsoft 4.51 conventions should be used (the previous version of the BASIC-80 interpreter that has some syntactic, phrasing, and functional differences from the current versions). With BASCOM, the user can also list the program with assembly language equivalents, regulate the size of the communication buffer(s), and perform debugging and error-handling codes in the program. Other options include the ability to ignore line numbers, except for statements that use GOTOs and GOSUBs (commands); store two-dimensional arrays in row order rather than column order; write strings (alphanumeric characters) to disk rather than accumulating and maximizing them; and compile the program for stand-alone use (not for use with the run-time package).

The extensive list of options is not discussed further in this book, but it should be noted that these options can increase or decrease both the size and execution speed of the program.

For an understanding of the two separate run-time libraries, the last compiler option must be examined. When the compiler transforms the ASCII version of the BASIC program, it changes the program into a specially formatted file. The format of this file is identical to an assembly language program produced by the Macro Assembler (covered later in this chapter). In this file, the now-converted BASIC program "calls" (uses) a common set of subroutines contained in one of the two .LIB files. The .LIB files actually contain the features and functions of the BASIC language. When linked by PC DOS' LINK.EXE, the compiled BASIC program is ready for use.

Each run-time library supports a different way of executing the program. If the run-time support library (BASCOM.LIB) is chosen, the linked program can be executed directly. It becomes a .COM file. If the name of this file is typed at system level (designated by the A>), PC DOS will load and execute the program.

If the run-time package is selected, LINK.EXE will join the BASIC program with the second library (BASRUN.LIB). However, BASRUN. LIB does not contain the full BASIC language. To remedy this problem, BASRUN.LIB calls subroutines in the run-time module (BASRUN.EXE), which contains the full language. When this version of the BASIC program is running, the run-time module, BASRUN.EXE, is loaded into the Personal Computer's memory. The program is then loaded and executed, using the core of subroutines in BASRUN.EXE for support. This is not the same as a pseudocompiler. The program produced by the BASIC Compiler is a native-language (machine-language) program executed by the Personal Computers' 8088 CPU.

There are advantages and disadvantages to both approaches. If a program is created that needs no additional support (i.e., BASRUN. EXE), the produced program is larger and requires more disk space for storage. In addition, certain features of BASIC concerning the loading and executing of additional BASIC programs (e.g., the CHAIN and COMMON commands) are sacrificed with this method. However, small BASIC programs need less total RAM memory space than programs that are linked with the run-time library (BASRUN.LIB), using the support module (BASRUN.EXE). A copy of the run-time module need not be on the system when this method is used.

The run-time package has several advantages. Programs take up less storage space, most features of "chaining" and the COMMON command are available, and less time is needed to link the program with the library. However, a copy of BASRUN.EXE must be available to the users of this program. If the program is solely for the use of the person who created it, there is no problem because BASRUN.EXE is provided with the BASIC Compiler. However, the author may not give the run-time module to other users unless a licensing agreement has been signed with IBM. This means that commercial versions of the program will cost more because IBM receives a royalty for each copy of BASRUN.EXE provided. The alternative would be for each user to purchase a BASIC Compiler and use BASRUN.EXE to run the program.

Despite these limitations, the rewards of the BASIC Compiler are great. Most features of Advanced BASIC are available. Programs are directly executed from PC DOS, and the BASIC interpreters are not required. The main advantage of the BASIC compiler is that a program developer can use the friendly, easy-to-develop resources of interpreted BASIC. When a program is perfected, it is compiled. The compiled program gains the advantage of all compiler-based languages: a significant increase in speed and protection for the program's source code. The BASIC Compiler gives the programmer the advantages of both programming worlds, interpreted and compiled.

Summary

Although the implementation of the BASIC interpreters and Compiler is somewhat unique to the IBM Personal Computers, it is still Microsoft BASIC. This means that most programs written for any version of Microsoft BASIC may be typed into the Personal Computer and executed with little or no modification. The majority of the modifications will center on the video display (CLS, LOCATE, CRSLIN, and color graphics commands) and commands that involve equipment which is unique to the Personal Computer (e.g., communications ports, special-function keys, etc.).

In spite of the limitations mentioned earlier, BASIC is an excellent, general-purpose programming language whose supporters are found in the personal, educational, entertainment, and business fields. This powerful language evolved from the many generations of Microsoft BASIC (starting in 1975). BASIC is not only a powerful language, but also a friendly one. Its evolution, as proved by IBM BASIC V1.1 and V2.0, is continual. More new features will be available in this language as time passes.

IBM FORTRAN and Pascal

Pascal was one of the first languages offered with the Personal Computers (August, 1981). FORTRAN was announced in December, 1981, and delivered in February, 1982. Both languages are available only under PC DOS. They require a minimum of 128K of RAM for PC DOS V1.1, possibly more for PC DOS V2.0, depending on the operating system's setup. Finished programs usually require less memory, however.

Pascal is the first programming language to be named after a person, Blaise Pascal, the noted seventeenth-century French mathematician. The name is not an acronym and is properly spelled in lower-case letters with a capital *P*. The Pascal language was created by the Dr. Niklaus Wirth (a professor in Zurich, Switzerland) in the early 1970s. It was conceived as a structured beginner's programming language that sharply resembled the PL/I and PL/M languages.

FORTRAN, an acronym for FORmula TRANslation, is a popular structured engineering and scientific language that was originally developed in the late 1950s. FORTRAN is, perhaps, the third most dominant programming language in the world, preceded by BASIC and COBOL, in that order. It evolved from version I to IV into the 1966 ANSI standard version (V-66). The current version comes from the 1977 ANSI standard (V-77).

Microsoft, the original author of the IBM languages including FORTRAN and Pascal, has two versions of FORTRAN: a subset of FORTRAN-66 for 8-bit microcomputers, and a subset of FORTRAN-77 for 16-bit microcomputers (including the Personal Computer). Despite the syntactical and operational differences between these two versions, they are, on the whole, compatible.

IBM Pascal is identical to the 8-bit Microsoft Pascal with no syntactic differences between the two. However, although IBM Pascal meets the International Standards Organization's standard for Pascal, Microsoft has added several useful enhancements to the language. (ISO is the only body that has issued standards for this language.)

Comparing Pascal and FORTRAN

Both Pascal and FORTRAN are structured, compiler languages. Their syntax is rigid and inflexible when compared to BASIC. As mentioned earlier, structured programs are more difficult to develop. Once developed, however, the long-term maintenance of these programs is easier and less costly in time than BASIC. The range of commands offered by the two languages provides broad and flexible programs. Because they are compiler based, programs developed under Pascal and FORTRAN execute much faster than comparable interpreted BASIC programs.

The skills developed while learning and using a structured language usually make a second structured language easier to learn. Thus IBM FORTRAN and Pascal programmers have an advantage over a BASIC programmer in learning other structured languages. Pascal was developed to teach students structured programming skills. It performs this task well. The skills learned while using either programming language are readily transportable into the commercial world.

Like the BASIC Compiler, the PC DOS linker, LINK.EXE, joins the compiled modules (subroutines) together. The FORTRAN and Pascal compilers produce a specially formatted file that is linked with the appropriate run-time subroutine library. Because IBM/Microsoft FORTRAN was written in IBM/Microsoft Pascal, one run-time library is used for both.

With the addition of the ANSI terminal control codes, programs written in IBM FORTRAN and Pascal can perform direct cursor addressing, screen manipulation, and medium- and high-resolution graphics. These can be done only if the program operates under PC DOS V2.0 and the ANSI.SYS file is used. Many PC DOS V2.0 features, such as hierarchical directories, are not fully used by the Pascal or FORTRAN compiler. A new release of the compilers (including the BASIC Compiler) will be required to update these languages so that they can use all the functions and features of PC DOS V2.0.

There are some disadvantages to the IBM FORTRAN and Pascal. Neither language offers double-precision numbers; the longest real number has only 7 digits. The FORTRAN is V-77 rather than V-66, which is the 8-bit microcomputer version. When Microsoft FORTRAN programs are transported from the 8-bit computers to the 16-bit Personal Computer, they must be rewritten to accommodate the function of V-77. This does not affect IBM Pascal, however, which is completely compatible with the 8-bit microcomputer version.

IBM/Microsoft FORTRAN is the full subset of the 1977 standard. The compiler does not handle complex (imaginary) numbers. Complex numbers (a + bi, where i is the square root of -1) are often used in engineering calculations, but the Personal Computers' FORTRAN cannot immediately handle these calculations. (It should be mentioned that no FORTRAN compiler that runs on a microcomputer today handles complex numbers.)

To the nonprogrammer, the features and limitations of Pascal and FORTRAN discussed above are of minimal interest. Those who program only in BASIC will also not be affected.

Summary

The educational and computer development fields have found Pascal to be a valuable language. Many colleges and high schools offer Pascal as the first structured language. Texas Instruments uses its version of Pascal for development work on its 9900 CPU series. Microsoft used its Pascal compiler to develop its FORTRAN compiler (although Microsoft has since switched to the C programming language for development). Similar uses are found in both areas. IBM Pascal is identical to the 8-bit Microsoft Pascal. Programs written in this Pascal may be transported freely to the Personal Computers.

IBM FORTRAN-77 gives scientific and engineering personnel localized control of their work. The use of the Personal Computers with FORTRAN represents a smaller, less expensive solution than costly time-sharing or mainframe facilities. Many FORTRAN programs can run on the Personal Computer, as long as they do not exceed its resources (the provided RAM and 20M disk storage). Programs that almost exhaust its resources, however, will run "better" on larger systems.

Because BASIC, FORTRAN, and Pascal operate under the umbrella of PC DOS, suitably formatted data can be shared by programs written under any of these languages. IBM FORTRAN and Pascal allow the user to take a significant step along the path to higher-powered computing with the Personal Computer.

UCSD FORTRAN and Pascal

The April, 1982, delivery of the UCSD p-System made a second operating system available to the Personal Computer. With the UCSD p-System came a second version of FORTRAN and Pascal.

Although UCSD FORTRAN meets the subset specification for V-77, it is not fully compatible with its IBM/Microsoft counterpart. This situation is also true of UCSD Pascal. Both IBM/Microsoft and the UCSD languages have some nonstandard commands, syntax, and extensions that, if used, will not be recognized by the other language. A program must, therefore, be altered to accommodate the other language's syntax and commands. (Most publishers follow the exact standard for a language, but add useful enhancements of functions and features. These enhancements become incompatible. This problem occurs frequently throughout the computing world, not just for microcomputers.)

Information stored by these two sets of languages is not compatible with the other set. For example, information stored under the UCSD p-System cannot be used by PC DOS or the reverse. An optional program, Xenofile™, available from SofTech Microsystems, can be used to transfer files between the two operating systems. However, numeric information is not guaranteed to be compatible, and some information must be made compatible with special user-written programs.

The UCSD languages on the IBM Personal Computers fall into the classification of interpreter compilers or pseudocompilers. Source code is translated into P-code (as discussed in the last chapter). The P-code is then interpreted by the P-machine CPU or P-machine interpreter. This procedure differs from that of IBM/Microsoft languages, which become directly executable programs (in machine language).

The disadvantage to the UCSD approach is that the UCSD FORTRAN and Pascal programs execute four to nine times slower than their IBM/Microsoft counterparts.

Features

There are three major advantages to the UCSD approach. Programs written under the p-System languages: (1) are smaller and take up less memory and disk space; (2) can be used on a variety of machines without change; and (3) can have greater-precision numbers than their IBM/Microsoft counterparts.

In the P-code approach to the p-System, the run-time support for the programs is part of the p-System itself. A separate set of run-time routines is not necessary for the UCSD languages; the run-time support is already in the operating system. Therefore, the compiled programs are smaller and take up less space. The p-System also supports the "swapping" of program segments. As portions (the segments) of the program are completed and will not be used further, the RAM memory these routines occupied is free for use by other portions of the program. The operating system, not the programmer (as with Microsoft languages), does most of the work necessary to support this *dynamic swapping* (the loading, executing, and discarding of program portions). As a result, larger programs can be constructed and used with less programmer effort under the p-System than under PC DOS.

Because the compiled programs are interpreted by the P-machine or P-machine emulator, the compiled code, not the source code, may be moved to another computer that uses the p-System and directly executed without change. This transportability is one of the major reasons for the popularity of the p-System. Only one copy of a program is maintained. This one copy, once it is moved to the other computer through disk storage or communicated through serial ports, can be used by any computer equipped with the p-System. This transportability is highly desirable for most program publishers.

The p-System has two different support subroutines for real, floating-point numbers. These subroutines are discussed in the UCSD documentation as the 4-byte and 8-byte versions. The 4-byte version allows six digits of precision, one less than IBM/Microsoft's FORTRAN and Pascal. The 8-byte version offers 12 digits of precision, five more than the PC DOS versions. (Of the IBM/Microsoft and UCSD languages, IBM/Microsoft BASIC has the most digits of precision, 16.)

Another attractive feature of the p-System is *long integers*. Most computer-language definitions of integers restrict the range of these numbers from -32,768 to +32,767. In some languages, long integers are in a range from -2,147,483,648 to +2,147,483,648 (an integer 10 digits long). The UCSD p-System allows integer numbers of 33 digits. Doing computations with long integers is understandably slow, but possible.

A major feature of the p-System languages is *turtlegraphics*. In BASIC, or through the ANSI cursor controls, the graphics screen is manipulated on a point-by-point basis. Turtlegraphics uses an imaginary turtle whose tail contains colors. The turtle is commanded to rotate a set number of degrees (based on a 360< circle), move a set distance, drop its tail, and paint; or walk with its tail up and not leave a trace. The turtle can be picked up and placed on another portion of the screen, if desired. The concept of turtlegraphics is easy to learn and makes graphics easy to manipulate.

With the Run-Time Package available for the UCSD p-System (as well as for the IBM Personal Computers and other operating systems), any program developed using UCSD FORTRAN or Pascal can run on a "foreign" operating system (non-p-System). The Run-Time Package extends the performance of computers that run p-System-based programs and makes the UCSD more desirable. However, the increase in program execution time is not diminished with the Run-Time Package.

The UCSD p-System languages offer highly transportable, powerful facilities for problem solving. The trade off in execution speed is a disadvantage that must be weighed. To choose between the two sets of languages, the user must weigh the advantages and disadvantages of the operating systems (PC DOS and the UCSD p-System) and the associated languages. The major factors in this decision may be transportability among different computer systems versus operating speed.

IBM COBOL

IBM offers the Microsoft COBOL compiler. COBOL is the acronym for *CO*mmon *B*usiness *O*riented *L*anguage. It is the language of business and the most common language on mainframes and mini-computers. Large installations run COBOL more than any other language.

In the microcomputer field, COBOL is one of the lesser languages, falling behind BASIC, Pascal, and FORTRAN. However, most sophisticated accounting and business operating packages are written in COBOL.

The COBOL language is regulated by two organizations in the United States. The first is the American National Standards Institute (ANSI). In 1974, ANSI issued the current minimum standards for COBOL, usually called COBOL-74. The COBOL standard has two sets: the high set, or Level II, and the lower set, called Level I, which is actually a subset of Level II.

(The ANSI subcommittee for COBOL has proposed a new standard, informally called COBOL-80. This standard has not been adopted, and there is significant controversy that may bar its final adoption because the many new commands introduced would force the rewriting of most COBOL programs in use.)

The second organization that regulates COBOL is a part of the General Services Administration. It validates the results produced by the compiler. Validition is based on standardized programs. The results of the validation are heavily influenced by the number of commands and functions built into the compiler. This means that a COBOL compiler with only Level I functions cannot receive the coveted High-Intermediate or High ratings because it does not have enough features.

IBM COBOL was originally written by Microsoft and tailored by IBM for the Personal Computers. It is a Level I COBOL with several Level II functions added. The compiler has received the GSA Low-Intermediate validation.

There are two reasons for using COBOL on a microcomputer. First, the COBOL compiler allows much of the current mature COBOL software to run on microcomputers. This gives the Personal Computer owner a larger base of software. Second, large companies can develop their COBOL programs on inexpensive microcomputers (four to six thousand dollars versus hundreds of thousands of dollars for mainframe computers) and transport the developed software back to the mainframe for actual use. This procedure is very attractive to data processing/management information departments that can purchase the Personal Computers for the approximate price of a sophisticated terminal.

IBM COBOL is a powerful COBOL. Its major Level II extensions are in the display and file area. COBOL is one of the few languages with built-in commands for managing the display. The *function* of the display commands is similar to that of their IBM BASIC counterparts. However, the *use* of the commands is not. Whereas in IBM BASIC users must concern themselves with many numbers that relate to colors and cursor position, COBOL programming "defines" the screen and uses the definition. In the case of IBM COBOL, colors are also available by names (RED, BLUE, etc.). IBM COBOL also supports many data file types that are appropriate for most Level II uses.

The Assemblers

An *assembler* is a software program that translates a narrow range of commands, called *mnemonics*, into instructions that are directly understood by the computer's CPU. Programming in assembly language is just two steps away from using the native on-and-off bits the CPU executes.

The next-to-the-last step is *hand coding*, the direct manual entry of hexadecimal, base 16, values that represent the commands and data for the CPU commands. The final step is informally called *toggling*, where toggle switches with l.e.d. lights, one for each bit, on the front panel of the computer are manually turned on or off to enter an instruction for the CPU. The latter method was popular in the microcomputer's "homebrew" kit-construction infancy. The former approach can be done with DEBUG or DDT; the latter cannot be done on the native Personal Computer. Fortunately, more productive software tools, such as assemblers and debuggers, have almost eliminated both procedures on most microcomputers.

There are three different sets of assemblers for the Personal Computer, one for each operating system. PC DOS' assembler is the Macro Assembler (MS-86) by Microsoft; ASM-86 and RASM-86 are Digital Research's assemblers for CP/M-86; and a program simply known as "the assembler" is provided with the UCSD p-System. Each assembler works with the 8088 of the Personal Computers to produce machine-language programs, except the UCSD assembler, which produces P-code. However, each assembler works with slightly different sets of mnemonics and operating systems and has different features.

Advantages

Assembly language programming is intended for those who are interested in writing programs that require little overhead, provide better performance, and use features that cannot be accessed through a high-level programming language.

Assembly language programs occupy the smallest amount of RAM space possible. High-level interpreter languages like BASIC may have small programs, but when the size of the program is added to the interpreter, the total RAM space is usually more. If a program does not use a function or feature of BASIC, the BASIC interpreter does not have a way to "shed" these functions and free the RAM space for program use. This is true of most interpreted languages.

High-level, compiler-based languages have a similar problem, but not to this degree. For example, some languages still include the larger floating-point subroutines, although only integers are used in the program. These subroutines remain in case an operator inputs a floating-point number when an integer should have been used. The only way to recognize that a noninteger number was used is through the floating-point routines. If a program simply opens and reads a disk file, all routines for disk file manipulation (opening, reading, and writing) are included. In effect, most compiler-based languages inject a small amount of nonused subroutines into the produced programs.

Assembly language programs do not have this problem. A language interpreter is not kept in memory to run the program; therefore, overhead is eliminated. The only subroutines included in the programs are those written by the programmer, which eliminates even more overhead. The programmer has complete control of the program in assembly language.

In some programs, speed is an important consideration. For example, subroutines written in high-level languages to sort information can be slow and inefficient. A subroutine to sort information can be written in assembly language and "called" (invoked) from the main program. This gives the subroutine the necessary speed and allows the programmer to develop the rest of the program in a high-level language. Another example is the Asynchronous Communications Support software, where the portion of the program that actually handles the communications adapter is written in assembly language. If communications are faster than 1200 baud (120 characters per second), the BASIC interpreter is too slow to handle the adapter. When speed has high priority, programs or subroutines are usually written in assembly language.

Assembly language programs give a high-level language additional capabilities. Several common examples are graphics plotting, some mathematical functions (such as the use of 20 or more digits of precision instead of the provided 7 or 16), and direct access to the keyboard or to an adapter. Assembly language allows the programmer close, intimate control of the facilities of the computer system. This type of programming is commonly called *system level programming*.

Many word-processing, data base management, and communications programs are written in assembler for these three reasons: faster execution time, exact control of the computer's resources, and smaller program size.

Limitations

Of all possible programming languages, assembler is the most difficult to learn, and assembly language programs are the most difficult to maintain. The programmer is responsible for keeping track of every machine location the program uses. Unlike high-level languages, which relieve the programmer of many mundane aspects, in assembly language the programmer must do most of the work. Most commands do not resemble English; they are mainly acronyms and abbreviations. One improperly phrased command that directs an unforeseen result can crash programs, memory locations, or disks.

At the speed of the IBM Personal Computers' 8088, the RAM memory could be filled with nonsense in less than two seconds. To erase the disk drives would take somewhat more time, but a fatal directive to a disk could take less than three seconds. However, it usually takes several wrong commands to produce these results. (The same is also true of high-level languages. A program line in BASIC stating "KILL *.*" would delete all files in the current directory.)

Assembly language programming is not dangerous, but some caution is advisable when learning and experimenting with assemblers. (A smaller degree of caution is also recommended to experienced assembly language programmers.)

The very low level of conversation between the programmer and computer requires major work in the creation and maintenance of assembler programs. Typically, assembler programs take 200 to 2000 percent more time to develop than high-level language programs.

Using Assembler

In Assembler, like high-level compiled languages, the instructions with the appropriate data are typed into a text file with a text editor, such as EDLIN, ED, or the IBM Personal or Professional Editor. This file becomes the *source code* file for the respective assembler. The assembler translates this text file into an intermediate file. A linker (like LINK.EXE) or loader (GENCMD.COM) transforms the intermediate file into the machine-executable *object code* file.

Because work takes place two levels above the native CPU level, any programming tools that reduce the entry and debugging time of the source code program are helpful. These tools are text editors, powerful assemblers, and high-powered symbolic debuggers.

Text editors give the programmer an efficient means of entering the program's text. Debuggers and symbolic debuggers also are available for each operating system (as discussed in chapter 4).

The powerful assembler equips the programmer with a range of commands that is larger than that of the set understood by the CPU. It produces machine-language programs that can be executed from any memory location (i.e., are relocatable), use powerful IF.. THEN..ELSE (conditional assembly) statements, use names (symbols) rather than numbers for memory locations, and add many lines of instructions (macros) to the program with one command.

Macro Assembler

The power of assemblers is judged by their ability to accept normal CPU commands called *ops* (shorthand for *op*erands, the mnemonic instructions) and *pseudo ops* (instructions translated by the assembler into appropriate machine-language statements or commands for the assembler). Pseudo ops usually control program printing, the interpretation of commands (IF..THEN..ELSE statements, for example), the beginning memory location for the program, and other elements.

Macro instructions are pseudo ops. A *macro* is like the defined function in BASIC (DEF FN). A set of assembler instructions, from one to hundreds of lines in length, is given a name. When the macro's name is encountered in the program, the assembler substitutes the set of named instructions for the single macro instruction. Like the defined function of BASIC, one or more variables may be used with the macro to increase its power and adaptability.

The IBM Relocatable Macro Assembler is the 8086 version of Macro-80™ (MS-80), the powerful Microsoft assembler for 8080 or Z80 CPUs. MS-86, its common name, provides extended aids for fast and efficient assembly language programs. MS-86 assembles instructions for both the 8086 CPU and the 8087 numeric coprocessor. This makes the Macro Assembler the only IBM language that can use the 8087. In addition, subroutines consisting of hundreds of program lines can be stored and later invoked by one command, the macro instruction. Complete cross-references of the program are produced with the commands ops and pseudo ops, the produced 8086 or 8087 instructions, and used memory locations unless otherwise indicated.

Because an assembler is not provided with PC DOS, MS-86 is a necessary program for anyone who wants to write assembler programs under PC DOS for the Personal Computers. MS-86 is also the most powerful assembler available for the Personal Computer.

The memory requirements for the Macro Assembler are 96K for PC DOS V1.1 and 128K for V2.0. A double-sided disk drive, two single-sided disk drives, or the Fixed Disk are also required. If the macro capabilities will not be used, a separate version is available that requires 32K less memory.

Other Assemblers

The CP/M-86 assembler is Digital Research's ASM-86™, a less powerful assembler that does not handle relocatable code (programs that can load and run from anywhere in memory) or true macro instructions. A restricted form of macros is allowed, however. ASM-86 has some pseudo ops. Its major advantage is that it is provided with the CP/M-86 operating system and, therefore, gives instant assembly language programming ability to the Personal Computer when CP/M-86 is purchased. For the use of ASM-86, a Personal Computer with one disk drive and 64K are required, but two mini-floppy disk drives or a hard disk are helpful.

Digital Research also sells RASM-86, its more powerful relocatable assembler. Like ASM-86, RASM-86 has very restricted macro capabilities, but it does produce relocatable programs. RASM-86's system requirements are identical to those for ASM-86. The program is available for both CP/M-86 and PC DOS.

The assembler provided with the p-System Development System (not the Run-Time Package) is modeled after the University of Waterloo's (in Waterloo, Michigan) TLA (The Last Assembler). This assembler provides a level of capabilities similar to the IBM Macro Assembler.

The UCSD p-System assembler can produce either standard P-code or a mixture of true machine-language code with a small amount of P-code. This allows for either slower-executing but transportable P-code programs, or higher-speed programs. Once this machine-language/P-code mixture is produced, however, the program loses its transportability to other systems that do not use the same CPU. For example, assembler programs produced on the Personal Computers would work with other p-System-equipped 8086 computers, but with no others. Because the assembler is part of the p-System, the requirements for using the UCSD assembler are identical to those for the p-System itself.

One advantage to the p-System is its optional cross-assemblers, available directly from SofTech Microsystems. A *cross-assembler* is a program that translates the source code written specifically for one CPU into the source code for a completely different CPU. This allows one assembly language program to fit all CPUs. Although this description is a simplification, cross-assemblers are extremely useful for machine-language programs that must run on a variety of computers using dissimilar CPUs. They are of little importance to those who do not need this capability.

Summary

Like a truck that moves cargo from point A to point B, each assembler produces a form of machine-language programs. The "comfort of the ride" (the ease, power, and speed) in arriving at the finish distinguishes these assemblers. The three assemblers mentioned in this section—the IBM Macro Assembler, ASM-86, and the UCSD assembler—work only with their respective operating systems. RASM-86 works on both CP/M-86 and PC DOS. The best advice for choosing the proper assembler is identical to that for choosing the proper high-level language. The user should examine the task or tasks to be performed and find the assembler whose capabilites best fulfill the tasks. The selection, however, of the operating system—PC DOS, CP/M-86, or the UCSD p-System—may override this decision.

Observations and Speculation
about Languages

Programming languages are tools that are combined with the rest of the computer system's resources to deliver a finished task or service. The tool should fit both the user and the task. As the homeowner's tool kit is different from the professional carpenter's or plumber's, the Personal Computers' tool kit of languages can be different from owner to owner.

Most users will find the three levels of the IBM BASIC interpreter, the BASIC Compiler, COBOL, FORTRAN, Macro Assembler, and Pascal to be ideal for their needs. Most Personal Computer owners will never use a programming language other than BASIC, if they need a language at all. Additional languages are available. Each language can fulfill a set of needs and should be selected and used with specific tasks (applications) in mind.

Many more languages and versions of languages, not sold by IBM, may be of interest to the reader. Both Digital Research and Microsoft sell languages that have potential for the Personal Computers.

Digital Research

Digital Research markets three versions of BASIC, a C, two versions of COBOL, a Logo, a Pascal, and PL/I.

Personal BASIC and CBASIC

Digital Research offers two types of BASIC: Personal BASIC and Commercial BASIC (CBASIC). CBASIC comes in two forms: a pseudocompiler version and a true machine-language version.

Personal BASIC, announced in May, 1983 (not available at the time of this writing), should function identically to IBM Advanced BASIC V2.0. It is available for CP/M-86, but not PC DOS. Programs written under PC DOS' BASIC may be moved to CP/M-86 and used with this interpreter.

The CBASIC and CBASIC Compilers are identical to their 8-bit counterparts for the 8080/Z80 CPUs. The CBASIC Compiler is a true machine-language compiler, whereas CBASIC-86 is an interpreted compiler. CBASIC-86 is completely compatible with CBASIC-80, and the CBASIC Compiler for the 8086 is compatible with its 8-bit counterpart. However, there are some slight differences in the syntax (phrasing) between CBASIC and the CBASIC compiler.

All versions of CBASIC (8080, 8086, pseudocompiler, and compiler) are written for commercial programming where the accuracy of numbers is vital. The CBASIC language uses binary-coded decimal (BCD) to handle real numbers. All real numbers are 14 digits long. BCD is a slower, but far more accurate, method of internally computing numbers than Microsoft's binary floating-point method. The speed of CBASIC-86 is slightly less than that of the IBM/Microsoft BASIC interpreters. The CBASIC Compiler operates at a speed comparable to the IBM/Microsoft BASIC Compiler.

In June, 1983, Digital Research will incorporate the kernel of its graphics system into the CBASIC Compiler and add 25 additional commands for graphics. This second version of the compiler will be available on both CP/M-86 and PC DOS. (CBASIC is available only for CP/M-86.)

COBOL

Digital Research, through an agreement with Micro Focus, Limited, of England, markets CIS COBOL and COBOL Level II. CIS COBOL is a GSA Low-Intermediate-rated complier. Level II is currently the only microcomputer-based COBOL compiler to receive the GSA's High-Intermediate validation. If complete compatibility with main-frame COBOL is desired, Level II COBOL is preferred. If this is not essential, the current version of IBM/Microsoft's COBOL or CIS COBOL is sufficient. (The improved Microsoft COBOL compiler is discussed below.)

Logo

The Digital Research DR Logo is based on the Logo language. The Logo language was developed initially as part of a National Science Foundation grant in 1968. Since then, most of the improvements to the language have come from the Massachusetts Institute of Technology (MIT); the University of Edinburgh, in Scotland; and Logo Systems, Limited, in Canada.

Logo is a structured, interpreted language. This combination is rare. Because Logo is a structured language, programs in Logo are organized into basic blocks, called *procedures* (the same name used for Pascal's basic blocks). Like the BASIC interpreter, the editing and execution of programs are interactive; programs may be constructed, tested, altered, and executed again.

Logo is a direct "descendant" of the LISP programming language. Both languages have been used extensively in artificial intelligence work. Both LISP and Logo are "natural" languages; programs are constructed in a method similar to the way people solve problems. With this approach, the educational field is moving to Logo to teach children how to program. Apple Computer and Texas Instruments, two major home and personal computer vendors, have versions of Logo available for some of their computers.

Logo is scheduled for delivery in the third quarter of 1983. It will run on both CP/M-86 and PC DOS.

Pascal/MT+86

Pascal/MT+86 is Digital Research's version of the Pascal programming language. It is comparable to both IBM/Microsoft Pascal and UCSD Pascal. Pascal/MT+ was originally written for the 8080/Z80 computers by MT Microsystems™ (which was later acquired by Digital Research). The 8086 version is similar to the 8080 version, but has some syntactical differences.

Pascal/MT+86 has several variable types that are not available in the current IBM/Microsoft version. BCD variables (18-digits long) and double-precision real numbers are allowed. Pascal/MT+86 uses the 8087 math coprocessor, but can also use a software emulation of the 8087 if this chip is not available. The optional Speed Programming Package, also by MT Microsystems, has several excellent tools that aid the Pascal programmer. Both Pascal/MT+86 and the Speed Programming Package are available on CP/M-86 and PC DOS.

PL/I

PL/I-80 and CP/M are almost synonyms. CP/M was developed to aid in the construction of Intel's PL/M™ language. As Digital Research evolved, most of PL/I's utility programs and parts of the operating system were written in the Digital Research version of PL/I-80. PL/I-86 is the 8086 version of the PL/I compiler. PL/I is a structured language that works with procedures, like Pascal. Unlike Pascal, PL/I is found on many mainframe computers. It runs on both CP/M-86 and PC DOS.

Tools

In addition to the Digital Research languages, several programming tools, such as Display Manager™ and Access Manager™, now available on CP/M-86, will be available on PC DOS by the third quarter of 1983. Both tools are sets of packaged routines for handling the display and disk storage, respectively. They can greatly reduce the amount of time required to develop visually oriented or file-management programs.

C

Both Digital Research and Microsoft market a C programming language. This structured, compiler-based language, developed at Bell Laboratories, has become almost the "universal" programming language for system level development. Both Digital Research and Microsoft have rewritten most of their programming languages from assembler (and PL/I for Digital's material) to C. Digital Research developed its own version of C, whereas Microsoft licensed its compiler for MS DOS from Lattice Associates of New York. Microsoft has enhanced this version of C with several additional functions and programming tools.

The Microsoft version of C, *not* identical to its Xenix version, is available only for MS DOS. The Digital Research version is available for CP/M-86 and PC DOS.

Microsoft

In addition to the C language, Microsoft markets a Business BASIC Compiler, COBOL, FORTRAN, and Pascal compilers.

Business BASIC

The Business BASIC compiler incorporates the best functions and features from the Microsoft interpreter and Digital Research's CBASIC language. Because the purpose of this compiler is to produce business programs, slower operating, but more accurate, binary-coded decimal (BCD) is used for math operations. This method is more precise for computing numbers with decimal fractions (numbers to the right of the decimal point).

The Business BASIC compiler has several features that are not found in the Microsoft BASIC Compiler. It can use alphanumeric names for subroutines rather than just line numbers. The program's source code is easier to maintain when a GOSUB CHECKDISK instruction is used instead of a GOSUB 10000. The Business Compiler also has multiline defined functions, extended "include" abilities, and dynamically dimensioned arrays.

Another new feature is the ability to compile programs separately, then link them together. This means that each major section of the program can take 64K of memory; then the sections can be joined into one program. However, all programs can use only a single bank of 64K for the data they create and use.

Thirty commands and functions have been added to Business BASIC. A program that translates CBASIC programs into Business BASIC programs is also included.

COBOL

A new version of COBOL has been released by Microsoft, and another version will be released by the end of 1983. Additional emphasis has been placed on the screen-formatting commands. COBOL is one of the few languages that has built-in facilities for formatting the screen. It uses highlighting or color to define the areas for the display and entry of information. The new release of COBOL is very similar to the Data General version and exceeds the Low-Intermediate standards for GSA validation. The version to be released by the end of 1983 will be further improved. Microsoft believes that this version will receive the High-Intermediate validation by GSA, becoming the second microcomputer compiler to obtain this rating. Microsoft also provides a highly useful interactive debugger with its COBOL.

Pascal and FORTRAN

Microsoft has new versions (V3.1) of the Pascal and FORTRAN compilers. The most significant difference for both compilers is the use of the IEEE standard for real numbers. The Microsoft compilers now use the same method for computing numbers that the 8087 coprocessor uses. Programs will use the faster 8087 coprocessor, if available. With the IEEE standard, FORTRAN and Pascal support double-precision real numbers. The FORTRAN compiler has also been improved; it operates at much faster speeds than in the past.

It is important to note that these language products by Microsoft are not marketed by IBM. To date, no language product for CP/M-86 has been marketed by IBM. Based on past history, it is likely that IBM will market the new versions of the Microsoft languages, but will probably not market any language products from Digital Research.

Summary

Many publishers market languages for the IBM Personal Computer. The list of languages runs from Ada (the official computer language of the United States Department of Defense) to THREAD (a FORTH-like language). Other versions of popular (and some obscure) languages also run on the Personal Computers, and the number of languages for the system will continue to increase.

A programming language is a tool. The right tool should be chosen to fit the final task: the application program. There is no shortage of good programming languages for the Personal Computers. The proper tools are available for almost any task.

CHAPTER 6

The Business Series Software

Applications Software

Applications software is the vehicle that turns computer hardware into a business tool. It is the fulfillment of the system software. For any particular hardware configuration, applications software is second in importance only to system software in assuring a productive system. Unfortunately, many of the users who can benefit most from small computers have not used computers before and, therefore, do not recognize the importance of knowledgeable applications software selection. This situation is complicated by the scarcity of specific information about software performance.

Applications software is the personality, brains, and power of the computer. Although prospective computer users often concentrate on hardware, which is more tangible (and more costly) than software, their success depends on placing equal emphasis on knowledgeable and deliberate software selection.

This chapter was written by Douglas Ford Cobb, general manager of software products for Que Corporation. Mr. Cobb received his B.A. degree, magna cum laude, from Williams College and his M.S. in accounting from New York University's Graduate School of Business Administration. After graduation, he worked for the firm of Arthur Andersen & Co. Before joining Que, he was president of Cobb Associates, Inc., a Boston-based microcomputer consulting firm. In addition, Mr. Cobb has conducted workshops for IBM Product Center personnel on the use of accounting systems on the IBM Personal Computer. Mr. Cobb is the co-author of SuperCalc SuperModels for Business *and* VisiCalc Models for Business, *both published by Que Corporation. He has also contributed articles on spreadsheets to the* IBM PC Expansion & Software Guide.

The IBM Personal Computer is a relatively powerful hardware system. Its ten special-function keys, high memory limit, high-resolution graphics, and 16-bit processor all contribute to its efficient performance. However, the eventual practical benefit to a nontechnical user depends on the applications software's personality and power.

The power of a computer lies substantially in the software. The Personal Computer has a wide variety of capabilities. For example, the same keyboard is used with most programs; but some use it efficiently, whereas others do not. The System Unit processes information from many programs; but some programs may be fast, and others may be slow. The software is what makes the difference. It determines the capabilities of the computer system.

Introducing Microcomputer Accounting

Today, more and more small businesspeople are finding that computerized accounting can bring tremendous benefits to their businesses. Computers were for many years the exclusive property of companies large enough to spend $ 50,000 or more for a complete system. Today, microcomputer systems costing between $3,000 and $15,000 are capable of performing all of the accounting tasks required by a small business. In general, small computers do the same things for small businesses that big computers do for larger companies. Computers help eliminate redundant and time-consuming activities. They eliminate tedious, error-prone clerical jobs. They reduce the flow of paper. But above all, computers help businesspeople control their businesses.

A manager who is "in control" knows exactly where his business has been and where it is now, but also has a good idea of where it is going. He has financial statements on his desk within a few days of the end of a month so that he can quickly evaluate the performance of his business. He has ready access to detailed information about his accounts receivable and accounts payable. If his business has inventory, he is able to track closely stock levels to avoid over- or under-investing in inventory. It is worth noting that the businessperson who can demonstrate present control over a business should be able to convince others, including bankers or investors, of his ability to manage it successfully in the future.

As you might expect, it is time consuming and difficult, if not practically impossible, to manage a business this thoroughly with traditional manual accounting techniques. In addition, the typical small businessperson is too busy working to generate revenue to devote the required time to tracking that effort. As a result, small businesses are rarely completely "in control." Many businesses are finding that computer-based accounting is the solution to the control problem. The two areas where computers particularly prove their worth to small businesses are cash flow management and general ledger.

Managing Cash Flows

One thing small businesses never have enough of is cash. Customers take advantage of the small business and string out their payments across 60, 90, 120, or more days, while creditors are waiting with past due notices after only 30 days. The result is a cash crunch, where outflows always seem to be ahead of receipts. Managing cash flows is therefore, by necessity, the most important function of a small business accounting system.

Computers cannot solve this problem, but they can give the small businessperson the tools needed to squeeze the best possible cash flow out of the situation. Accounts receivable management systems help track and collect amounts owed to the business. Accounts payable packages help plan cash outflows and aid the manager in the attempt to earn discounts through early payment.

Accounts payable software must be able to store records of purchases and retrieve those records for payment. Between these steps, it must generate reports for the manager, showing how much is owed, to whom it is owed, and when it is due. Such software should be capable of printing checks when payment is made, and of producing detailed reports showing what was paid to whom. The system should also be able to pay automatically amounts owed based on due-date information.

The flip side of cash outflow management is the management of cash receipts. Accounts receivable software helps to achieve that end. A good accounts receivable program must be able to record credit sales as they occur and track the dollars represented by receivables to the point where they are either collected or written off as bad debts. It must be able to produce detailed reports that "age" the receivable amounts (aging involves categorizing outstanding balances according to the total number of days between the report date and the date the balance was originally entered into the system). Other important features include the ability to: charge interest on items that are outstanding for more than a predetermined period of time, compute and retain records of sales tax collected, produce invoices and invoice registers, and track and record cash collections.

Inventory control systems help managers keep the optimum amount of inventory on hand at any time. Inventory in the warehouse can be thought of as an investment of cash in an "unspendable" (or illiquid) asset. Every dollar that is tied up in inventory is a dollar that cannot be used to pay off creditors or buy new capital equipment. Mismanaging inventory can thus lead to two serious problems. If a firm overstocks, or invests too heavily in inventory, there is a chance that there will not be enough free cash to meet the other needs of the business. On the other hand, the business that underinvests in inventory runs the risk of losing sales because it is unable to fill rush orders. Mismanagement of inventory also makes accurate income reporting difficult because the change in a firm's inventory in any given period is equal to the firm's cost of goods sold for the period.

Payroll systems are not primarily cash flow management systems. They are a tool for automating the repetitive task of preparing payroll checks. For small businesses with a large number of employees, frequent pay days, or unusual pay policies, payroll systems can save hours of time each week. For the average small business, however, the biggest benefit of computerizing the payroll function is simplifying the clerical nightmare of tracking withholding tax obligations to the government.

The general ledger is the tool that ties together an accounting system. It maintains the company's chart of accounts and records the details of every transaction entered into by the company. In well-planned families of accounting software, the general ledger automatically receives summary information from the other modules in the system (e.g., accounts receivable). This helps minimize clerical errors common to multiple-posting manual systems. At the end of an accounting period, the general ledger prepares and prints the financial reports, including a balance sheet and income statements, and detailed subsidiary schedules and journals. Therefore, one of the best measures of the power of a particular general ledger is its ability to produce a wide range of useful management reports. For the businessperson who requires timely information about sales, profits, or budgets, the general ledger is indispensable.

A variety of software is available to assist the small businessperson in managing other areas of his operation. For example, inventory software tracks stock levels to help the manager optimize inventory levels. Payroll packages streamline the time-consuming payroll process. Job costing programs help managers in construction and other job-oriented industries track performance on a job-by-job basis. The availability of a diverse group of accounting software packages means that nearly every business can configure a network of packages to suit its particular needs.

The Other Side of the Coin

Although computerized accounting can bring tremendous benefits to a small business, it also introduces a significant risk factor. The following major features of accounting software are designed to combat those risks.

Systems Security and Data Integrity

When a small businessperson decides to computerize his operation, he is deciding to entrust valuable records to a piece of hardware and a few software packages—a serious step! Because computerized accounting has the potential for catastrophic losses, accounting software usually includes features designed to protect the user's valuable data from accidental loss. *Systems security* and *data integrity* are convenient terms to describe those security devices. The small businessperson seeking a family of accounting software should be careful to choose software that provides an adequate level of security.

User Friendliness

Businesspeople buy computers to save time and increase efficiency, and thus save money. However, if weeks are wasted struggling through the introduction of the computer into the business, and if the day-to-day process of using the system turns out to be a battle against the software, the computer can end up costing the business a small fortune. This is where the term "user friendly" becomes important. *User friendly* simply means that the software is easy to learn and use, and helps the operator do the required tasks. User friendliness is achieved through such features as comprehensive manuals; handy reference cards; menu-driven programs; screen-oriented input (i.e., input handled through logical, clearly laid out screens); and, ideally, the availablity of on-line instructions. A word to the wise: computerizing an accounting system is difficult enough without having to fight with the system itself.

System Flexibility

Off-the-shelf software has one major limitation: it is always written for the "average" small business, which, as every small business-person knows, does not exist in the real world. Every business has its own peculiarities. Some have more than one division. Some need comparative financial statements. One business may have 1,000 inventory items and only 25 accounts receivable, while another has 500 accounts, but only 50 items. Most importantly, some businesses process a large number of monthly transactions, whereas others post only a few. For these reasons, off-the-shelf software should be as flexible, or as adaptable, as possible. The businessperson choosing accounting software must take care to buy software that is capable of stretching to accommodate the special characteristics of the business.

Accounting as an Art

Computerized accounting involves, as the name suggests, a combination of computers and accounting. Whereas the computer side of the combination is important, a generally strong accounting environment is essential to the success of any system. A computer cannot change a poorly managed company into a well-managed one. There is no substitute for a bookkeeper/operator with good accounting skills. Finally, promptly delivered information is useless unless it is accurate. To get accurate information out of the computer requires putting accurate information into it. To have accurate information to put in, the business must have a well-organized accounting system. A computer is just one of the resources that a small businessperson should rely on for building a powerful information system.

Accounting with the IBM Personal Computer

The introduction of the IBM Personal Computer gave millions of small businesses the opportunity to go with Big Blue for their computer accounting systems. In the nearly two years since the machine was introduced, thousands of small businesses have chosen the Personal Computer.

Because the first version of the IBM Personal Computer was strictly a floppy disk-based system, it could offer only a limited solution to the accounting needs of all but the smallest business. The first disk drives could store only 160,000 bytes—enough space for a small inventory or accounts receivable system. Even when the drives were expanded to 320,000 bytes, they were only barely adequate for the volumes of transactions required by many businesses.

In addition, at first IBM published only a few modules of accounting software. Although the original line (licensed from Peachtree Software of Atlanta, Georgia) included a general ledger, an accounts receivable module, and an accounts payable module, it had no inventory control, payroll, or job costing software.

Neither of these factors made the IBM Personal Computer a poor accounting tool. Together, they simply put a serious limit on the volume of transactions the machine could support, and thus on the size and complexity of the business that could use the Personal Computer as its primary accounting system.

The disk storage limitations have been overcome, thanks to the introduction of the Personal Computer XT. The 10-megabyte Fixed Disk drive available with the Personal Computer is more than adequate for most small business accounting needs.

Along with the XT, IBM has introduced several new modules of accounting software, including a payroll package and an inventory system from Peachtree, and a complete new family of accounting applications licensed from BPI Systems. The BPI system includes a general accounting module; accounts receivable, inventory, and payroll packages; and a job cost system.

Final Comments

Computerizing an accounting system is a complex task. Careful planning is the most important part of the process. The business that chooses to automate must evaluate both its current condition and its plans for the future in order to arrive at a precise definition of the type of system required. Then, and only then, should the search for suitable hardware and software begin. The following software reviews are designed to help with both steps.

IBM/Peachtree Accounting Software

The IBM Personal Computer accounting software is a version of the popular Peachtree software from Retail Sciences in Atlanta, Georgia. The Peachtree software family has been available for several years on CP/M-based computers and has developed a reputation for quality.

Five modules of the Peachtree family are available for the IBM computer: General Ledger, Accounts Receivable, Accounts Payable, Inventory Control, and Payroll. Each module has a retail price of $595.

The IBM/Peachtree programs have an outstanding combination of features that makes them user friendly and adaptable. They can produce most of the reports and statements needed by a small business. Because the modules (except for inventory control) are completely integrated, transactions entered under one program are automatically transferred to all other relevant modules at the end of the accounting period, saving time and helping eliminate errors that are common with multiple posting. Most importantly, the software includes features that help to ensure systems security and data integrity.

General Characteristics

IBM/Peachtree software includes two levels of password protection: one that restricts access to the system files; and another, the operator password, that generally protects the data files from unauthorized access. The system maintains detailed transaction information and prints transaction control reports after each set of entries has been posted.

The IBM/Peachtree family also provides checks that help exclude erroneous information from the system. These features are part of the IBM/Peachtree software's unique data input process, which combines on-line data input with batch-like security features.

Computer data input is typically handled in one of two ways. Either data is entered *on-line*, meaning that all input is immediately processed and posted to the relevant master file; or, it is entered in *batches*, where all input is held in a temporary file until the end of the input session, then posted to the master file.

IBM/Peachtree software uses a *session-oriented on-line* input format. All data entered are posted immediately to the master files, but certain information, such as the total amount of all entries, is maintained for every input session. This compromise method captures many of the data integrity advantages of batch processing while maintaining the input speed of an on-line system. Ideally, a batch-oriented system will print an edit list prior to posting transactions to the master file. This helps assure that no erroneous data enter the central records. This software does not print such an edit list, but it does allow deletions and modifications of transactions based on the information in the transaction report. In addition, the user can specify account-number hash totals and transaction-number counts to further ensure data integrity. This software also allows the user to select forced-entry balancing, which prevents out-of-balance entries from being posted to the master files.

The user can edit any screen of data prior to posting by responding "no" to the software's question, "OK (Y or N)?." A "no" response allows the operator to go back and change any incorrect item on the screen. Once the user gives approval, the software does some checking on its own, screening any erroneous input, such as account or source numbers.

The Peachtree accounting software includes a routine called "restore," which is designed to recover information apparently lost on bad or damaged diskettes. Given the nature of floppy disks and the seeming reluctance of most small businesspeople to follow a strict backup schedule, this feature alone can be worth its weight in gold.

At several points in each module, we attempted to "clobber" the software by typing spurious responses to requests for user instructions. We were not able to do it. The software appears to be well protected against the possibility of an accidental keystroke destroying several hours of work.

Each software module has a clear, comprehensive manual. The manuals begin with a general description of the package, include detailed instructions to assist the user in configuring the system to specific needs, and conclude with examples and detailed descriptions to assist the user in the day-to-day operation of the software. The manuals also have examples of the reports generated by the modules. These examples enable the user to find out quickly which report is the source of some needed piece of information. Provided with the manuals is a handy reference card, ideal for quick checks when the user is not certain of a particular command.

Inside the software, clear, logical menus and easy-to-follow input screens assist the user in running the programs.

The ability to delete entries is one feature of the IBM/Peachtree combination that may best be described as a necessary evil. Although this feature provides a simple way to solve several problems that arise in systems without a preposting edit function, it would be better to restrict deletions and force users to correct errors by posting mirror-image reversing entries. The risk that comes with the ability to delete entries is that transactions may be lost, without any record of their ever having existed. Because deleted transactions do not appear on the transaction register, the only audit trail is the control report generated at the time the entry was made. This software does prevent the deletion of entries in the accounts receivable module, however, where the loss of an entry could mean no record of cash owed to the business. The user can restrict the use of the transaction deletion function when the system is configured. We recommend that you consider doing so.

Unfortunately, the Peachtree software does not take advantage of one of the most exciting features of the IBM computer: the special-function keys. Ideally, these keys could assist the user in making choices, thereby avoiding some of the lengthy menus in the software. As it stands, these keys are used only to edit information on input screens. This is not an unfriendly feature, but rather the absence of a feature that we would like to see supported with this package.

The IBM/Peachtree software has only one major unfriendly feature. To make backup copies of data disks, the user must use the IBM Disk Operating System. The accounting software has no built-in provision for making copies. The need to use the operating system adds an unnecessary level of complexity to the software.

Another problem is the limited transaction capacity of the IBM/-Peachtree software when used with 5 1/4-inch floppy disks. Although the current configuration has sufficient capacity for many small businesses, a growing business should beware of outpacing the introduction of new expanded hardware. We recommend that you consider purchasing the Fixed Disk drive if accounting is the primary or an important function for your Personal Computer.

General Ledger

The IBM/Peachtree General Ledger uses a flexible chart of accounts with broad ranges for each major type of account. However, most users will need to modify their chart of accounts to suit the required format—a common problem with off-the-shelf software. The account numbers are 5- or 6-digit numbers, with the first 3 or 4 digits representing the account number and the last two the divisional designation.

One slightly confusing characteristic is the use of account numbers for account group headings and totals. This feature requires careful planning to ensure that the accounts are arranged properly. The advantage of this arrangement is that financial statements can be formatted to the user's taste, with up to three columns and nested subtotals.

General Ledger allows the user to set up 100 separate divisions, which can be arranged in up to 10 groups. This feature is so powerful that it can be used as a job costing system, with each division representing a separate job. Divisional reports, including balance sheets and income statements, can be produced.

The user can specify statements that will compare current period activity to prior period or to budgeted amounts.

The general ledger package allows the user to designate "source codes" to differentiate entries. Up to nine source codes can be used. Code 6 represents a repeating journal entry, which is automatically posted each month by the system. The other codes can be used to set up a cash receipts journal, cash disbursements journal, general journal, or other subsidiary detail ledgers. This software can produce reports of all transactions with a particular source number. The General Ledger package also allows the user to define income-statement supporting schedules. These schedules allow the user to develop a detailed financial statement package, with summary balance sheet and income statements, and whatever additional schedules are required to present the results of the business in sufficient detail.

This software also prepares depreciation and loan amortization schedules. Although these capabilities are not interrelated to accounting functions, they are a valuable tool that is "icing on the cake" for a good accounting system.

Accounts Payable

IBM / Peachtree Accounts Payable performs all of the tasks expected from an accounts payable package, plus others that make it better than average.

Accounts Payable produces variations of the standard accounts payable reports. The accounts payable trial balance can be sorted on either the due date of the bill or the last date a discount is available. A cash requirements report, which details all amounts owed sorted by due date, can also be produced. The vendor file (containing detailed information about each vendor) can be printed and sorted on vendor name (alphabetic) or number (numeric).

The Accounts Payable system is capable of handling a variety of nonstandard conditions. For example, sometimes discounts are taken that are subsequently disallowed by the creditor. The IBM / - Peachtree software solution to this problem is to delete the old, incorrect, invoice from the system; then replace the invoice with a new one. Although this solution is not ideal, it works. Similarly, sometimes it is more convenient to pay a bill with a manually prepared check than with the computer. The computer, however, does not usually remove an item from the open invoice file until that bill is paid and a computer-generated check is written. A good accounts payable program should be able to handle such an eventuality. The IBM / Peachtree manual suggests that the user either print and void the check related to that payment or delete and reenter the relevant invoice as a prepaid item. Once again, this is not the best solution, but it is a satisfactory one.

Another valuable feature of the IBM Accounts Payable package is its ability to pay selectively open invoices. The user can choose to pay all or some invoices within a range of due dates, a range of discount dates, or for a selection of vendors. When paying vendor by vendor, the user can choose to pay all, none, or some of the invoices for each vendor. This feature allows the small businessperson to avoid paying certain invoices, those under dispute, for example, thus increasing his power to carefully manage cash flows. CRT account inquiries provide quick access to the status of a particular vendor's account.

This system also allows the user to preprogram repeating payments. These payments are then automatically posted each month. This feature is handy for expenses such as monthly rent payments.

Accounts Receivable

The IBM/Peachtree Accounts Receivable package allows accounts receivable information to be maintained on either an open-item or a balance-forward basis. *Open-item* means that each invoice is maintained as a discrete open item from period to period until it is paid. *Balance-forward* accounting groups all the invoices for a given customer into one amount, which is carried forward into the next month. Open-item accounting gives the user more detail, whereas balance-forward saves disk space. In some situations, balance forward accounting is unacceptable, for example, if invoice-by-invoice records are required. Other companies that are interested in the net amount owed by a particular customer, can use balance-forward accounting. For open-item accounts, the software condenses all open items with the same invoice number into one record at the end of every accounting period to conserve disk space. Because most transactions in the system are handled on an invoice-by-invoice basis, little, if any, sacrifice is involved in this loss of detail. If a particular customer account is a balance-forward account, the monthly transactions are further condensed into one accounts receivable amount, which is carried forward to the next period.

Accounts Receivable combines order entry, invoicing, and accounts receivable in one package. When printing invoices, the system will either automatically number them or let the user individually number each one. Automatic numbering is a handy device that helps the small businessperson keep track of sales.

The Accounts Receivable software uses 14 transaction codes to record and track entries into the system. The major transaction codes handle sales, cash receipts, and bad debt write-offs. These codes would be adequate to handle most transactions arising in an ideal world. But real-world software must be able to handle sales returns, credits, adjustments, and service charges as well. Peachtree's transaction codes allow for all of these types of entries. In addition, this program has codes for state, county, and city sales taxes; freight; and early payment discounts so that sales records can contain the detail of every relevant charge. Finally, each of the major codes can be subdivided into as many as 37 detail codes, allowing product-by-product tracking of sales data.

Occasionally, customers will overpay invoices or submit payments that cannot be readily matched to open items. IBM/Peachtree includes a routine to apply these amounts to the subsequent open balances incurred by a customer. The system also generates a report of open credits applied, a valuable piece of paper when disputing a balance with a customer.

Sales tax information is calculated and retained automatically by the software. A bracket rate scheme is used to compute sales tax for state, county, and city jurisdictions. The user defines maximum amounts for county and city taxes. Although an unlimited number of sales tax jurisdictions can be established, each additional one reduces the disk space available for recording transactions.

Finance charges are handled the same way. The system allows four interest rates and five sets of terms for individualized customer arrangements. A minimum balance for finance charges can be specified by the user, and interest can be computed on the month-end balance or the average daily balance. Finance charges are billed to customers on the account statements prepared each month for every account with an open balance.

Although the accounts receivable customer files allow the user to input a credit limit for each customer, the software does not check invoices against this amount to ensure that no customers exceed their credit limits. The user can always check the printed customer list to verify credit limits, but on-line credit checking would stream-line the system even further.

Inventory Control

IBM/Peachtree Inventory Control uses the LIFO, FIFO, and Average Cost conventions to maintain cost data on inventory items. It can also use a user-defined Standard Cost for each item. These options should meet the needs of most small businesses.

This program allows the user to expand inventory data files onto a second or third floppy disk. If this technique is selected, each disk becomes, in effect, a separate inventory system that generates its own reports.

A single input screen is used to post all transactions. Each transaction is given one of four codes to determine its purpose. These codes are SAL (Sale), REC (Receipt of Merchandise), RET (Return of Merchandise), and ADJ (Adjustments). This single-screen format makes the software very easy to use.

Inventory Control generates a Physical Inventory Report, which includes space for penciled-in adjustments and comments. This report is a useful tool for consolidating information about end-of-year inventory adjustments.

IBM/Peachtree Inventory Control retains both reorder point and reorder quantity information for each part. The software also prints a reorder report that includes information about each item which is at or below the reorder point. Unfortunately, the system does not have the capability to reorder automatically items that are below their reorder points.

The software allows the user to specify a preferred vendor for each part number. That vendor's part number can also be kept on file.

Unfortunately, IBM/Peachtree Inventory Control is a stand-alone inventory system. It cannot automatically link with the General Ledger and Accounts Receivable modules of the family. This weakness seriously reduces the usefulness of this software package.

In addition, the system has no facility for tracking back orders. If the user attempts to "sell" units that are not in stock, the software returns an error message: "QUANTITY EXCEEDS AVAILABLE BALANCE; CURRENT BALANCE IS XXXX UNITS; PRESS ENTER KEY." Because back-order tracking is one of the most important features of computer inventory control, the lack of that capability is a significant problem for this program.

Finally, the software does not generate purchase orders. All purchases are handled outside of the system and are posted only when the merchandise is actually received.

Payroll

IBM/Peachtree Payroll is one of the best small-business payroll systems available. The software calculates employee payroll on a weekly, biweekly, semimonthly, and monthly basis. It maintains complete records on all employees, including the number of vacation days allowed (up to a maximum of 320 days per year!).

Up to six miscellaneous deductions and three miscellaneous earnings accounts can be specified. These accounts can be used to record special withholdings from pay (like insurance or employee payroll savings plan) and unusual income items (like bonuses). The system keeps track of the employer's Earned Income Credit liability, records taxable tips, and allows two different overtime rates to be defined in the system.

Like all the IBM/Peachtree modules, Payroll has password protection. This protection is especially important in the payroll area because of the extremely confidential nature of payroll records.

The system computes pay based on an hourly, hourly by exception (for part-time workers), salary, or commission basis. Payroll checks can be printed each period.

The Payroll program also produces a payroll register and a deduction register at the end of each payroll period. A payroll summary is produced monthly.

The Peachtree Payroll module has the additional benefit of interacting with the General Ledger module.

Users of computer payroll systems often have difficulty keeping up with changes in state and federal tax rules and implementing those changes in their systems. In an effort to avoid these problems, IBM provides exceptionally good support for its users in this area. The manual includes a thorough explanation of all current state tax laws and instructions on how to build the needed data into the system. A telephone service is available for ongoing assistance.

Conclusion

The IBM/Peachtree software is a good choice for a small-business accounting system. This user-friendly and flexible system provides an adequate level of system security, with the possible exception that transaction deletions are allowed. Each module can perform the basic tasks expected of an accounting system, and all have additional features that allow them to deal with the less common situations which arise in managing inventory, payroll, accounts receivable, accounts payable, and central general ledger accounting.

The first-time user of the IBM/Peachtree software should have few problems learning and implementing the system. Because the programs are so flexible, considerable thought should go into the configuration process. The user would be well advised to read the manuals several times before embarking on that process. All in all, however, this remarkably user-friendly software should present no problems to the small business user.

In the first edition of *IBM's Personal Computer*, we listed two major limitations of the IBM/Peachtree accounting system: the limited disk size of the IBM PC and the limited number of accounting applications that were available. Both of these limitations have been corrected. The introduction of 320,000-byte floppies and the IBM Fixed Disk drive has virtually eliminated any storage capacity constraints. The addition of payroll and inventory control systems has rounded out the IBM/Peachtree family.

IBM/BPI Accounting Software

IBM/BPI accounting software is a vastly improved version of the popular BPI Systems Apple II accounting series. This software is a well-designed and executed small-business accounting tool. In fact, the General Accounting module is perhaps the best single-volume accounting system available for a microcomputer. The other modules available for the Personal Computer include Inventory Control, Accounts Receivable, Payroll, and Job Costing. Each module costs $425, except Job Costing, which costs $550.

General Characteristics

The IBM/BPI system is well documented. The manuals begin with a general description of the software and include sections on installing and using the system. Each manual contains a full glossary and examples of all the reports generated by the system. The reference card provided with each module allows quick location of needed information.

The system is batch oriented. The user is offered the option of reviewing, editing, and even deleting any transaction before posting it to the disk. A batch total is computed for each group of transactions. Unfortunately, batch control reports cannot be printed after batches are posted.

The IBM/BPI system includes several important data integrity features. The software will not accept an out-of-balance accounting transaction. It also rejects invalid keyboard responses and is resistant to being "clobbered." Adequate protection ensures against data being sent to a printer that is turned off.

Unfortunately, the system does not include *enough* data-integrity protection. The software is not password protected, and it is not possible to force printing of control transaction reports.

The user can set up "prompts" to assist in posting frequently used account numbers. Nearly all input in the five modules can be prompted in this manner. Input is handled through clear, logical screens.

The General Accounting, Inventory Control, Accounts Receivable, Payroll, and Job Costing modules are interactive. Transactions are passed automatically among the modules by the computer.

The system fully utilizes the IBM Personal Computer's function keys in processing and editing transactions.

The most important weakness of the IBM/BPI system is its limited accounts payable function, which is integrated into the General Accounting system.

Another weakness is the lack of sufficient storage space for large volumes of transactions when the system is used with 5 1/4-inch floppy disks. This can lead to two problems. First, the user can become swamped with disks—each module requires four disks, so three modules would require a total of twelve, plus backups. Second, there is an increased chance of disk-full probems with 5 1/4-inch floppies. We recommend that you obtain a Fixed Disk drive.

The program's manual uses a large number of accounting terms, such as register, ledger, journal, and post. This may be confusing to users without accounting experience.

General Ledger

The IBM/BPI General Accounting module is a self-contained accounting system. This one package has all of the basic tools needed to automate the accounting function of many small companies. The module includes a simple payroll ledger; an accounts receivable ledger; an accounts payable ledger; and, of course, a general ledger.

The system's payroll ledger helps simplify the payroll withholding and reporting process. Payroll expenses can be distributed to up to eight ledger accounts.

The General Accounting program can also print checks. This rare feature helps further automate both the payroll and vendor payment processes. It also sets this software apart as a truly comprehensive general accounting system.

Because the General Accounting data can be divided between two diskettes, the module is not as capacity constrained as other 5 1/4-inch disk-based systems. When data is divided, the system can contain far more than the basic 1,000 accounts. Up to ten divisions can also be created for separate profit and loss reporting.

One limitation of this system is that it does not let the user customize the basic financial statements. It also does not produce comparative reports or income statement detail schedules.

Another drawback is the requirement that the user modify the chart of accounts to meet the system's account-number range requirements.

Accounts Receivable

The Accounts Receivable system produces a variety of accounts receivable reports, including an aged trial balance, a list of all overdue accounts, a report of all accounts that have been delinquent at some time during the current year, and a cash collections report.

Customers can be divided into two groups and stored on two separate data disks, or retained on one disk, as the need arises. Four types of customer accounts are allowed: regular accounts receivable, fixed payment accounts, repeating charge accounts, and revolving credit accounts. Two levels of finance charges may also be specified by the user.

Grouping codes can be assigned to customers. These codes can be used to assign each customer to a salesman or sales territory, or to group customers according to size or credit standing.

This program also prints monthly customer statements and sends notices to overdue accounts.

The IBM/BPI Accounts Reveivable program has some limitations. For example, it allows customer accounts to be maintained on either an open-item or balance-forward basis, but not both.

Accounts Receivable will not print invoices. Invoice transactions can be entered directly to the invoice register, but the invoice form can be printed only from the Inventory Control module. This prohibits the Accounts Receivable system from being an effective stand-alone system.

Finally, this system has no formal method of accounting for over-payments and the partial payments that can arise in open-item accounting.

Inventory Control

The IBM/BPI Inventory Control system uses the FIFO, LIFO, or Average Cost method of valuing inventory, at the user's discretion. It retains the three most recent costs for items in stock and can produce a report detailing these "cost layers."

This program can also accommodate multiple branch locations. Each branch location can invoice and receive inventory. The system then transfers data between branch locations.

Back orders and low-balance items are processed automatically. Inventory Control prints invoices for the products sold and automatically transfers accounts receivable data to the Accounts Receivable module. Cash sales as well as credit sales can be accommodated. This software also allows the cancellation of open purchase orders, if necessary.

Inventory Control produces a variety of useful reports, including price lists, price labels, inventory lists, low-balance lists, back-ordered reports, and invoice registers.

Although the system can print invoices, it has no facility for recording cash collections. The Accounts Receivable module is required if the user needs to track collections. This reduces the value of IBM/BPI Inventory Control as a stand-alone system.

In addition, the system cannot be configured for manufacturing inventory control (raw materials, work-in-process, and finished goods).

Payroll

The BPI Payroll program prepares payroll for weekly, biweekly, semimonthly, or monthly payroll periods. It prints checks, W2 forms, and the following reports: payroll register, check register, earnings record, and withholding tax reports.

The Payroll system retains detailed information on each employee, including all tax withholding information and the number of vacation and sick days taken. At the end of each pay period, the program computes pay and withholdings for each employee. Pay can be computed using any of the following methods: hourly, salary, commission, and draw against commission.

Up to six miscellaneous deductions can be specified in the system. The system will also track Earned Income Credit liability and record taxable tips. Two separate overtime rates can be established.

The BPI Payroll system interacts with the BPI General Accounting module and the Job Cost system.

Like the Peachtree Payroll program, BPI Payroll offers a tax update service to help keep users up to date on tax law changes.

This program comes with a superior manual, which includes a full discussion of the payroll process (with flow charts), a glossary, a set of sample reports, and a group of templates that can be used while installing the system.

Job Cost

The BPI Job Cost module is the unique element of the BPI family. This program can be used by many professional firms (e.g., accountants, consultants, and lawyers) and many small businesses (such as contractors).

Because the program is very flexible, it can be tricky to install. A great deal of preparation is required to accumulate the data required by the program. For each job, the program maintains hours, units, and rates data for every task that is part of the job.

The Job Cost system maintains both budgeted and actual cost data for each job. When the job is first defined, a job estimate report showing the budgeted cost of each task can be printed. Later, a job status report can be printed, comparing the budget to the actual costs on a percentage of completion basis.

This program also retains budget and actual cost data on completed jobs. The data can then be used to compute estimates on future jobs—a very convenient feature.

The user can print job status reports as required. At month end, a report can be produced, summarizing the activity for all active jobs, along with a job-by-job summary of income received and expenses incurred.

The Job Cost system allows job income to be computed by either of the two accepted methods: percentage of completion or completed job. It also interacts with the BPI Payroll and BPI General Accounting modules. Labor cost data can be transferred directly from the Payroll system to the Job Cost system.

Choosing a System

The choice of one system over another depends primarily on the particular needs of the user. For example, if a simple, but comprehensive, general accounting system is required, the BPI General Accounting module would probably be the ideal system. It has a good combination of a general ledger with simple payroll, accounts receivable, accounts payable, receiving, and check writing functions. It also has enough power to handle the needs of many small businesses.

Similarly, if Job Costing is a requirement, the BPI system would get the nod.

On the other hand, if accounts payable accounting is the primary requirement, the BPI system's lack of a separate accounts payable makes Peachtree the choice. In addition, because BPI cuts invoices in the Inventory module, the BPI Accounts Receivable module does not stand alone well. If a complete accounts receivable system is required, BPI may not be the best choice.

Because the Peachtree Inventory module does not integrate with the General Ledger and Accounts Receivable systems, it is not a good choice unless it will be used as a stand-alone system.

Both systems have some limitations. For example, neither system is capable of doing sophisticated manufacturing inventory with raw materials, work in process, or finished goods.

Conclusion

Overall, the BPI and Peachtree systems are two of the best implemented small business accounting systems available. These programs are similar in many ways. For example, both systems require the same hardware: a Personal Computer, at least two floppy disk drives, and a printer. The BPI system also allows the use of a color monitor and a serial printer.

Thanks to IBM's attention to quality, both systems have excellent documentation: complete manuals, reference cards, and installation templates. Even users with little or no prior computer experience should have little trouble installing the systems. Either system would be a good selection for most small businesses.

Introducing Electronic Spreadsheets

What Is a Spreadsheet?

A *spreadsheet* program is an electronic replacement for traditional financial modeling tools: the accountant's columnar pad, pencil, and calculator. In some ways, electronic spreadsheets are to those tools what word processors are to typewriters. Spreadsheet programs offer dramatic improvements in the ease of setting up and using financial models.

The typical electronic spreadsheet resembles an accountant's columnar pad, except that the spreadsheet is much larger. Most electronic spreadsheets have 254 rows and 64 columns. As a general rule, each row is assigned a number, and each column a letter. The intersections of the rows and columns are called *cells*. They are identified by their row-column coordinates (for example, cell A15 or cell X55). These cells can be filled with three kinds of information: text (or labels), numbers and mathematical formulas, and special spreadsheet functions. A cursor allows the user to write information into the cells much as a pencil lets you write on a piece of paper.

Electronic spreadsheets allow mathematical relationships to be created between cells. For example, if a cell named C1 contained the formula:

C1 = A1+B1

then C1 would display the sum of the contents of cells A1 and B1. The cell references serve as *variables* in the equation. No matter what numbers are entered in A1 and B1, cell C1 will always return their sum. Of course, spreadsheet formulas can be much more complex than this simple example.

Spreadsheet functions are shortcuts that help the user perform common mathematical computations with a minimum of typing. Most sheets have mathematical functions (like SUM), statistical functions (like MAX, MIN, and AVERAGE), financial functions (like Net Present Value), and special functions (like IF...THEN). Newer spreadsheets such as Multiplan™ and SuperCalc2™ include more advanced functions.

Spreadsheets offer advantages at every phase of building and using a model. Because spreadsheet programs hold the model in the computer's memory while it is being built, the user is not bound by the physical limitations of the printed page. Do some of your formulas repeat across time? Use the your spreadsheet's *replicate* feature to project quickly your assumptions from one cell to another. Did you forget a row or a column? Simply *insert* it at the appropriate point. Is one of your assumptions or formulas incorrect, or is there a typographical error in one of your headings? Correct the error instantly with the *edit* command.

The very act of building a model on a spreadsheet defines all of the mathematical relationships in the model. Until you decide to change them, every sum, product, division, subtraction, average, and net present value will remain the same. Every time you enter data into the model, computations will be calculated at your command with no effort on your part. All of these computations will be calculated correctly—spreadsheets don't make math errors. And next month, when you decide to use the same model again, the formulas will still be set, ready to calculate at your command.

Even more important, spreadsheet software allows you to play "What if...?" with your model after it has been developed. If you use paper, pencil, and a calculator to build your models, every change to the model will require recalculating every relationship in the model. If the model has 100 formulas and you change the first one, you must make 100 calculations by hand to flow the change through the entire model. If, on the other hand, you use a spreadsheet, the same change requires only the press of a few keys; the program does the rest. This capability makes possible extensive "what if" analysis.

Because of their versatility, VisiCalc and Multiplan, like other visible numeric processors, are important tools for both small and large businesses. More and more companies of all sizes are using VisiCalc, Multiplan, and other spreadsheets to help speed and simplify financial analysis.

Applications for Spreadsheets

Spreadsheets are sometimes called *planning tools*, and one of their major uses is financial projection. However, spreadsheets can be configured to solve almost any problem that used to be attacked with a pad and pencil. A spreadsheet can also be an auditing tool to assist accountants in the preparation of reports and financial statements. It can analyze collections on accounts receivable, inventory stock level, and employee performance. A well-designed spreadsheet program can even function as a limited accounting system for a small business, helping code disbursements into budget categories and track collections.

The Future

The popularity of spreadsheets is growing significantly. The development of increasingly sophisticated spreadsheet applications has led to a separation between spreadsheet builders and spreadsheet users. No longer is a spreadsheet program used exclusively by the manager who developed it. Instead, it is being used by clerks and secretaries who see it only as a preconfigured tool. For example, a bookkeeper in one office we know of uses a checkbook balancing template developed by her boss. Every month, she loads the master template from disk, fills in the blanks, then prints a hard copy of her work. This tool saves her several hours of work every month, but she has no idea of how the program works. As spreadsheets become more flexible and powerful in the future, this trend should continue.

This same trend has created opportunities for third-party providers of preconfigured models. Buying models that have already been planned and executed by a spreadsheet professional can save busy managers hours of time. Some of these model builders specialize in vertical market applications, such as real estate. Others offer a wide range of templates in such areas as cash management, tax calculations, and budgeting.

There is no question that the development of spreadsheet programs will continue as the needs of individual users become more complex. As the power and capability of the basic programs expand, there will be no limit to the applications of spreadsheets.

IBM / VisiCalc

With the exception of a few games, VisiCalc is by far the largest selling microcomputer program in the history of the industry. It was also the first substantial electronic spreadsheet program. Interestingly, VisiCalc has survived the competition of the many look-alike spreadsheets that have been introduced since its success became widely recognized. It continues to be enhanced by the original publisher, VisiCorp, and has been converted for many popular personal computers. (A new version of VisiCalc, called VisiCalc Advanced Version, has been announced, but was not available for review.)

The version of VisiCalc implemented on the IBM Personal Computer is the same as most other versions of VisiCalc. The only exceptions are a few features that result from the fundamental characteristics of the IBM Personal Computer (e.g., the use of the PC's keyboard).

Because VisiCalc was the first spreadsheet program, and thus the "one to beat," most of its outstanding features have been copied extensively, making them commonplace. Keep in mind, though, that VisiCalc is still the standard by which all spreadsheets are measured. Most of what is said about VisiCalc can be said about the other programs, but most of these things were said first about VisiCalc.

Perhaps VisiCalc's greatest feature is that it is *visual* software. The program emulates a sheet of paper; data is entered in the sheet just as it would be written onto an accountant's pad. This feature helps decrease model building time and increase the user's comprehension of the model.

VisiCalc is *programmable* software. The basic program is like an empty sheet of paper. The user "programs" in the data and equations to create a meaningful financial model. Unlike programming languages, however, VisiCalc is easy to use. However, sophisticated use of VisiCalc requires at least a knowledge of algebra, because each variable cell is defined by an equation.

The primary application for VisiCalc is financial planning and analysis. A variety of built-in arithmetic, financial, trigonometric, and logical functions are provided to aid the user in these tasks. VisiCalc also includes commands that insert, delete, and move rows and columns in the worksheet. This makes setting up a new sheet, or modifying an old one, simple.

One of VisiCalc's most powerful commands is "REPLICATE," which allows a user to quickly install formulas, constants, or labels (alphabetic characters) in almost any cell.

VisiCalc offers a great deal of flexibility in formatting the display of data in the worksheet. Users can format *globally* (all cells at once) or one cell at time. Formats include integer, dollars and cents, left justified, right justified, and graph.

When VisiCalc is used, the screen of the computer becomes a "window" onto the large worksheet. VisiCalc allows this window to be divided into two parts. This feature allows the user to look at any two sections of the worksheet side by side, even though they may be located far apart on the overall worksheet. The two windows may also be synchronized for scrolling.

From the beginning, VisiCalc has included a LOOKUP function. This tool was originally designed to retrieve tax rates for making calculations from tax tables. Its use has been expanded, however, to include maintaining inventory lists and employee pay rates. VisiCalc's LOOKUP function has several limitations, including the requirement that all data be arranged in ascending order and the inability to "lookup" text.

One VisiCalc option, the Data Interchange Format (DIF), can be used to store files in a universal format. Because DIF is being adopted by several other software publishers, the users of their application programs, such as plotting, data management, or accounting programs, will be able to exchange files with VisiCalc.

Thanks to the use of the 8088 processor, VisiCalc recalculates much faster on the IBM Personal Computer in comparison with most other personal computers. If the 8087 math coprocessor is added to the basic IBM system, the program is even faster.

Another advantage of the IBM's 16-bit microchip is increased modeling area. Prior to the IBM Personal Computer, most VisiCalc models had to be less than 30K in size. The Personal Computer can process VisiCalc models of more than 500K.

When used with the IBM 80 CPS Printer, VisiCalc has an option that allows the user to create special typefaces to emphasize and condense printed characters.

Some of the IBM keyboard features can be used by VisiCalc, such as the HOME and PrtSc (print screen) keys. These features are quite convenient and, therefore, speed up program use.

IBM's VisiCalc manuals (documentation) are outstanding. They are the best yet in the personal computer industry, offering step-by-step explanations of virtually all operations.

VisiCalc is a copy-protected program. However, the IBM version comes with two disks: one for regular use, and one to be stored for use in case the first one fails. Some non-IBM versions of the program come with only one disk.

IBM's keyboard has the cursor-control keys on the numeric section. As a result, the NUM LOCK key must be depressed twice for each cell entry if a numeric keypad is used. Unfortunately, the NUM LOCK key does not respond quickly, making this process clumsy.

In addition, the IBM's special-function keys are not implemented for VisiCalc. This feature is unfortunate for new VisiCalc users, but, of course, is of little consequence to those who are already familiar with VisiCalc's command keystrokes.

VisiCalc's printing command is awkward to use for some printers. It requires that some users become more involved in the printer setup characters than they may prefer.

VisiCalc uses a simple linear form of recalculation. The model recalculates by beginning at the upper right corner of the spreadsheet (cell A1) and proceeding either row by row or column by column through the sheet. The user must be very careful to build dependencies in the worksheet to avoid *forward references* (a cell whose value depends on other cells below it in the recalculation order) and *circular references* (two or more cells defined by each other) which can create calculation nightmares.

Multiplan

Multiplan, by Microsoft, is one of the "new generation" electronic spreadsheets. It offers all of the functions, formats, and commands of the first generation spreadsheets like VisiCalc and adds several exciting new features as well.

The experienced VisiCalc or SuperCalc user would have no problem recognizing most of the features of Multiplan (or most any other spreadsheet). In its basic spreadsheeting capability, Multiplan is very similar to VisiCalc. Like VisiCalc, Multiplan uses a 255-row by 63-column spreadsheet. However, Multiplan numbers both rows and columns in the sheet. Thus cell reference A1 in VisiCalc becomes cell r1c1 in Multiplan.

Multiplan's new method of cell referencing and unique functions require some getting used to. The serious spreadsheet user will not be bothered by the learning curve. In fact, Microsoft has shown concern for prior users of VisiCalc by including a file import feature that will read a VisiCalc file directly into Multiplan.

Multiplan comes with extensive tutorials, a comprehensive manual, and a diskette of useful examples of Multiplan's unique functions. The program itself has on-line help available at a keystroke. It comes with an extensive shirt pocket guide that spans most topics of concern to the Multiplan user. In fact, the reference card is the largest we have seen thus far for any program. Because of its size, it can be cumbersome.

Probably the hardest thing to get used to is Multiplan's elimination of the "/" key for initiating commands. The average VisiCalc or Super-Calc user will continue to reach for that key for a while after converting to Multiplan.

Multiplan goes well beyond the first generation electronic spreadsheets by including a long list of descriptive error messages. Multiplan's error messages fully describe the nature of the difficulty and are much less insulting than the traditional cryptic "ERROR" or "FORMULA ERROR" messages. Especially handy are the #REF! message, which warns the user that a formula refers to a cell that doesn't exist, and the #DIV/0! message, which indicates that a division by zero has been attempted. Multiplan's error messages are a major improvement over those of the older spreadsheets.

Multiplan requires a minimum of 64K RAM. On a 64K RAM system, only 15K of RAM is left for spreadsheet use. Even though Multiplan uses RAM memory very efficiently, this is only enough memory for a very small model. When used with the largest amount of memory Multiplan can handle, only 53K is fully available.

Multiplan addresses this problem by using overlay files to "park" unneeded sections of code on diskette. As the program runs, sections of code are swapped back and forth between RAM and diskette. This swapping slows Multiplan down. The delays are more severe in computers with 64K than in computers with 128K.

Fortunately, Multiplan allows several sheets to be linked together, allowing interaction among the linked sheets. Multiple sheet linking is probably the most exciting new feature of Multiplan, because it helps relieve the program's memory shortage problem and allows the user to link logically the parts of several complex models.

Multiplan can link only one single-cell value at a time from one model to another. For example, cell r1c1 on sheet A could refer to cell r1c1 on sheet B for its value, but it could not access a LOOKUP table or SUM range from sheet B.

Multiplan's LOOKUP tables are true tables rather than single rows or columns. For example, suppose you have a table with the following column headings:

Employee Number	Name	Age	Length of Service	Marital Status

Using the employee number as the key variable, the user could LOOKUP either name, age, length of service, or marital status. If age is the key variable, you can look up length of service or marital status. Name *cannot* be used as a key variable because the key variable must be numeric.

Another new information management feature of Multiplan is the ability to retrieve information from an indexed table. Unlike a LOOK-UP table, which allows the user to search a range of indexes for a data item, an index table requires the user to specify the exact coordinates of the data item being retrieved. For example, in Multiplan, the function INDEX (TABLENAME,R2,C3) returns the value located in row 2, column 3, of the indicated table. Experienced programmers will recognize this as a type of array.

MultiPlan offers several new arithmetic, logical, and special functions. One handy new function is @STDEV, which computes standard deviations.

Multiplan includes a number of interesting functions for working with text. The text functions of Multiplan are similar to those of Microsoft's biggest selling product, the Microsoft BASIC language. (Microsoft BASIC is also the biggest selling microcomputer language in the world.) The FIXED function converts a numeric entry to a text entry. Conversely, the VALUE function converts text entries made up of numerals into numeric entries. "Converted" numbers can be concatenated (linked together) with text to embed numerical data in the middle of sentences. The function MID considers either text, or a cell reference containing text, and returns the specified portion of the total text string. Another text function, LN, simply returns the number of characters in a cell.

Multiplan also allows text to serve as the object of a LOOKUP or IF...THEN function. This ability, when combined with the other functions above, makes Multiplan a clear winner in the area of text operations.

As in other advanced spreadsheets, Multiplan allows areas inside the sheet to be referred to by user-specified names. A named range can be a single cell or a rectangular area of any size. The names can be designed to describe the contents of the cell or the range being named. For example, a range might be named "SALES," or "TOTAL EMPLOYEES."

Multiplan supports up to eight windows on the screen at one time. It numbers each window as it is created. Like VisiCalc, windows can be set to scroll together (synchronized) or separately (unsynchronized).

Multiplan's F(ormat) command provides extensive options for the formatting of text or numbers within a cell. Text may be aligned to be centered or left- or right-justified within a cell. Numbers may have a fixed number of significant digits. The user has a wide range of possible formats available, including floating dollar signs, commas, asterisks (or other graphics characters), exponents, integers, and percentages.

Column widths may be chosen individually, as a group, or globally with the F(ormat) W(idth) command.

Multiplan can sort columns and tables of data within the spreadsheet. The user must specify the range to be sorted (one or more columns of data), the column by which the sort is to be performed (the sorting "key"), and whether the sort is to be in ascending or descending order. Sorting can be performed either numerically or alphabetically.

Multiplan addresses the recalculation problems of the first generation of spreadsheets. It offers a "natural" mode of recalculation. Natural recalculation begins by discerning the most fundamental cell in the sheet (i.e., the cell on which most other cells are based). This cell is evaluated first. Next, the program searches for the second most basic formula in the sheet and evaluates it. This process continues until the entire worksheet is recomputed.

Accompanying natural recalculation in Multiplan is the ability to perform iterative calculations. In Multiplan, the number of iterations can also be determined by some predefined limit of change in a given cell.

Conclusion

VisiCalc and Multiplan are both exceptionally flexible and powerful programs. VisiCalc is a legend. It has probably had more effect on the microcomputer industry than any other software package. All other spreadsheets, including Multiplan, owe VisiCalc a tremendous debt for opening the spreadsheet doors. And after five years of leading the industry, VisiCalc is still one of the best programs available for a microcomputer.

Multiplan offers extensive capabilities that should satisfy even the most demanding spreadsheeter. Its extensive features allow large amounts of data to be linked relationally. Although a minor sacrifice of speed is encountered initially in the model's development, Multiplan can provide very sophisticated operations once the model is in place.

Multiplan is close to being the ultimate spreadsheet program, although its large number of functions, formatting options, and commands also bring it close to the limits of usability. However, the features of Multiplan far outweigh its minor flaws and represent very high quality in a spreadsheet format.

Because of its flexibility, ease of use, and power, spreadsheet software is probably the most widely used application for microcomputers. Most exciting of all, the limits of spreadsheet software are still nowhere in sight.

Introducing Data Management

Data management is one of the most popular applications for computers of all sizes. This is true for several reasons. First, computers store data very efficiently. A single IBM floppy disk can store 360,000 bytes of data, roughly equivalent to 180 pages of typewritten text. An IBM Fixed Disk can store 10 million bytes of data—a file cabinet full—on a five-inch platter.

In addition to being very efficient in storing data, computers can quickly retrieve stored information. Some programs are capable of selecting a single piece of data from among thousands of records in a matter of seconds. This is a substantial improvement over the retrieval speeds of manual systems.

Most manual filing systems allow each record to be stored under only one index. For example, a personnel file system might have the employee records arranged by name, by employee number, or by length of service. Each of these arrangements might be helpful at one time or another.

Unlike manual filing systems, computer files can have more than one index for each record. This means that a file can be "rear-ranged" at will to conform to the user's immediate need. After the user is finished, the file can be returned to the original order or any other desired order. This feature makes computer file management vastly superior to manual filing.

The overriding reason for the popularity of file management programs, however, is that most people have a need to store vast amounts of data efficiently, then retrieve that data quickly and easily.

This is especially true of businesses. Almost every business has a need to store efficiently vast amounts of information. In fact, most business applications for computers involve data management. Accounting systems are really specialized data managers; so are calendar programs.

The problem of "data overflow," however, also occurs at home. Managing recipes, address lists, and inventories of personal property are all file-oriented tasks.

These needs have created tremendous demand for a wide variety of data management programs. The data management programs selected by IBM for the Personal Computer are pfs: FILE and pfs: REPORT.

pfs:FILE and pfs:REPORT

The two modules, pfs:FILE and pfs:REPORT, work as a team to store, retrieve, and present data. The FILE module stores and retrieves data, and the REPORT module allows the data to be formatted for display and printing.

These two programs, introduced in 1981 by Software Publishing Corporation, became best sellers, despite heavy competition from programs like VisiDex. They were originally designed to run on the Apple II computer.

Although pfs:FILE and pfs:REPORT are not super-sophisticated data base managers (like dBase II, FMS-80, Condor, and MDBS), they are more than adequate for many business and personal filing needs. Both programs come with excellent documentation. Even the beginning computer user will have no problem learning to use the pfs programs.

pfs:FILE

The first module, pfs:FILE, can be thought of as an index card box filled with 3" by 5" cards. The user designs input forms that allow data to be written onto these cards. (Naturally, the program does not really use cards. The data is stored on diskettes.) Designing the forms is a simple process. These forms can also be used to retrieve, modify, and print data.

The user retrieves information from the disk by selecting certain criteria that apply to the stored data. The criteria can be general or very specific. In addtion, "wildcard" characters can be used to retrieve the data. For example, a search using the criteria "Doug" would result in a list of all records where the first name was "Doug." A search with "D....." as the criterion would retrieve all records that included the names David, Donald, etc.—all names that begin with a D.

Data can also be retrieved with a "Not" search. This type of operation returns all the records that do not match a certain criterion.

One of the best features of pfs:FILE is its flexibility. The program can be used equally well at home or at work for simple data management chores.

Like most microcomputer file management programs, pfs:File has a limited storage capacity on 5 1/4-inch diskettes. If you have a great deal of data to store, you should consider acquiring IBM's Fixed Disk, or another Winchester-type drive, for your computer.

pfs:REPORT

The second module, pfs:REPORT, increases the power and flexibility of the pfs family by enabling the user to produce reports using the data in files created by pfs:FILE.

The program offers a number of options that can be used to create custom reports. A report can include up to 16 columns of data. The user defines the contents and sequence of each column. Columns can be filled with data from a file, or, by using the program's arithmetic features, with the results of calculations on other columns. The math functions also allow reports to contain column statistics (such as averages and counts) and column subtotals and totals.

A report can include retrieval criteria that indicate which records should be printed. These criteria can include wildcards, "not" cases, and numeric ranges.

Reports are easy to create, thanks to pfs:REPORT's report generator. Once a report is created, the program automatically spaces all of the columns, centers the report on the page, and numbers all of the pages as it prints. Report forms can be stored on disk and reused later. This allows "standard" reports to be defined and used over and over on a periodic basis. Old reports can be modified as it is necessary.

Furthermore, pfs:REPORT allows the data in a report to be sorted in ascending or descending order, using the data in the first two columns as keys. For example, a personnel report might have the following data columns: Employee Name, Address, Telephone Number, and Years Employed. This report could be arranged so that the records were in alphabetical order by employee name.

Like pfs:FILE, REPORT can be used both in the office and at home to simplify file management chores.

Conclusion

The pfs in the names of these two programs stands for *personal filing system*. These programs are personal tools, not heavy duty business data base managers. As personal tools, however, they are excellent. They are well designed, well documented, and easy to use. These programs are appropriate for many home and office data management applications.

Introducing Word Processing

What Is a Word Processor?

A *word processor* is much like a typewriter; both machines have a keyboard and a printing device. But a word processor is much more than a typewriter. The magic of a word processor is the device that lies between the keyboard and the printer: the computer. All of the capabilities of word processing result from the ability of the computer to store, manipulate, display, and print the characters it receives from the keyboard. Whatever the operator enters into the word processor is captured and stored by the computer. Once stored, data can be retrieved for editing at any time.

The implications of this simple principle are remarkable. Because the text is "saved" for future use, the operator can enter text at full speed without regard for typing errors. Once the text is in the system, errors in spelling, punctuation, and usage can be edited out of the document.

A document stored on a word processor can be used again and again. For example, a form letter stored on a word processor can be printed any number of times with just a few keystrokes.

Another benefit of word processing is realized in text revision. Before word processing, revising a document required retyping it. Word processing makes revision incredibly simple. For writers, attorneys, and other professionals who produce long documents that require constant revision, word processing is indispensable.

What Do You Need in a Word Processor?

Most word-processor buyers want the most powerful program available. However, this may not be the best approach for every application. The *conditions of use* that should influence software selection include frequency of use, type of documents, formatting requirements, and special uses.

If the purpose of word processing is *high volume* text production, such as in a legal office, typing pool, or publishing house, then power is the major requirement, assuming that the same operator will be using the word-processing equipment. In such applications, the ability to jump directly to a given page, dynamically insert text without limit, move blocks of text (sentence, paragraph, page, or several pages) anywhere within a file (or even better, from any file to another), search and replace any number of times with or without case conversion, dynamically format with multiple margins at any point in the text, set decimal tabs, print two columns, alternate layout for binding, and do the many other functions of powerful word-processing software, will be well worth the capital and time invested.

If, on the other hand, the word processor will be used less frequently, the overall friendliness of the program and the quality of the documentation should be weighed heavily.

The *length of the documents* produced will help determine the software functions that are important. *Short documents*, usually memos, are the least demanding. They seldom require complex formatting or sophisticated printing, such as boldface or overstrike. Normally, the operator's priority is to get the text in and out (printed) as fast as possible. Editing time is low because the operator can usually remember all of the text, including text that is not displayed on the screen. In addition to the important "electronic editing" functions, it is desirable to have the "text displayed as printed" and "print from editor" functions, making "saving" the last edited version before printing unnecessary. Of course, saving is available if the operator wants to file the document for future use. It is simply not required before printing. This arrangement increases the efficiency of draft production because the operator can save the last version after printing when leaving the machine.

Medium length documents are more demanding. They are often reports (sometimes technical) and, therefore, require superscripts and subscripts. More powerful "block" and "search and replace" operations are useful, but are not as important as they would be for long documents. On-screen "display as printed," including page breaks, reduces the number of draft copies required before final copy. Stronger tab functions, particularly "decimal tab" for financial reports, are very helpful. More powerful formatting and printing capabilities (such as electronically centered and boldfaced headers) add quality to the document's appearance.

Long-document production requires powerful software. Long texts are often rearranged, necessitating strong block-move functions. The ability to lift (read) or place (write) any size block of text within a document (or from any document to the "work" document) is very convenient.

"Search and replace" functions become important with long documents. Functions such as "search backwards" and "search all times" are significant to operator efficiency. However, "search all times," "search for a partial match," and "replace-query" functions also contribute to document quality. They provide an improved probability of finding all occurrences of a word or phrase, and a better likelihood of not replacing a word out of context.

Certain types of documents (or more accurately, the types of documents produced by certain industries) have unusual and extensive *formatting requirements*. Headers and footers are important in most long texts, particularly in legal text. Special characters, such as paragraph or subsection symbols, are also important in legal text. In addition, courts have different paper-size requirements, resulting in multiple-standard page formats.

"Merging text files" is helpful in boilerplating documents or otherwise inserting standard clauses, paragraphs, or pages. Boilerplating is helpful in the preparation of proposals and quotations to assure that essential conditions are not omitted. The same function can be used to convey special messages, such as a vacation-shutdown schedule. The essential benefit of a text merging capability, beyond the obvious labor saving for the typist, is that well-prepared text is used each time without risking typographical errors or omissions by the typist.

Multiple margins can be used to emphasize a passage of text or to identify quoted text. Some programs allow within a document any number of margins the operator may want. Alternating layout may also be useful for documents that will be bound.

Special printing functions, such as boldface, underline, double-strike, superscripts, and subscripts, are normally considered part of the word-processor printing functions. For general purposes, however, they are formatting functions. The clarity and legibility achieved through boldfacing headers and key words in the text add to the professional look of any document.

Many other special formatting options are available. When selecting a word processor, the prospective buyer should inquire about any special formatting that will be required for a particular application.

Word processors can be utilized for such *special purposes* as generating collection letters, personalized promotional or invitational mailings, printing multiple originals of a document, printing invoices and statements, and building reports from standard sections. It is important to identify each of these special uses before selecting software. Special-use capabilities differ substantially from one software package to another.

The special uses listed above, except for "building reports," result from the capability to merge data files. This capability means that, in the case of collection letters, a separate file is loaded with the names, addresses, and amounts of the debts. The word processor is then commanded to produce the letters, inserting the appropriate data as necessary. Some word processors can produce such letters while unattended.

The ability to sort a data file and select certain records is also helpful. For example, if a person wants to send collection letters to only those debtors who have an outstanding balance above $50.00, a program with the sorting or selection capability could automatically generate letters to only those debtors.

Keep in mind that word-processing needs may change. Typically, word-processing users who have taken the time to understand the subject find unexpected uses as they become more familiar with the system. These users also commonly use the system more than they originally expected simply because jobs that seemed difficult and time consuming before word processing no longer seem so.

IBM's Word Processors

IBM publishes two word-processing programs for the Personal Computer: EasyWriter and Peachtext. EasyWriter is a fairly simple word processor that can be used for many less complex applications. Peachtext is a more powerful program that is best suited for certain "heavy-duty" tasks.

EasyWriter Version 1.1

EasyWriter was the first word-processing program published for the IBM Personal Computer. Like some of the other business series software packages, EasyWriter was first published for the Apple II™ computer. On the Apple II, EasyWriter enjoyed a series of firsts: first word-processing program to use an 80-column video board (the Apple native mode is 40-character lines); first dynamically displayed text to be shown as it will be printed; and the first Apple program that permitted incremental spacing with suitable letter-quality printers.

The IBM version of this program maintains the best of the Apple program's features and adds many more. Unfortunately, version 1.0 of the program suffered from a number of serious problems, such as a tendency to behave erratically. Version 1.1 has solved many of these problems, and owners of EasyWriter 1.0 can upgrade to 1.1 at no cost. (Another version of the program, Easywriter II, is published by Information Unlimited Systems. It differs significantly from version 1.1.)

EasyWriter is user friendly. It includes many powerful features that give the operator a wide variety of formatting options. As a result, EasyWriter is suitable for many types of formats and documents.

The EasyWriter system was written in the FORTH programming language by John Draper, the author of the 1.7 version of FORTH for the Apple II. Although FORTH provides faster disk operations (than Apple's DOS) and program transportability between computers, EasyWriter sacrifices direct compatibility with files created under any other operating system.

Like all IBM Personal Computer software, EasyWriter comes with an excellent manual. In addition, the system is fully menu driven, so novice users can quickly gain proficiency with the system. Special help commands display the correct keystrokes for commands while an operator edits a document. All of these features combine to make the program easy to learn and use.

EasyWriter makes full use of the Personal Computer's special-function and cursor-control keys for efficient entry and editing of documents.

The program's menu-driven printer configuration program greatly aids the setup of the EasyWriter system for IBM and non-IBM printers (both parallel and serial).

Extensive printing-format flexibility is available through menu-selected margin and page settings, and placement of embedded commands for dynamically altering the page's appearance.

Text being edited by EasyWriter is displayed exactly as it will be printed, except for special printer commands, such as boldfacing or underscoring. This feature reduces the number of draft copies required to perfect a document's appearance.

Documents may be printed while in the editing mode and previewed on the video screen. The latter feature reduces the number of draft copies required to perfect the text.

An "un-delete" command allows the recovery of most inadvertent deletions while in the editing mode. This feature is extremely important for those users who do not practice careful file backup procedures.

This program supports multiple titles/footnotes and allows titles to be placed anywhere on a given page.

Powerful user-defined and special printer characters permit the use of special printer characteristics (such as foreign language characters, reverse line feeds, and alternate character sets). Examples and directions are supplied in the manual for the special printer characters for both the IBM 80 CPS Printer and non-IBM supplied printers.

Commands are provided to make backup copies of data diskettes while in the program, or to use both disk drives for document storage.

A programmable end-of-line character allows special features to be used on some printers (i.e., underscore characters on the IBM or other dot-matrix printers).

The FORTH programming language makes EasyWriter relatively inflexible in communicating with other programs (such as mail list managers, accounting systems, etc.) created under PC DOS, CP/M-86, or the UCSD p-System. Version 1.1 includes a translation utility that allows EasyWriter files to be converted into ASCII text files. Unfortunately, this utility is cumbersome and not completely reliable.

Some editor-mode operations in EasyWriter are slow. These include aligning text, moving to the beginning or end of a large document, and scooping text into the block movement buffer. Fortunately, Version 1.1 corrects the problem of the system hanging when attempting to align text. Alignment (right justification) of the text still involves additional keystrokes if portions of the on-screen text have different margins or the document is less than 20 lines long.

In Version 1.0, the Search and Search/Replace commands did not always function properly. Version 1.1 corrects this problem. Searching for a specific phrase that occurs a number of times in the text can still be troublesome, however.

Version 1.1 also improves EasyWriter's block move and block copy functions, but block size is still restricted. The amount of usable memory that the program can access is also increased. With a 128K chip, the program can edit a file of up to 24,000 characters (about 12 pages).

EasyWriter does not automatically create a backup copy of a text file at the conclusion of an edit. However, the system does have the ability to create backup diskettes.

Peachtext

The IBM Peachtext word processor is a direct descendant of the popular CP/M word processor Magic Wand™. Although Peachtext is similar to Magic Wand, the IBM version offers several significant improvements over the older versions.

The Peachtext program operates from two modes, edit and print, which are accessed through a menu. As the names imply, the edit mode is used to create and revise documents, and the print mode is used to create printed text. Each mode has a command screen that provides basic information about the currently active document.

The program is remarkably easy to learn, thanks in part to a manual that meets IBM's high documentation standards. Even novice word-processor users should have no problem using Peachtext.

Peachtext includes the full range of print formatting commands, including superscript, subscript, boldface (with up to ten different intensities), underlining, variable margins, indentation of text, page length, left and right alignment of text, and justification of text (both margins flush). With the conditional command, all formatting commands can be issued (or omitted) based on a condition.

When used with a suitable specialty printer, Peachtext is capable of producing proportionally spaced text. This feature allows documents to be produced that appear to be typeset.

This program supports the full range of block operations, including block move, block copy, block read and write to disk, and block delete. Global and selective search and replace commands are also included.

IBM has taken several steps to improve the user friendliness of Peachtext. First, the program is accompanied by an excellent manual, which is supplemented by a handy user reference card. In addition, on-line help screens are built into the program. A function-key template is also included.

Peachtext can read and write standard IBM PC ASCII text files. Up to 128 variables can be created within a document, then filled from an ASCII file (or from the keyboard) during printing. Thanks to Peach-text's "IF" (conditional) command, data can be retrieved from a data file based on certain predetermined conditions. This feature makes Peachtext exceptionally flexible in creating and printing merge-print form letters.

Peachtext takes full advantage of the Personal Computer's key-board. All ten function keys are used.

Peachtext's editor includes a program utility mode, which can be used by programmers to create code.

Peachtext can perform simulated print spooling, allowing one doc-ument to be printed while another is being edited. Using this feature, however, slows both the printing and editing processes signif-icantly.

Peachtext also has some limitations. For example, its editor does not display text in a "what you see is what you get" format. This may be uncomfortable for users who are familiar with WordStar or Bench-mark. The program does, however, allow the user to "preview" the print format of a document before printing it.

This program does not provide a built-in page break indicator, making the design of a document difficult and tedious. It also does not allow the user to specify variable tab settings.

With Peachtree, it is inconvenient to print less than a full document. This limitation can be very troublesome when the finishing touches are being added to a document.

Conclusion

When EasyWriter is combined with the Personal Computer, the result is a word processor with good capabilities to produce simple documents. Text can be entered rapidly, just-typed mistakes are easily corrected, insertions are readily made, and cursor movement is straightforward. However, some of the characteristics of this program make it less suitable for longer documents.

Those users who anticipate producing larger and more complex documents may want to consider Peachtext. Peachtext's conditional functions, block operations, and search and replace capabilities make it a match for almost any word-processing task.

CHAPTER 7

Communications
with the IBM PC

Since the announcement of the IBM Personal Computer in August, 1981, a wide variety of hardware and software products for communications has been developed for this computer. These communications capabilities distinguish the IBM Personal Computer from other microcomputers on the market.

Today, more communications products are available for the IBM Personal Computer than for other microcomputer systems, making it a good choice for corporations that provide personal computers to managerial and other professional personnel.

Balanced Computing

As computer resources in organizations evolve into a *balanced computing* structure, more communications capabilities in personal computers are needed. The new low-cost desktop computers, particularly the IBM Personal Computer XT, greatly increase the productivity of managers and other professionals.

This chapter on Communications with the IBM PC was written by P. D. (Pete) Moulton, a nationally and internationally recognized authority on small computer systems and data communications. He uses an IBM Personal Computer extensively in his consulting and business activities. Moulton is communications editor of Personal Computer Age magazine and has published more than 20 papers in computer and communication trade journals. His professional career totals 14 years' experience planning, designing, and implementing computer communications systems. Here, Moulton describes the communications capabilities of the IBM Personal Computer and Personal Computer XT, and explores the benefits of Personal Computer-Mainframe interaction.

The focus here is not on technical benefits realized from off-loading mainframe computer processing. The focus, instead, is on increased productivity from desktop workstations, where microcomputers are provided to managerial and other professional personnel in many business organizations.

Managers are finding that personal computers can eliminate much of the drudgery of day-to-day work, such as the reading of numbers and the completing of forms.

It is no longer necessary to ask the computer center or MIS Department for a programmmer to develop analyzing and formatting programs to simplify workloads. Also, one no longer has to wait for the programmer to be assigned to the program development task. Now, with an IBM Personal Computer system that costs from $5,000 to $7,000, professionals can quickly do the job themselves.

Although incorporating features of both distributed processing and office automation, balanced computing is more comprehensive than either of these systems.

In *distributed processing,* functions resident in overburdened mainframe computers are moved to smaller, less costly computers connected to the host computer. The purpose is to distribute processing functions to remote systems while maintaining dependence on a mainframe computer. These remote systems perform limited data editing and formatting. As remote batch systems and information display terminals, they are allowed to update the mainframe computer's data bases.

Office automation systems are an outgrowth of word processing. Related filing and retrieval functions eventually became bundled into these word-processing systems, transforming them into office automation systems. But because these systems primarily emphaize the efficient creation of paper work, they only address the paper-shuffling functions performed in offices.

Balanced computing is based on matching an organization's structure and work functions with necessary computing power. Thus, for any organization, an appropriate balance of computing resources exists for the organization's particular structure and functions.

Balance does not come from solving technical problems in the distribution of computing resources (distributed processing) or from automating paper work functions (office automation). Balance is achieved by providing the right amount of computing power to meet the needs of the working environment.

Also, balanced computing focuses on the work activities of each individual in an organization. In the past, many of these activities could not be supported cheaply by computers. The only available alternative, which was to extend access to mainframe computers, was an expensive solution. Today, however, low-cost personal computers make it possible for almost all work activities to be supported by computer processing power.

This power is not derived from distant mainframes, but from micro-computers placed at appropriate organizational levels, e.g., a personal computer on an employee's desk.

From a technical viewpoint, a balanced computing structure requires that corporate and personal data bases be interrelated so that data can be exchanged between corporate and personal computers. Consequently, balanced computing makes the communications capabilities of microcomputers, such as the IBM Personal Computer and Personal Computer XT, increasingly important.

Business Communications Requirements

With today's microcomputer systems, like the IBM Personal Computer and Personal Computer XT, managers and other professionals can extract data from an organization's central computer systems for processing in desktop microcomputers.

To prepare reports and perform daily work activities effectively, these professionals can use turnkey software, such as electronic spreadsheet programs; time management and scheduling programs; information storage and retrieval programs; graphics creation and display programs; text-processing programs; and other programs provided with these microcomputer systems.

Consequently, three kinds of communications capabilities are required for the IBM Personal Computers:

1. Transmitting and receiving of text files for sending electronic mail and retrieving information from external timesharing sources, such as The Source™, CompuServe™, and the Dow Jones Information Service™. This capability is also the primary means of communication used by hobbyists to exchange programs and

text files and to establish their computers as bulletin boards or clearing houses for specific types of information.

2. Accessing the central, or mainframe, computer to extract (but not update) information from the organization's central data files. Personal Computers, then, are supported as terminals on a mainframe so that executives can access corporate data.

3. Sharing of files among several interconnected Personal Computers in an office working environment. This capability permits employees in the same organizational unit to share secretarial and administrative resources without leaving their desks to deliver floppy disk resident files.

Both business users and hobbyists are interested in performing text file transfers for electronic mail. Only business users, however, desire the additional capabilities of accessing and extracting data from corporate data bases on IBM mainframe computers and of sharing data among several workstations assigned to a single organizational unit.

Transfers of mainframe/personal computer files are becoming increasingly important, as demonstrated in a recent survey entitled "Policy for the Personal Business Computer."

This survey, prepared by Advanced Office Concepts Corp., was conducted to determine the extent to which personal computers have penetrated corporations. Of the nearly 250 corporate users responding, 26% were among the 1,000 largest U.S. companies, with 60% having 1,000 or more employees. Over 75% of the corporate users had IBM mainframe computers, and 50% used other mainframes.

Accessing of mainframe files occurred in one-third of the participating companies. An additional 14.7% planned to permit accessing in the future. Over three-fourths of the companies did not allow data base updating from personal computers, and only 5% planned to permit updating in the future.

This restriction may reflect only the large amount of off-line, departmental work currently done on personal computers, rather than a firm bias against permitting personal computer users to update mainframe data bases.

The Evolution of
IBM's Personal Computer
Communications Products

IBM first supplied the Asynchronous Communications Support program to meet the electronic mail needs of its Personal Computer owners.

In its first release, the package was incomplete, lacking the ability to transfer files automatically to and from the Personal Computer's floppy disks; to the asynchronous communications interface; and, thus, to a remote computer system. Because the first release provided a few added features over the COMM.BAS program that accompanied PC DOS, IBM should have upgraded the original version of the Asynchronous Communications Support program for a nominal fee to those purchasers of the original program.

IBM, however, did not offer this option, probably because of the belief that the buyer would not have purchased the program for a Personal Computer that needed to communicate only as a dumb terminal.

Version 2.00, the current release of the Asynchronous Communications Support program, provides the disk file transfer functions.

Before the Personal Computer's first year was completed, IBM announced several enhanced communications capabilities: the second release of the Asynchronous Communications Support program; an asynchronous communications program that allowed the Personal Computer to emulate the functions and communications of the increasingly popular IBM 3101 terminal; and System Network Architecture (SNA) support, including both 3270 and 3770 terminal emulation capabilities.

Terminal *emulation* allows the Personal Computer to duplicate the operations and features of the selected terminal device through the addition of special communications hardware adapters and software products. The IBM 3101 terminal emulation package does not require a new communications interface adapter. The program uses the Asynchronous Communications Adapter (#1502074). However, the SNA support software does require the purchase of a special SNA communications adapter (#1502090), in addition to the SNA support programs thenselves.

Today, IBM provides a complete line of communications hardware and software products for Personal Computer owners who desire electronic mail and text transfer capabilities, as well as access to corporate IBM mainframe computers.

Within the next year, IBM's announcements of communications products will probably address the last area of communications, linking together Personal Computers with a local area network (LAN), which is coaxial cable based and has token passing protocol.

One reason for including more expansion slots and a separate expansion chassis for the Personal Computer is that those users implementing all three kinds of communications capabilities (text file transfer, host access, and local area networking) require a precious expansion slot for an Asynchronous Communications Adapter, the SNA communications adapter, and the LAN communications adapter.

Use of this expansion slot, along with slots for the standard Diskette Drive Adapters, the Fixed Disk Adapter, the Monochrome Display/ Printer Adapter, and the Color Display Adapter, nearly exhausts all the expansion slots in the Personal Computer XT chassis.

Because such a fully expanded system usually runs with more than 256K of memory (requiring the addition of a memory expansion card), all the Personal Computer XT's expansion ports are being used.

The independent manufacturers that make combination adapter boards for the Personal Computer will solve this problem by developing a combination board that provides asynchronous, synchronous, and SNA communications support, as well as clock/calendar functions. True multifunction adapters that support local area networks will not appear for several years because the chips needed to place all functions on a single card are not manufactured in sufficient quantities at this time.

Personal Computer
Data Communications Components

In a discussion of the IBM communications products, it is necessary to use some technical terminology in data communications.

These terms describe how communications channels work and how communications hardware and software use these channels, or telephone lines. Unfortunately, many of these terms are misused (and abused), just as many computer terms, like *system,* are used inappropriately. Such misuse adds to the confusion and the mystique surrounding computer technology when, in fact, computers may be no more complex than the ordinary household food processor.

Three elements are required to set up the Personal Computer for data communications with other computers: computer communications hardware, communications software, and telephone services. (See Figure 1A.) In the figure, the computer hardware includes the Personal Computer Monitor, Keyboard, and System Unit.

To these are added either the IBM Asynchronous Communications Adapter card or one of the independent vendor combination cards (e.g., one that provides expansion of RAM), plus—all on the same card—an Asynchronous Communications Adapter, a modem cable, and a modem.

The *modem* (MOdulator / DEModulator) is a device that converts the digital voltage signals in the Personal Computer into analog tones (frequencies) that travel over telephone lines. (See Figure 1B.) Modems are connected to the Personal Computer using an industry-standard RS-232 bit serial interface. (See interfaces below.)

Communications software, the second element required for setting up data communications between the Personal Computer and other computers, is provided with the Personal Computer. For example, the COMM.BAS program, as part of the Personal Computer's operating system, allows communications for the Personal Computer as a dumb terminal.

Another example is the Asynchronous Communications Support program (Version 2.00) with added disk file transfer capabilities. This program supports PC to PC, PC to TSO, and PC to VM communications—all capabilitites not provided by the COMM.BAS program.

Having a telephone, or a communications, line installed next to the Personal Computer is the third essential element for data communications.

This telephone line can be a switched line (normal telephone), a leased line (full-period, 24-hour communications channel connecting two specific points), or a private line (user-installed, twisted-wire

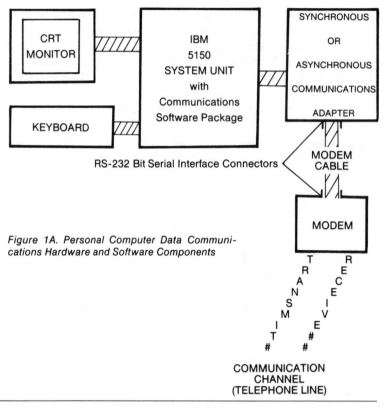

Figure 1A. Personal Computer Data Communications Hardware and Software Components

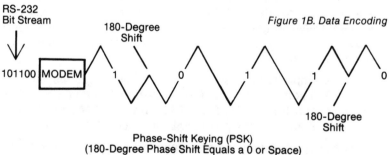

Figure 1B. Data Encoding

RS-232
Bit Stream

101100 MODEM   1   0   1   1   0

180-Degree
Shift

180-Degree
Shift

Phase-Shift Keying (PSK)
(180-Degree Phase Shift Equals a 0 or Space)

Bits are encoded by shifting the phase angle of the transmitted data signal. In this case, a
phase shift of 180 degrees signals a 0 bit. Differential phase shift keying uses several
different phase shifts to represent the four possible combinations of 0 and 1 bits (00, 01, 10
and 11). This encoding is used by the Western Electric 212 modems, the most commonly
used 120 cps modem.

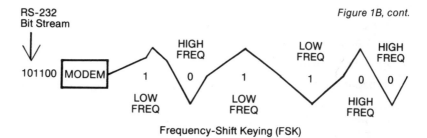

Frequency-Shift Keying (FSK)

Bits are encoded in analog signal by shifting between HIGH and LOW frequencies for 0's and 1's, respectively. This encoding is used by the Western Electric 103 modems, the most commonly used 30 characters per second (cps) modem.

pairs or coaxial cables from several thousand feet to a few miles in length). All these telephone lines provide both transmit and receive pathways for communicating with a remote computer, regardless of whether 2-wire, dial-up service or 4-wire, full-period service is used.

The Communictions Buzz Words

The terminology required for understanding the communications features of the IBM Personal Computer and Personal Computer XT includes the following:

Duplex
   Half
   Full

Communications channels
   Two wire
   Four wire

Codes
   ASCII
   EBCDIC

Synchronization
   Asynchronous transmission
   Synchronous transmission
   Character and message synchronization
   Synchronous vs. asynchronous modems
   Transmission speed

Interfaces
  RS-232
  Parallel

Uploading/Downloading

Transparency

Error checking
  Parity
  CRC

Compatibility and emulation

These terms are described below in greater detail as they pertain to the IBM Personal Computer.

Full vs. Half Duplex

There are three types of communications pathways. A *simplex* path is a one-way channel between the transmitting and receiving devices (as in a lecture). A *half-duplex* path is also a one-way channel that occurs only once, with information flowing in the opposite direction permitted in a subsequent time period (as in a conversation in which one person speaks and another answers). In a *full-duplex* path, data flows in both directions simultaneously (as in an argument). Full-duplex channels are formed using two simplex, or one-way, channels.

Most communications channels are electrically, or physically, full duplex. For example, all asynchronous communications occur over electrically (physically) full-duplex channels. These channel characteristics are determined by the telephone line and the electrical operation of the modem on that line. (See Figures 2 and 3.)

Because full-duplex transmission provides two separate one-way paths over which data flows, this kind of transmission is required for *echoplex* communications in which characters are displayed when echoed by the host in the Asynchronous Communications Support program menu selections.

During echoplex communications, data typed on the Personal Computer's keyboard travels on the inbound pathway and is then returned by the host over a separate outbound pathway to be displayed on the Personal Computer's CRT monitor. Echoplex communications are used to permit the Personal Computer operator to verify that the data sent to the remote computer system has been received correctly.

In physical, half-duplex transmission, only one data pathway is provided by the modem. This pathway must be alternately used to communicate inbound data to the host and to receive outbound data from the host. At speeds of 1,800 bits per second (bps) and above, two-wire modems operate in half duplex.

Message transfer using communications protocols is either full duplex or half duplex, regardless of the type of electrical channel available. (Obviously, in cases employing a half-duplex electrical channel, the protocol message transfer must be half duplex as well.) For example, the Asynchronous Communications Support program's teletypewriter protocol only provides half-duplex message

Figure 2. Modem Signaling on Telephone Lines

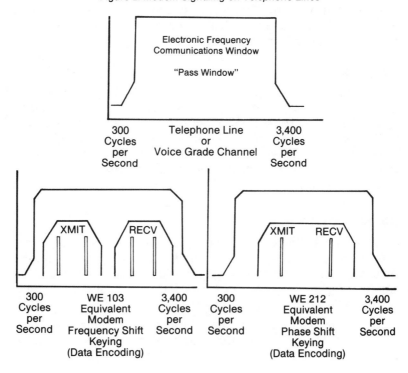

transfer despite operating on a full-duplex electrical channel. A message terminated by a carriage return (CR) character must be sent to the receiving computer before it responds with a reply to the Personal Computer.

The electrically full-duplex channel is used to echo the characters transmitted back to the Personal Computer as a mechanism for the operator to verify the accuracy of the data transmitted and received by the host computer.

Two- vs. Four-Wire Communications Channels

Full-duplex or half-duplex operation is independent of the telephone line interface to the modem. The telephone line interface can be either 2-wire (equivalent to dial-up, switched-network service), or 4-wire, leased-line, full period service.

Typically, the Western Electric 103 equivalent modem (the most common 30 cps modem) offers full-duplex transmission capability over 2-wire, switched telephone service (Direct Distance Dialed), as does the increasingly popular Western Electric 212 equivalent modems (the slightly less common 120 cps modem).

When data is transmitted at 1,800 bps and above on 2-wire service, modems operate with switched carriers. The carrier frequency signal is turned on and off by the modem to transmit data. With switched carriers, the transmission mode is half duplex. Modems on 4-wire, leased channels generally operate in full duplex with a separate carrier on each set of wires, one set for transmit and the second for receive. (See Figure 2.)

Character Codes

ASCII (American Standard Code for Information Interchange) is the most common character set used in microcomputer systems, including the IBM Personal Computer. This data code set is used for representing text characters in Personal Computer storage, as well as for displaying and printing the data.

The ASCII standard defines the character representations for 7 information bits, permitting 128 unique bit patterns to be represented by different combinations of 7 of the 8 bits in a single byte.

The IBM Personal Computers use a unique 8-bit version of ASCII (in which the eighth bit is a 1) for internally processing data, and a standard 7-bit version for communications. Although the full 8-bit version characters can also be transmitted over the communications interface, the 7-bit ASCII provides a universally accepted format for translating characters to binary form, and vice versa.

EBCDIC (pronounced Eb-SEE-Dick) is an acronym for Extended Binary Coded Decimal Interchange Code. In this code, all 8 binary positions are used to represent characters. This code is used internally in all IBM mainframe computers and in communications with these computers. The Personal Computers translate the ASCII characters to EBCDIC characters for transmission to IBM host computers during IBM 3270 terminal emulation and sometimes during 3770 terminal emulation.

Synchronization

Synchronization refers to the type of *bit synchronization* used by both the transmitting and receiving devices to assure correct detection of each distinct bit in the serial stream. The two major types of bit synchronization are *asynchronous* transmission and *synchronous* transmission. Other types of synchronization required to coordinate activities between sending and receiving devices on a communications channel are *character* synchronization and *message* synchronization.

Asynchronous Transmission

In *asynchronous* transmission, which is the kind used by the Personal Computer's Asynchronous Communications Adapter, AST combo boards, and similar products, there is a clock on the card that is used to time the sampling of the incoming communications line and to record the bits at each sample time. This clock is set in response to the Asynchronous Communications Support program's transmission-speed parameter setting.

During data transmission the communications line is operated in an idle state; i.e., no data is transmitted. Whenever a character is sent, it is preceded by a start bit that causes the electrical voltage on the RS-232 interface to change from its idle state value. On sensing this voltage transition (the voltage varies between + and -15 volts), the asynchronous adapter card starts its clock and begins sampling the voltage value on the line. If the initial voltage change is not as long as a single bit should be for the designated transmission speed, the adapter card resets itself and continues to look for a correctly sent bit (proper voltage).

At the end of a transmitted character, a stop bit is appended to cause the communications channel to return to its original idle state. The receiving device can then search for additional characters. Because of the added start and stop bits, all asynchronous communications characters have 10 bits when they travel over the communications channel. Asynchronous transmission is simple, requires the least expensive modems, and is used with teletypewriter protocols.

Synchronous Transmission

In contrast, *synchronous* transmission communications adapters use a clock signal provided by the modem to detect the bits being received. A master clock signal for the entire communications circuit is input by the host computer to its attached modem. The modem then sends both the clocking signal and the serial stream of 0's and 1's to the receiving Personal Computer's modem, which, in turn, decodes both signals and provides them to the computer on separate RS-232 interface lines (pin 3 and pin 17).

This type of transmission requires more complex and, consequently, more expensive modems; is comprised of blocks of characters (instead of a single character at a time); and is used with all the remaining protocols previously identified.

Because synchronous transmission uses blocks of characters, these blocks must first be buffered by the terminal, then a transmit key must be struck before the characters are sent to the host computer. During synchronous transmission, each character is comprised of only 8 bits, because of the character blocking and the clocks provided by the modem. Added start and stop bits are not required for synchronous data transmission.

Synchronous block transmissions require more complex protocol handshaking to complete the transfer of data between the terminal and the host computer. These handshaking procedures usually involve some form of polling, with the host computer controlling the communications channel and inviting the terminal device to send its data, when ready. Or the handshaking involves selecting the terminal device to receive a transmission from the host computer, assuming the terminal is active and on the communications channel.

The handshaking procedures differ, depending on whether point-to-point channels (one terminal per line) or multipoint channels (several terminals sharing the same line) are used to connect the terminal to the host computer. Point-to-point channels are used mainly for remote batch (file transfer) terminals and time-sharing terminals (usually asynchronous teletypewriter protocol), whereas multipoint channels most often connect inquiry response (data base transaction processing) terminals to the host computer system.

Character Synchronization and Message Synchronization

Besides bit synchronization, communications devices need to break the received stream of bits into characters and messages. Therefore, these devices perform character and message synchronization functions.

Character synchronization is performed by counting the number of bits per character. The receiving device can break up the incoming serial stream of 0's and 1's into alphanumeric characters. For asynchronous transmission the number of bits per character is most often 10 (a start bit, 7 information bits, a parity bit, and a stop bit), whereas for synchronous transmission the number of bits per character is 8.

The Personal Computer's communications adapter adds or strips the asynchronous start and stop bits. Consequently, the Personal Computer always stores 8 bits in memory.

Message synchronization is performed using communications control characters (or with SDLC and HDLC, special flag bytes comprised of a 0, six 1's, and a 0).

In asynchronous communications, some communications control characters are common to each manufacturer's variation of the teletypewriter protocol. These characters include carriage return (CR), and the XON (DC1) and XOFF (DC3) characters. For example, the IBM Asynchronous Communications Support program can vary the line-turnaround characters sent to the host with CR, DC1, DC3, end of transmission (EOT), or line feed (LF).

The different protocol variations all use their own specific sequences of handshaking control characters (or bits, in the case of the fourth and fifth generation protocols) to implement the data exchange and communications control procedures between the Personal Computer and the host computer system. Only in a few cases are these procedures widely enough implemented for them to be called standard, as with the BSC, the SDLC, and the asynchronous teletypewriter protocol variations for the IBM 3101, DEC VT52, and VT100 terminals.

Synchronous vs. Asynchronous Modems

The major difference between synchronous and asynchronous modems is that the synchronous modems provide the receiving terminal with a timing signal (a clock signal) used to sample the incoming stream of data and recreate the 0's and 1's.

The timing signal for asynchronous transmission is on the Personal Computer's Asynchronous Communications Adapter. (See the Personal Computer *Technical Reference* manual, pp. 2-124 and 2-135; and the Personal Computer *XT Technical Reference* manual, pp. 1-183, 1-193, 1-197, and 1-198.) The data stream sampling is begun under asynchronous transmission when the start bit transition is detected by the adapter card.

In synchronous transmission, synch characters, or flag bytes, are used to signal the beginning of a block of data, to resynchronize the transmit and receive clocks, and to begin the data sampling. In Synchronous Data Link Control (SDLC) transmission, Non-Return To Zero Inverted (NRZI) bit stream encoding is sometimes used to provide sufficient bit transitions to maintain the clock synchronization between the transmitting and receiving modems. Synchronous Communications Adapters expect a clock signal from the modem. (See the Personal Computer *XT Technical Reference* manual, p. 1-221.)

Some modems can be configured for either synchronous or asynchronous transmission, such as the Western Electric Model 212 modem.

Transmission Speed

Transmission speed is commonly referred to as the *modem baud rate*. This rate is not strictly accurate, but close enough for estimating transmission times. When transmission speed is stated as 300 baud, it indicates a transmission speed of 300 bps, or 30 cps, because 10 bits comprise each character transmitted asynchronously.

Low and medium speeds (0 through 1,200 bps) indicate asynchronous transmission.

High speeds (anything above 1,200 bps) indicate synchronous transmission. Synchronous protocols transmit 8 bits per character because the communications synchronization overhead is incurred when blocking or framing the data for transmission. Thus, synchronous transmission at 4,800 bps is equivalent to 600 cps.

Interfaces

An interface is the point where two devices connect, such as a computer and a peripheral. In general computer usage the peripheral may be a printer, monitor, or some other device. The important interface in data communications is the interface with a modem.

Technically, the term *interface* refers to the style of connection and the associated electrical signals that are utilized in connecting two devices.

The most common communications interface for personal computers is the EIA (Electronic Industries Association) RS-232C interface. This interface operates at data transmission speeds of up to 20,000 bps, over a cable that is usually less than 50 feet long, and functions independently of any communications protocol. (A protocol is similar to a spoken language.) Twenty-five pins are defined, e.g., transmit data pin 2 and receive data pin 3. However, typical equipment configurations use only about 9 of the pins.

The interface to connect the Personal Computer to an 80 CPS dot-matrix printer is an industry-standard parallel interface. This is often referred to as a Centronics interface because Centronics, the first major manufacturer of dot-matrix printers, sold many printers with this interface. The IBM Personal Computer RS-232 serial interface, Centronics-equivalent parallel interface, and the floppy disk industry-standard parallel interface are identified in Figure 3. Figures 4 and 5 describe two common configurations of the RS-232 interface.

The RS-232 serial interface is sometimes used to connect a printer to the IBM Personal Computer. When this happens, both the Per-

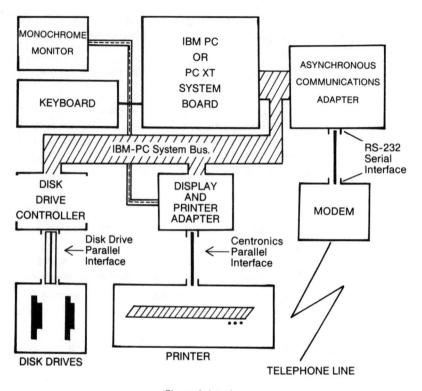

Figure 3. Interfaces

sonal Computer and the printer operate as Data Terminal Equipment (DTE), transmitting data on pin 2 and receiving data on pin 3. (The pin numbers are locted on the RS-232 connector.)

Modems operate as Data Communications Equipment (DCE), receiving data on pin 3 and transmitting data on pin 2. Consequently, when two DTEs are connected with the RS-232 interface, pin 2 and pin 3 must be cross-connected for them to transfer data successfully. If the RS-232 pins are not properly set, the connection simply will not work.

A second RS-232 cable configuration, shown below, illustrates the pin changes required to make auto-dialing modems that perform

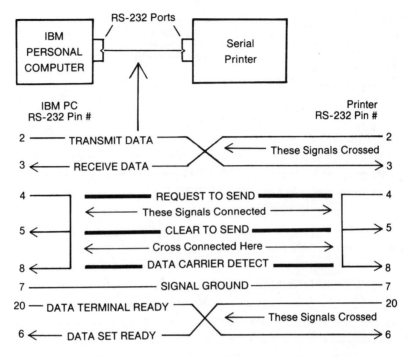

Figure 4. RS-232 (Modem Eliminator) Cable Configuration for Printer

auto-dialing through the RS-232 interface operate with the Personal Computer. The Hayes Smartmodems have this pin configuration set internally, with configuration switch settings inside the modem. Other manufacturers do not necessarily have configuration switches for the RS-232 interface signals.

In the following configuration the data-carrier-detect, data-set-ready, and clear-to-send lines are cross-connected because the Personal Computer will halt communications if it does not receive these signals, and the modem cannot supply data carrier detect until it has established contact on an operating channel with a remote modem. This RS-232 configuration can make almost any modem work with the Personal Computer.

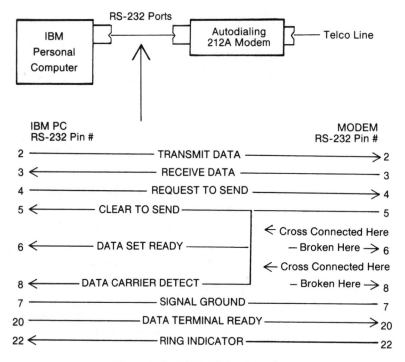

Figure 5. RS-232 Cable Configuration

Uploading and Downloading

Uploading and downloading are processes of communication between a personal computer and a remote computer (often the host).

Uploading communicates a file or program from the IBM Personal Computer to a remote computer. *Downloading* communicates a file or program from the remote computer to the Personal Computer.

Some communications programs permit uploading and downloading only if the files to be transmitted or received are resident in the Personal Computer's random access memory (RAM). In other communications programs the files may be stored either in RAM or on the Personal Computer's disks. These two processes are significant to some users of the IBM Personal Computer who communicate with remote bulletin boards; information service computers; and on public packet, switched-data networks.

Transparency

Data transparency is a key communications capability. Most data communicated to The Source and CompuServe consists of plain text files—alphanumeric data blocked into records of up to 255 characters by carriage-return (CR) and line-feed (LF) characters.

The alphanumeric data is stored and transmitted using ASCII, with 7 information bits. Internally, the IBM Personal Computer uses the ASCII code but allows all 8 information bits to define the characters. When 8 information bits are used, the parity bit is always set to 0 for the normal ASCII interpretation of the data being transmitted, and set to 1 for an additional 128 characters. (Note that characters are stored in the Personal Computer's memory using 9 bits, with the ninth bit being the parity bit.) These extra 128 characters are used to provide foreign alphabet letters such as "beta."

Some files are stored on the Personal Computer's disks in a condensed, or compressed, binary format. For example, BASIC programs are only stored on disk in standard ASCII code when BASIC's save command is issued with the *,A* suffix. Otherwise, programs are stored in compressed format.

Since most communications use control characters to perform message synchronization, if one of these control characters were, by chance, to occur in the binary file of data stored on disk, and if that file were sent over a data communications channel, the remote computer would incorrectly interpret the message synchronization and would malfunction, thus aborting the transmission. To transmit binary data, therefore, it is necessary either to translate the data into standard ASCII codes or to have a special communications feature that makes the communications process transparent (invisible) to the data being transmitted.

IBM's Binary Synchronous Communications and Synchronous Data Link Control protocols provide transparent transmission capabilities that permit transfer of binary data files.

Error Checking

During data communications different methods of error detection and correction are used. The two primary methods encountered today are parity error detection with echoplex data transfer and cyclic redundancy checking.

Parity error detection uses the eighth ASCII bit as a parity bit to make each character transmitted contain an odd number of 1 bits. Other parity bit conventions are even, no parity, mark (always a 1) and ignore any parity.

If changes in a character's bits occur during transmission because of communications errors, then the parity bit is not likely to match up with the other bits in the character. Such a mismatch signals a transmission error. This error detection technique is about 95% effective because a parity mismatch (not having an even, or odd, number of 1's in the character transmitted) can catch only an odd number of bit changes in the character transmitted. Consequently, if 2, 4, or 6 bits change, parity does not detect it.

Parity is used in the Personal Computer to detect bit changes in RAM because RAM tends to drop only single bits. For this use, parity's effectiveness is much greater than 95%. But in data communications, when a transmission error occurs, several bits are scrambled, making parity practically useless as a mechanism for detecting errors.

To detect and correct transmission errors for asynchronous teletypewriter protocol communications, echoplex operation should be used, in which the operator views the data transmitted (echoed by the receiving computer).

Cyclic Redundancy Check (CRC) divides the binary stream of 0's and 1's with a polynomial to generate a quotient and a remainder. A *polynomial*, which can be written as a mathematical formula, is a number comprised of powers of X (e.g., X to the sixteenth power plus X to the thirteenth power plus X to the fifth power plus X plus 1). The remainder becomes the Block Check Character (BCC), which is compared to an equivalent remainder that the receiver develops.

If the remainders match, then the block has been received correctly. Otherwise, a transmission error has occurred, and the receiver signals the transmitter to resend the block of data. Error correction is provided by retransmission of the data in error. The polynomial remainder technique makes CRC error detection about 99.99% effective in detecting data transmission errors.

CRC error detection is not used only for data communications. Many disk systems generate a CRC for each sector of data stored. Along with the data, the CRC is stored on the disk. When the data is read from the disk, an equivalent CRC is developed and compared to the stored CRC. A match signals OK, and a mismatch causes the disk to register a read error.

The technique is highly effective for both disks and data communications because when errors occur, more than one bit is changed. This change is readily detected by the CRC calculation.

CRC bytes can be calculated by the communications interface hardware in the IBM Personal Computer or, in some cases, by the communications software. When the calculation is performed by software, system performance may degrade, depending on how the CRC is calculated.

In all cases, CRC is the superior method of error detection. It also requires the most expensive communications hardware and software.

Compatibility and Emulation

Five levels of data communications compatibility can be identified: transmission speed; code; protocol; functional, or feature; and operational. With the first three levels (transmission speed, code, and protocol), mismatches can be readily resolved with a variety of equipment available today.

For slow-speed asynchronous transmission, Automatic Baud Rate Detection (ABRD) matches the transmission speed of a terminal to the speed of a receiving computer. Selection of the same modems and transmission speeds for both a terminal and a computer easily resolves any mismatch for high speed asynchronous and synchronous transmission.

The major codes used in this country today are ASCII (used by most microcomputers, including the IBM Personal Computer) and EBCDIC (used by IBM mainframe computers). A simple conversion algorithm and translation table allows conversion from one code to the other.

Other less frequently used codes can be similarly translated into ASCII and EBCDIC. Several vendors offer microcomputer systems that convert asynchronous teletypewriter protocol to 3270 BSC protocol. Converters for other protocols can be similarly constructed. Achieving compatibility at the functional and operational levels is, however, a different matter.

Functional compatibility requires that the features of a microcomputer system (e.g., the number and types of keyboard keys, and the display formatting and editing features) exactly match the terminal features expected by the mainframe computer software. Thus, the microcomputer must provide display features expected by IBM's Customer Information Control System (CICS) or Information Management System (IMS) software in the mainframe computer to achieve functional compatibility.

When functional incompatibilities exist, the user must either develop software to resolve them or restrict the use of the systems. For example, if an exact match of the keyboard is not possible because a microcomputer lacks function keys, then either a function can be left unused, or multiple keystrokes can be substituted for the single function key.

Functional compatibility may not duplicate on the terminal the exact operation that is expected by the mainframe computer software, but does provide equivalent features.

At the highest level of compatibility, the operational level, file formats used by programs in both a host computer and a microcomputer system must match. How is data identified? What is its structure? Does a file have VisiCalc formulas or straight text? Who is the sender? These questions are resolved when operational compatibility is achieved.

Emulation is the duplication of the functions of a specific communications device by another communicatons device. For example, the Personal Computer's 3270 data communications option assigns Personal Computer keys to the IBM 3270 display PF and PA key functions. This duplication allows the Personal Computer to retrieve and update data resident on IBM mainframes, just as an IBM 3270 terminal might perform these tasks with the same keys. Here, the IBM Personal Computer is said to emulate the operation of the IBM 3270 display system.

Protocols

Protocol applies to the rules established for exchanging information between computers. A *communications protocol* is the mechanism, or procedure, which the computer that sends and receives must follow to exchange data accurately over the communications link.

The protocol defines message formats, devices for detecting and correcting transmission errors, and the commands and responses needed to coordinate the activities of the transmitter and receiver.

The primary data communications protocol families, which are incorporated into most data communications products, include the following:

> Teletypewriter Protocol
> Binary Synchronous Communications (BSC)
> Synchronous Data Link Control (SDLC)
> Digital's Data Communications Message Protocol (DDCMP)
> LAN Protocols (CSMA/CD and token passing)

These protocols vary in sophistication, from the simplest (asynchronous teletypewriter protocol) to the most complex, like fourth generation protocols. These include IBM's SDLC; the X.25 level II HDLC (High level Data Link Control protocol); and DEC's DDCMP (Digital's Data Communication Message Protocol). Fourth generation protocols, developed in the late sixties and early seventies, were first delivered in products in 1974.

Local area networks (LAN), using fifth generation protocols, allow each station attached to the LAN transmission medium to function on an equal status with all other attached stations. The two LAN protocols most often used in new LAN products are Carrier Sense Multiple Access with Collision Detection(CSMA/CD), and token passing.

To identify a protocol precisely, it is necessary to state first its family name and then the manufacturer and product model number that implements the protocol. For example, four major variations of the BSC protocol are the IBM 2780, IBM 3780, IBM HASP workstation, and IBM 3270.

Each of these variations has a different set of commands and responses that are exchanged between the transmitting and receiving devices. Consequently, if the transmitting device uses the IBM 3780 BSC protocol for data transmission, and the receiving device uses the IBM 2780 protocol, then transmission errors are likely to result. One of the more recent communications software offerings uses the teletypewriter IBM 3101 protocol.

Before examining the IBM Personal Computer communications products, it is important to identify the communications protocol families and their operations. This information is necessary for the explanations that follow of the IBM communications software packages. The salient features of the protocol families are summarized in Table 1.

The table summarizes the technical characteristics of each protocol. In addition, information is presented on the number of variations of the protocol, the capability of imitating or emulating the operation of other IBM terminal products supported by communications software in the host computer, and examples of products for the IBM Personal Computer that use certain communications protocols.

The table also identifies the asynchronous teletypewriter protocol family as the one used in most communications products and software for the Personal Computer because of this protocol's simplicity.

The teletypewriter protocol's simplicity, however, is both a benefit and a burden. The benefit is that the protocol is easy to use for developing communications products that will exchange ASCII text data between computers using the asynchronous teletypewriter protocol. The burden is threefold: transfer of binary files isn't supported; error detection is minimal; and several hundred product-specific variations of the protocol exist because it is so flexible.

Some software products that use the teletypewriter protocol for data transmission provide the ability to transfer binary data files over a communications channel and also provide mechanisms to detect transmission errors and to correct them through retransmission of the data in error.

Although highly desirable, these features are not implemented by product developers in any consistent fashion. Consequently, each product used on one Personal Computer cannot exchange binary files with a different manufacturer's product used on a second, connected Personal Computer. In other words, both Personal Computers must operate with identical communications software. This requirement severely limits the usefulness of the binary file transfer features.

TABLE 1. PROTOCOL SUMMARY

Protocol Family	---------- Traditional Data Communications ----------					------ LAN's -------	
Feature	TTY	BSC	SDLC	HDLC (X.25)	DDCMP	CSMA/ CD	Token
Bit Synchro- nization	Asynch	Synch	Synch	Synch	Synch	Synch	Synch
Transmission Bits Per Char	10 Bits	8 Bits	8 Bits	8 Bits	8 Bits	8 Bits	8 Bits
Half/Full Duplex Message Flow	Half	Half	Half or Full	Half or Full	Half or Full	Ether —Net Half	Half or Full
Error Checking	Parity (none)	CRC	CRC	CRC	CRC	CRC	CRC
Data Trans- parency	No	Yes	Yes	Yes	Yes	Yes	Yes
Pt. to Pt. Vs. Multipoint	Pt. to Pt.	Both	Both	Pt. to Pt.	Both	Both	Both
Year Introduced	50s	1964	1974	Mid 70s	1974	Late 70s	Late 70s
Relative Equipment Cost	Low	Medium	High	High	Medium	High	High
Number of Variations	Several Hundred	Around 4	Under 10	LAP & LAPB	Under 10	Under 10	Under 10
Terminal Emulation Capability	Principally IBM 3101, & Others	IBM 3270, 3780, & Others	IBM 3270 & 3770	No	No	No	No
Used in IBM Communi- cation Products for the PC	Yes IBM ASC V2.0 DowJ Rpt	Yes IBM 3270 BSC	Yes IBM 3270 & 3770	No	Micro- Comp. Prods.	Orchd Tech LAN & Others	No

IBM provides a solution to this problem with its Release 2.00 of the Asynchronous Communications Support program. The new program is accompanied by a utility program that translates binary files to ASCII text files, and vice versa. This utility is similar to the one provided with the second release of the EasyWriter text-processing program.

The problem here is that once the data is received, it must be processed again by the utility program so that it can transform the data back into its original binary form.

The file conversion program (FILECONV) also checks for transmission errors. This checking indicates only that errors were encountered during data transmission and that those errors affected the data received. This information does not appear until some time after the file transmission has occurred. To correct the error through retransmission requires manually reestablishing communications, then retransmitting the entire file that was affected by the errors.

IBM announced a new asynchronous teletypewriter protocol communications package for the Personal Computer that allows it to emulate the operation of the IBM 3101 terminal. This package should make it easier to interface the Personal Computer with minicomputer systems and protocol converters supporting this particular variation of the asynchronous teletypewriter protocol.

Communications hardware and software products using the IBM BSC and SDLC protocols are now available from IBM. These products have strong appeal because they provide a means for ready access to corporate data bases on IBM host computers without necessitating modification of the host computers' application software. Since the cost of the Personal Computer is only slightly more than the cost of an IBM 3270 terminal, Data Processing shops are beginning to supply managers and other professionals with Personal Computers instead of 3270 terminals.

Personal Computers can be used to great advantage by professional employees because of the additional spreadsheet, word-processing, and stand-alone data base software now available.

HDLC protocol products will probably appear for the Personal Computer within the next year.

HDLC is part of the X.25 interface between terminals (and host computers) and packet-switched data networks, such as Telenet™,

Tymnet™, the less familiar Uninet™, and American Bell's Net-1000™ communication service.

The X.25 interface is very popular in Europe but is seldom used in the United States. It is mainly used as a high-speed interface for host computers connected to packet-switched networks, but not for terminals connected to these networks.

The DDCMP protocol is used in MicroCom's Professional Communications System products that perform electronic mail, as well as modem, printer buffer, and LCD time-of-day clock functions. The PCS is a microcomputer-controlled, intelligent modem that performs the more common auto-dialing functions and additional automatic electronic message transfers.

The local area network CSMA/CD protocol is used in the Orchid Technology local networking products, as well as those LAN products offered by 3COM. This protocol will be used in many other LAN products for the Personal Computer.

The second LAN protocol, token passing, is not presently used in any products for the Personal Computer. However, when IBM announces a LAN capability for the Personal Computer, it is likely to be based on the token passing protocol.

IBM Data Communications Products

The IBM-offered communications products for the Personal Computer allow it to function as a dumb terminal; to perform text file transfers with remote computer systems and computer-based information services; and to extract data from IBM mainframe computers. These IBM products include the following:

Dumb Terminal
COMM.BAS

Text File Transfer
Asynchronous Communications Support, Rev. 2.0
IBM 3101 Emulation Program
Dow Jones Reporter™

Corporate Data Extraction
BSC 3270 Emulation
SNA 3270 + 3770 Emulation

IBM does not currently market local area network products for the Personal Computer. Such products, however, permitting many Personal Computers in a single facility to be interconnected and to share data files, will likely be announced within a year.

Minimum Configurations for the Personal Computer

These communications products all require either an IBM Personal Computer or the IBM Personal Computer XT. The packages that are based on the asynchronous teletypewriter protocol and that provide text file transfer all operate with a minimum of 64K of RAM. In contrast, the more complex BSC and SDLC protocol packages, which are aimed at extracting data from IBM host computers and which emulate 3270 Information Display System terminals, require, as a minimum, 128K of RAM.

All packages work with one single-sided, 160K diskette drive and will function with the Personal Computer XT's hard disk system. In addition, these packages all operate with the Personal Computer's Monochrome or Color Displays, using the 80-column display format, although some of these packages support the 40-column display format.

To use the IBM communications products more effectively, system configurations with memory and disk storage capacities greater than the minimum configurations are recommended. In every case, better performance will be realized if twice the minimum recommended RAM memory is used. However, memory exceeding twice the minimum configuration, or greater than 256K, is not likely to improve performance with these communications software packages.

Recommended system configurations for the Personal Computer and Personal Computer XT are given below:

Computer Hardware

IBM Personal Computer
+ 128K to 256K of RAM
+ Dual 320K (360K with DOS 2.0) Floppy Disk Drives
+ Monochrome or Color Monitor (with 80-column capability)
+ IBM 80 CPS Dot-Matrix Printer

IBM Personal Computer XT
+ 256K of RAM
+ Single 320K (360K with DOS 2.0) Floppy Disk Drive
+ Single 10M Hard Disk Drive
+ Monochrome or Color Monitor (with 80-column capability)
+ IBM 80 CPS Dot-Matrix Printer

Software

DOS 2.0 or 1.1
Disk BASIC language extensions

Personal Computer Communications Software/Hardware

Dumb Terminal Operation

+ COMM.BAS

Asynchronous Communications Adapter (#1502074); Modem Cable (#7347005); asynchronous WE 103 or 212 equivalent modem on switched line

Text File Transfer

+ Asynchronous Communications Support, Rev. 2.0
+ IBM 3101 Emulation Program
+ Dow Jones Reporter

Asynchronous Communications Adapter (#1502074); Modem Cable (#7347005); asynchronous WE 103 or 212 equivalent modem on switched line

Mainframe Computer Data Access

+ BSC 3270 Emulation

BSC Communications Adapter (#1502075); Communications Adapter Cable (#1502067); host computer system with compatible BSC IBM 3270 display system software support; synchronous communications modem with clocking up to 4800 BPS on a switched line or up to 9600 BPS on a leased line

+ SNA 3270 and 3770 Emulation

SDLC Communications Adapter (#1502090); Communications Adapter Cable (#1502067); host computer system with compatible SNA 3270 or SNA 3770 software support; synchronous communications modem for up to 4800 BPS on a switched or leased line

These hardware/software configurations for the Personal Computer fulfill requirements for simple dumb terminal communications, text file transfer, and host computer data base access.

Dumb Terminal Communications

The Personal Computer's Disk Operating System comes with a simple communications program labeled COMM.BAS. This program runs under the BASIC interpreter and permits the Personal Computer to function as a simple asynchronous communications protocol terminal.

The operator can use the program to access remote information services, such as The Source or Compuserve, and to communicate as a terminal with other microcomputer bulletin boards. The COMM.BAS program, however, does not support text file transfers from memory or disk. Furthermore, when a printout of the information received is desired, the operator must use the print-screen feature of the Personal Computer to make the printout.

Regardless of the shortcomings of the program, the price of COMM.BAS is appealing. (It comes free with the purchase of DOS 1.1 and DOS 2.0.)

Text File Transfers

More serious users of the Personal Computers soon find the capabilities of the COMM.BAS program inadequate because they want either to transmit files of data to remote computer systems or to receive them from these systems. Such file transfers can be performed with files in RAM or in disk memory.

Transmission of larger files is best performed using disk memory because of its larger capacity. Personal Computers with only 64K of RAM are usually limited to file transfers of about 30K before the RAM must be written to disk. This memory writing process often involves operator interaction with the Personal Computer and substantially increases the total time that the Personal Computer and the remote system must be connected.

As a result, this procedure is undesirable when transferring data from information services that require payment based on the amount of time connected to the remote computer system, or when communicating with bulletin boards in making a long distance telephone call.

Asynchronous Communications Support Program, Version 2.0

The Personal Computer's Asynchronous Communications Support program, Version 2.0 (#6024032), with a price of $60.00, not only provides the file transfers from disk to remote computer, but even more. The Asynchronous Communications Support enables the IBM Personal Computer to function as an asynchronous (start/stop) TTY ASR 33/35 terminal. Also, the program transforms the Personal Computer into an interactive terminal and allows the IBM Personal Computer to exchange program and data files with remote systems.

Programs and data may be sent from a disk file on the Personal Computer to a remote system and/or received from a remote system and stored in a disk file on the Personal Computer.

Binary files may be converted on the Personal Computer to ASCII text files, and vice versa, for uploading or downloading, through the use of a utility program supplied with the Asynchronous Communications Support program. However, this file translation process must be performed as a separate procedure before communications are initiated.

The Asychronous Communications Support program provides an operating mode for two IBM Personal Computers to communicate with one another, allowing the transfer of program and data files between them. This data exchange mode from Personal Computer to Personal Computer does not, however, include CRC error detection and correction via retransmission of blocks containing errors. These features are provided by some independent manufacturers' packages.

Flexibility in specifying protocol options for the TTY ASR 33/35 terminal aids attachment to a variety of manufacturers of host computers. When starting the program, Personal Computer users interactively specify the following communications operating parameters:

+Bit rate of 75 BPS to 9600 BPS
+Parity
+Number of stop bits
+Line turnaround characters (usually carriage return)
+Local character echoing or host character echoing
+XON/XOFF, RDY/BUSY support

Pre-set, menu-selectable communications parameter options are provided for the following:

+VM/370, MVS/TSO
+Dow Jones News/Retrieval Service (Dow Jones News/Retrieval Service is a registered trademark of Dow Jones & Company, Inc.)
+The Source (The Source is a service mark of Source Telecomputing Corporation, a subsidiary of The Reader's Digest Association, Inc.)

Other parameter specifications for transmission with specific hosts may be stored in Personal Computer disk files for subsequent use.

The program functions with either of the two Asynchronous Communications Adapter ports, if they are installed. A program operating option permits printing while receiving data from a remote computer system.

In summary, the Asynchronous Communications Support program is intended by IBM to be the workhorse for asynchronous TTY protocol communications.

The program does not provide two features found in independent vendors' asynchronous communications programs: file transfer with CRC error checking and text editing, and communications in the same program.

Crosstalk™ and ASCOM™ are two programs that provide error checking for file transfers to remote microcomputers which are running the same programs. Others, like DataCapture/pc™ and Microterminal™, perform dual functions of text editing and file transmission. However, there are as yet no asynchronous communications programs that put all three features together.

IBM 3101 Emulation Program

The 3101 Emulation Program (#6024042) with a price of $140.00, emulates many of the communications features of the IBM 3101 Model 20 asynchronous TTY protocol terminal. This program facilitates communications with a variety of minicomputer systems and information services.

Similar to the Asynchronous Communications Support Program, the 3101 program also permits disk-resident text file transfers to and from remote systems. A utility that converts binary diskette files to and from ASCII text format for communications with remote computer systems is also provided with the program.

Emulation of the IBM 3101 Display Terminal is set according to user-selected options stored in disk-resident specification files. Users may specify line characteristics and keyboard mapping or use popular 3101 configurations described in one of several specification files that are provided with the program, including the following:

+VM/370, MVS/TSO
+IBM 7426 Terminal Interface Unit (TIU) for IBM 8100
+Yale IUP for Series/1
+3101 Pass-through (PVM)
+Communications with another IBM Personal Computer
+Dow Jones News/Retrieval Service
+The Source

The 3101 Emulation Program does not precisely emulate the IBM 3101 Model 20 communications. Below are listed functions of the IBM 3101 that are not supported:

+Transparent mode
+Half-duplex modems
+Reverse channel and controlled request to send
+Non-EIA RS-232C interfaces
+Nonblinking cursor
+Highlights via IBM Color/Graphics Monitor Adapter
+Program mode and ATTR keys
+Local mode
+Print line function
+Print and send message functions and send mark function
+Foreign Language features

These asynchronous communications programs provide limited ability to access IBM mainframe data files. However, additional mainframe programming is usually required to prepare the data for access by the Asynchronous Communications Support and IBM 3101 Emulation programs.

Emulation of IBM's ubiquitous 3270 Information Display System terminal allows access to IBM mainframe resident data with minimal mainframe programming.

The IBM Dow Jones Reporter Program

The Dow Jones Reporter (#6024031), with a price of $100.00, is an asynchronous communications program designed to operate specifically with the Dow Jones Information Service.

The program, which is classified by IBM as a professional tool and not a communications program, is designed to allow the Personal Computer user to gather raw financial data from the Dow Jones Information Service and to store this data on disk files for subsequent analysis. Thus, a Personal Computer user can manage particular finances and stock portfolios.

The program also assists the Personal Computer user to follow the latest financial news and to review historical data on stocks and companies.

Since the Dow Jones Reportor is designed for communications primarily with the Dow Jones Information Service, the program's communications features have been specifically tailored for that purpose. The program can communicate with other remote computers, but it is not as flexible as the Asynchronous Communications Support program.

Mainframe Computer Data Access

The primary IBM communications tools for accessing data resident on IBM mainframe computers are the Binary Synchronous 3270 Emulation program and the SNA 3270 Emulation and RJE Support program.

Binary Synchronous 3270 Emulation, Version 1.0

The Binary Synchronous 3270 Emulation program (#6024037), with a price of $700.00, is the workhorse of IBM mainframe data base access programs. This program permits the transferring of data retrieved from the IBM mainframes to the printer and, more importantly, to disk. The program must be used with the IBM Binary Synchronous Communications (BSC) Adapter.

With the 3270 program, the Personal Computer transmits and receives BSC 3270 data streams with a host system performing necessary code conversions from ASCII to EBCDIC.

A configuration utility is used to set up the Personal Computer and to tailor JJ and C communications features for the specific mainframe environment.

Communications capabilities include:

+Communications over both switched and leased lines
+Half-duplex message flow over half- or full-duplex channels
+Transmission at speeds up to 9600 BPS
+External clocking input from a synchronous modem
+Constant line trace, error logging, and communications statistics accumulation

The IBM Personal Computer appears to the IBM mainframe computer system as one of the following IBM 3270 BSC devices:

3271-2/3277-2	Leased line
3274-51C/3278-2	Leased line
3275-2	Switched or leased line
3276-2	Leased line

The IBM Personal Computer provides the same screen display formats as those supported by the 3275, 3276, 3277, and 3278 terminals. The only difference is that the Personal Computer uses the 25th line to display terminal status information. The following 3270 features are provided.

+12 program function keys
+Local print key
+Audible alarm
+EBCDIC code transmission
+Keyboard numeric lock
+Status line messages
+IBM 3279 Base Color Mode Support
+Printer support
    * 3284-3 (when configured as a 3275)
    * 3284-2
    * 3286-2
    * 3288-2

The IBM Personal Computer connects to host subsystems that support the above BSC 3270 devices, features, and options. BSC 3270 functions that are not supported include:

+Structured fields and attributes
+Extended highlighting
+Extended color
+Programmed symbols
+Transparent BSC transmission

Additional communications and operational features provided by
the BSC 3270 Emulation program are listed below:

+User-definable 3270 keys
+PRINT command that allows the user to route printer-directed
 data to a disk file or the printer
+SEND command that allows ASCII file data to be written to the
 unprotected fields on the display for modification and/or
 transmission to the host
+TRACE command that formats and prints or displays the communications line trace
+STATS command that displays communications statistics

When the user desires a stand-alone workstation that functions like
a 3270 terminal, this package provides the solution.

The BSC 3270 Emulation program allows the user's terminal to
communicate as a simple BSC 3270 terminal in an emulation-
operating mode and to prepare 3270 data screens off line in command mode. Once screens are prepared, they can be transmitted to
the IBM mainframe computer.

Responses received from the computer and displayed on the
screen can be directed to the printer or a disk file. This program
probably provides the most flexible means of accessing data resident on IBM mainframe computers.

IBM Personal Computer SNA 3270 Emulation and RJE Support

Extraction of data from the program host computer is somewhat
more cumbersome with the SNA 3270 Emulation and RJE Support
program (#6024036), with a price of $700.00, because the 3270
Emulation capability does not provide a direct means to save
responses received from the mainframe computer in a disk file.
Consequently, to extract data from mainframes, the user must first
access the data as a 3270 terminal and construct a 3770 terminal
output data file.

Then in a separate session, the user must log on as a 3770 remote batch terminal and transfer the data to a Personal Computer disk file. Both the SNA 3270 Emulation and the RJE 3770 Emulation can run on the same communications channel (at alternate times).

Thus, the same Personal Computer and a single communications line can perform both types of SNA terminal operations.

A configuration utility tailors the Personal Computer communications features for the specific SNA communications environment. Communications capabilities or the SNA 3270 Emulation and 3770 Remote Job Entry Support program include the following:

+ Communications over both switched and leased lines (including multipoint lines)
+Half-duplex message flow over half- or full-duplex channels
+Transmission at speeds up to 4800 BPS
+Constant request to send and line turnaround
+External clocking input from a synchronous modem
+On-line diagnostics with line trace, error logging, and analysis

SNA 3270 Emulation capabilities make the Personal Computer appear to the IBM SNA host system as an IBM 3274 Model 51C, Logical Unit Type 2 Control Unit. The Personal Computer provides the same screen displays as the 3278 Display Station except for the status line.

The IBM Personal Computer connects to SNA IBM mainframe systems that support the following 3270 emulation devices, features, and options:

+Twenty-four 3270 program function keys
+Local print key
+Audible alarm
+EBCDIC code communications
+Keyboard numeric lock
+3279 Base Color Mode Support
+Status line messages
+User-definable 3270 keys
+3287-1, -2 printer support
   * For local copy and
   * Host-initiated screen print

This product also provides SNA 3770 RJE terminal emulation capabilities for remote batch file transfers. The RJE 3770 operation allows the Personal Computer to submit batch jobs to the SNA mainframe computer using SDLC communications protocol over switched or leased lines.

After the job is processed by the SNA host computer, the resulting output can be directed back to the Personal Computer, to other RJE 3770-emulating Personal Computers, to another RJE terminal, or to the mainframe computer's input/output peripherals.

In the 3770 emulation mode, the Personal Computer appears to the host system as an IBM 3770 communications terminal with the following features:

+Logical Unit Type 1 (LU1)
+FM Header Type 1
+TS Profile 3 and FM Profile 3
+Data compression for transmissions outbound from the host
+ASCII or EBCDIC code communications
+Transparency
+3770 Devices Emulated
  Console
  Printer
  Card/Punch

The IBM Personal Computer connects to IBM SNA mainframe computers that support the devices, features, and options identified above. Following are additional communications and operational features provided by the SNA 3770 Emulation subprogram:

+Transmit and receive source and object data in PC DOS compatible files
+Print formatting includes setting
  *Channel control
  *Page size
  *Tabs
  *Line density (1 to 72 LPI)
+Diskette drive selection
+Directing print data streams to diskette or printer
+End-of-job statistics
+Multiple dataset print/punch output
+Maintaining multiple job files from keyboard or diskette

The major disadvantage of the SNA 3270 Emulation and 3770 Remote Job Entry Support program is that in order to extract data from SNA host computers, the Personal Computer user must have the SNA mainframe set up with files to transfer to the Personal Computer using the 3770 RJE Emulation subprogram.

The SNA 3270 Emulation subprogram does not permit the Personal Computer to capture data retrieved from the SNA mainframe to Personal Computer disk files.

Micro-to-Micro Networks

IBM does not currently market local area networking products for the Personal Computer. Since this is the next communications capability desired by business users, IBM will soon fulfill this need with local area networking hardware and software products for the Personal Computer. In the interim, local area networking products from independent manufacturers fill the gap. However, buyer beware.

With the announcement of the Personal Computer XT, IBM has, in effect, made some of the currently offered LAN products obsolete because they were designed to operate with DOS 1.1. This system was, in most cases, modified to include hard disk support for an independent vendor's hard disk. Such hard disk-based systems allowed Personal Computers to share files resident on the hard disk, making Personal Computers responsive to service requests from multiple users.

DOS 2.0 now sets the product mainstream for interfacing the IBM Personal Computer to hard disk subsystems. If the previously designed LAN and applications software is not moved to DOS 2.0, or if the LAN Communications Adapter interferes with the hard disk drive controller interface as it is used by DOS 2.0, then the Personal Computer must upgrade those components (i.e., switch them for compatible components) to maintain compatibility with future Personal Computer hardware and software products.

The Final Word

The IBM Personal Computer and Personal Computer XT are premier microcomputer systems for business applications. They provide managers and other professionals with computer workstations that can significantly enhance productivity by implementing balanced computing within both large and small organizations. The

IBM Personal Computer and Personal Computer XT desktop computer systems are competitively-priced, open-designed systems, making them the hottest selling microcomputers.

IBM has correctly foreseen that the next capabilities required for professional workstations must be those of communication. IBM has responded with a set of communications hardware and software products that meet the current requirements to transfer text files between computers and to access IBM mainframe resident data bases. Also, independent vendors are providing similar and, in some cases, better and more flexible communications products.

The need for micro-to-micro communications is rapidly growing. IBM should soon respond with hardware and software products that meet this need.Such communications products will keep the IBM Personal Computer and Personal Computer XT in the mainstream of the microcomputer marketplace for the next five years.

REFERENCES

Datamation, November, 1982, page 106, "We're Not Sure Really How Many We Have." This survey was prepared by Advanced Office Concepts Corp. to determine the extent to which personal computers have penetrated corporations. Of the almost 250 corporate users responding, 26% came from among the 1,000 largest U.S. companies, with 60% having 1,000 or more employees. Over 75% of the corporate users used IBM mainframe computers, and 50% used other mainframes.

APPENDIX A

Key:

X   =   available in level or version
—   =   not available in level or version
N   =   new function added
C   =   function/command change in this version
D   =   function/command works differently in compiler version
1   =   double precision available in V2.0
2   =   cassette portion does not work with XT
3   =   command/statement accommodates V2.0 paths
4   =   command/statement accommodates V2.0 I/O redirection
5   =   command also works with V2.0 VIEW command
6   =   additional keys available in V2.0

BASIC Commands

Command Name	Level of BASIC Cas.	Disk	Adv.	Comp.	Version 1.0	1.1	2.0	Comments
ABS	x	x	x	x	x	x	x	
ASC	x	x	x	x	x	x	x	
ATN	x	x	x	x	x	x	C	1
AUTO	x	x	x	—	x	x	x	
BEEP	x	x	x	x	x	x	x	
BLOAD	x	x	x	x	x	x	x	2, 3
BSAVE	x	x	x	x	x	x	x	2, 3
CALL	x	x	x	D	x	x	x	
CDBL	x	x	x	x	x	x	x	
CHAIN	—	x	x	x	x	x	C	3
CHDIR	—	x	x	—	—	—	N	
CHR$	x	x	x	x	x	x	x	

Command Name	Level of BASIC				Version			Comments
	Cas.	Disk	Adv.	Comp.	1.0	1.1	2.0	
CINT	x	x	x	x	x	x	x	
CIRCLE	—	—	x	x	x	x	C	5
CLEAR	x	x	x	D	x	x	x	
CLOSE	x	x	x	x	x	x	x	
CLS	x	x	x	x	x	x	x	
COLOR (text)	x	x	x	x	x	x	x	
COLOR (graphics)	x	x	x	x	x	x	x	
COM(x) ON, OFF, and STOP	—	—	x	D	x	x	x	
COMMON	—	x	x	D	x	x	x	
CONT	x	x	x	—	x	x	x	
COS	x	x	x	x	x	x	C	1
CSNG	x	x	x	x	x	x	x	
CSRLIN	x	x	x	x	x	x	x	
CVI	—	x	x	x	x	x	x	
CVS	—	x	x	x	x	x	x	
CVD	—	x	x	x	x	x	x	
DATA	x	x	x	x	x	x	x	
DATE$	—	x	x	x	x	x	x	
DEF FN and FN	x	x	x	x	x	x	x	
DEF SEG	x	x	x	x	x	x	x	
DEFtype	x	x	x	D	x	x	x	
DEF USR	x	x	x	x	x	x	x	
DELETE	x	x	x	—	x	x	C	
IDM	x	x	x	D	x	x	x	
DRAW	—	—	x	D	x	C	C	5
EDIT	x	x	x	—	x	x	x	
END	x	x	x	D	x	x	x	
EOF	x	x	x	D	x	x	C	4
ERASE	x	x	x	—	x	x	x	
ERL	x	x	x	x	x	x	x	
ERR	x	x	x	x	x	x	x	
ERROR	x	x	x	x	x	x	x	
EXP	x	x	x	x	x	x	x	1
FIELD	—	x	x	x	x	x	x	
FILES	—	x	x	x	x	x	C	3
FIX	x	x	x	x	x	x	x	
FOR..NEXT..STEP	x	x	x	D	x	x	x	

Command Name	Level of BASIC				Version			Comments
	Cas.	Disk	Adv.	Comp.	1.0	1.1	2.0	
FRE	x	x	x	D	x	x	x	
GET (files)	—	x	x	x	x	C	C	
GET (graphics)	—	—	x	x	x	x	x	
GOSUB	x	x	x	x	x	x	x	
GOTO	x	x	x	x	x	x	x	
HEX$	x	x	x	x	x	x	x	
IF..THEN..ELSE	x	x	x	x	x	x	x	
INKEY$	x	x	x	x	x	x	x	4
INP	x	x	x	x	x	x	x	
INPUT	x	x	x	x	x	x	x	4
INPUT#	x	x	x	x	x	x	x	2, 4
INPUT$	x	x	x	x	x	x	C	2, 4
INSTR	x	x	x	x	x	x	x	
INT	x	x	x	x	x	x	x	
KEY ON, OFF, LIST and program	x	x	x	D	x	x	C	6
KEY(x) ON, OFF, and STOP	—	—	x	D	x	x	C	6
KILL	—	x	x	—	x	x	C	3
LEFT$	x	x	x	x	x	x	x	
LEN	x	x	x	x	x	x	x	
LET	x	x	x	x	x	x	x	
LINE	x	x	x	D	x	x	C	5
LINE (w/style)	—	—	x	—	—	—	N	5
LINE INPUT	x	x	x	x	x	x	C	4
LINE INPUT#	x	x	x	x	x	x	x	2
LIST	x	x	x	—	x	x	x	
LLIST	x	x	x	—	x	x	x	
LOAD	x	x	x	—	x	x	x	2
LOC	—	x	x	x	x	x	C	
LOCATE	x	x	x	x	x	x	x	
LOF	—	x	x	x	x	x	C	
LOG	x	x	x	x	x	x	C	1
LPOS	x	x	x	x	x	x	x	
LPRINT	x	x	x	x	x	x	C	4
LPRINT USING	x	x	x	x	x	x	C	4
LSET	—	x	x	x	x	x	x	
MERGE	x	x	x	x	x	x	C	2, 3

Command Name	Level of BASIC				Version			Comments
	Cas.	Disk	Adv.	Comp.	1.0	1.1	2.0	
MID$	x	x	x	x	x	x	x	
MKDIR	—	x	x	—	—	—	N	3
MKI$	—	x	x	x	x	x	x	
MKS$	—	x	x	x	x	x	x	
MKD$	—	x	x	x	x	x	x	
MOTOR	x	x	x	—	x	x	x	2
NAME	—	x	x	x	x	x	C	3
NEW	x	x	x	—	x	x	x	
OCT$	x	x	x	x	x	x	x	
ON COM	—	—	x	D	x	C	C	
ON..GOSUB	x	x	x	x	x	x	x	
ON..GOTO	x	x	x	x	x	x	x	
ON KEY	—	—	x	D	x	x	C	
ON PEN	—	—	x	D	x	x	x	
ON PLAY	—	—	x	—	—	—	N	
ON STRIG	—	—	x	D	x	C	x	
ON TIMER	—	—	x	—	—	—	N	
OPEN	x	x	x	D	x	C	C	2, 3
OPEN"COM	—	x	x	D	x	C	C	
OPTION BASE	x	x	x	x	x	x	x	
OUT	x	x	x	x	x	x	x	
PAINT	—	—	x	D	x	x	C	5
PEEK	x	x	x	x	x	x	x	
PEN ON, OFF	x	x	x	D	x	x	x	
PEN STOP	—	—	x	x	x	x	x	
PLAY	—	—	x	D	x	C	C	
PLAY(n)	—	—	x	—	—	—	N	
PMAP	—	—	x	—	—	—	N	
POINT	x	x	x	D	x	x	x	
POINT(n)	—	—	x	—	—	—	N	5
POKE	x	x	x	x	x	x	x	
POS	x	x	x	x	x	x	x	
PRINT	x	x	x	x	x	x	C	4
PRINT#	x	x	x	x	x	x	x	2
PRINT USING	x	x	x	x	x	x	C	4
PRINT USING#	x	x	x	x	x	x	x	2
PSET	x	x	x	x	x	x	C	5
PRESET	x	x	x	x	x	x	C	5

Command Name	Level of BASIC				Version			Comments
	Cas.	Disk	Adv.	Comp.	1.0	1.1	2.0	
PUT (files)	—	x	x	x	x	C	C	
PUT (graphics)	—	—	x	x	x	x	x	
RANDOMIZE	x	x	x	D	x	x	C	1
RANDOMIZE TIMER	—	x	x	—	—	—	N	
READ	x	x	x	x	x	x	x	
REM	x	x	x	D	x	x	x	
RENUM	x	x	x	—	x	x	x	
RESET	—	x	x	x	x	x	x	
RESTORE	x	x	x	x	x	x	x	
RESUME	x	x	x	D	x	x	x	
RETURN	x	x	x	x	x	x	x	
RETURN line#	—	—	x	x	x	x	x	
RMDIR	—	x	x	—	—	—	N	3
RND	x	x	x	x	x	x	x	
RSET	—	x	x	x	x	x	x	
RUN line#	x	x	x	D	x	x	x	
RUN filename	x	x	x	x	x	x	C	1, 3
SAVE	x	x	x	—	x	x	C	3
SCREEN(x, y)	x	x	x	x	x	x	x	
SCREEN (mode)	x	x	x	x	x	x	x	
SGN	x	x	x	x	x	x	x	
SIN	x	x	x	x	x	x	C	1
SOUND	x	x	x	x	x	x	x	
SPACE$	x	x	x	x	x	x	x	
SPC	x	x	x	x	x	x	x	
SQR	x	x	x	x	x	x	C	1
STICK	x	x	x	x	x	x	x	
STOP	x	x	x	D	x	x	x	
STR$	x	x	x	x	x	x	x	
STRIG ON, OFF	x	x	D	D	x	C	x	
STRIG(n) ON, OFF, and STOP	—	—	x	D	x	C	x	
STRING$	x	x	x	x	x	x	x	
SWAP	x	x	x	x	x	x	x	
SYSTEM	—	x	x	x	x	x	x	
TAB	x	x	x	x	x	x	x	
TAN	x	x	x	x	x	x	C	1
TIME$	—	x	x	x	x	x	x	

Command Name	Level of BASIC				Version			Comments
	Cas.	Disk	Adv.	Comp.	1.0	1.1	2.0	
TIMER	—	x	x	—	—	—	N	
TRON	x	x	x	D	x	x	x	
TROFF	x	x	x	D	x	x	x	
USR	x	x	x	D	x	x	x	
VAL	x	x	x	x	x	x	x	
VARPTR	x	x	x	x	x	x	x	
VARPTR$	—	x	x	x	—	N	x	
VIEW	—	—	x	—	—	—	N	
WAIT	x	x	x	x	x	x	x	
WHILE..WEND	x	x	x	D	x	x	x	
WIDTH	x	x	x	D	x	C	x	
WINDOW	—	—	x	—	—	—	N	
WRITE	x	x	x	x	x	x	x	
WRITE#	x	x	x	x	x	x	x	2

Index

Que Microcomputer Products

BOOKS:	ISBN No.	Date Available
The Osborne Portable Computer	0-88022-015-5	Currently
VisiCalc Models for Business (S)	0-88022-017-1	Currently
SuperCalc SuperModels for Business (S)	0-88022-007-4	Currently
IBM PC Expansion & Software Guide, 2nd ed.	0-88022-027-9	Currently
C Programming Guide	0-88022-022-8	Currently
Timex/Sinclair 1000 User's Guide, Vol. 1	0-88022-016-3	Currently
Timex/Sinclair 1000 User's Guide, Vol. 2	0-88022-029-5	Currently
Timex/Sinclair 1000 Dictionary	0-88022-041-4	Currently
IBM's Personal Computer, 2nd ed.	0-88022-026-0	Currently
Timelost—Timex/Sinclair Version	0-88022-030-9	Currently
Timelost—TI-99/4A Version	0-88022-053-8	Currently
Timelost—Atari 400, 800, 1200XL Version	0-88022-056-2	Currently
Timelost—VIC 20 Version	0-88022-054-6	Currently
Spreadsheet Software: From VisiCalc to 1-2-3	0-88022-035-X	Currently
TI-99/4A Favorite Programs Explained (S)	0-88022-050-3	October '83
Real Managers Use Personal Computers!	0-88022-031-7	September '83
PC DOS User's Guide (V.1 & 2)	0-88022-040-6	October '83
MS DOS User's Guide (V.1 & 2)	0-88022-061-9	October '83
CP/M Programmer's Encyclopedia	0-88022-043-0	October '83
CP/M Software Finder	0-88022-021-X	August '83
Multiplan Models for Business (S)	0-88022-037-6	September '83
1-2-3 for Business (S)	0-88022-038-4	October '83
Using 1-2-3	0-88022-045-7	September '83
Using InfoStar	0-88022-044-9	October '83
Using KnowledgeMan	0-88022-046-5	November '83
C Programmer's Library (S)	0-88022-048-1	November '83

(S) — Denotes companion software available.